PETER MANUEL,

Hector MacLeod is a former solicitor who served as a director of several Chinese companies while living in Hong Kong. Having returned to the UK, he continues to act as a business consultant in liaison with China.

Malcolm McLeod is the former vice principal and professor of African Studies at the University of Glasgow. Now retired, he is currently a trustee of the National Museums of Scotland.

PETER MANUEL

SERIAL KILLER

HECTOR MacLEOD
AND
MALCOLM McLEOD

EDINBURGH AND LONDON

First published in Great Britain in 2009 by
MAINSTREAM PUBLISHING COMPANY
(EDINBURGH) LTD
7 Albany Street
Edinburgh EH1 3UG

ISBN 9781845963972

All internal photographs courtesy of The Herald & Evening Times picture archive unless stated otherwise

A catalogue record for this book is available
from the British Library

Typeset in Garamond and Trixie

Printed in Great Britain by
CPI Mackays of Chatham Ltd, Chatham, ME5 8TD

In memoriam Anne Kneilands and all those who perished at the hand of Peter Thomas Anthony Manuel, and for those who mourn them

ACKNOWLEDGEMENTS

The authors would like to thank all those who gave so freely of their assistance in researching and writing this book, and in particular The Hon. Lord Cameron of Lochbroom, The Rt. Hon. Lord Rodger, The Hon. Lord Sutherland, Sheriff R.D. Ireland, QC, Joseph Beltrami, Ross Harper, Leslie Wolfson, David Pirrett, the Ferns family, Bill Niven, Peter Anderson (of the National Archives of Scotland and son of Dr Anderson), Morag Fyfe, Jennifer Duffy, Victoria Brown, Ruth Jones, John Bruce and the rest of the staff of the West Reading Room of the NAS, who have helped so very much, Carol McDivitt of the Crown Office, Sir David McNee, Superintendent (rtd) Alastair Dinsmor and Superintendent (rtd) Alec MacLean of Glasgow Police Museum for their unfailing generosity, Sandra Brown, the Pitt family (and a special thanks to Mhairi for all her invaluable assistance), Bishop Joseph Devine and Canon Gibbons, Dr Rajan Dargee, Professor David Holmes, Dr Peter Gordon and Dr S.E. Avons for their guidance in matters psychiatric and psychological, Sir Michael Bond for his amazing contribution, Dr Richard Goldberg, Frankie Fraser, Thomas Christie, Michael McGuinness of the Smith Art Gallery and Museum, Stirling, and of Viewpark, David Cornwell, A.M. Bean, Ian Robertson, Jacqui Henrie, Paul Tucker, Emma Sanders and Patsi MacKenzie for their support and encouragement, Andrew Primrose, George Horspool and, of course, our families, who have cheerfully suffered our neglect and preoccupation. We are grateful to the National Archives of Scotland for permission to reproduce Crown copyright material from its files. A list of the documents consulted can be found in the bibliography.

FOREWORD
BY DR DAVID HOLMES

Factual accounts of serial killers more often than not leave their fictional counterparts a long way behind in terms of the brutality and inexplicable motivation contained in their details. What is invented for Hollywood and the small screen rarely lives up to the intriguing facets of a real case. In the following account, the authors not only provide rich detail but also sift through the evidence to make sense of the notorious life of Manuel.

Through painstaking, detailed research, MacLeod and McLeod have not only created a gripping replay of the crimes of Manuel but also provided intelligent and well-considered views on his case. That he was notable for having a clear head in the face of danger and being tenacious in verbal combat, as well as becoming Scotland's most industrious serial killer, would tend to confirm rather than disprove Manuel's psychopathic propensities. However, it would be a very limited explanation for his crimes to dismiss them as solely the logical product of such a dangerous and severe personality disorder, as most psychopaths do not kill people. Further threads of Manuel's sexual and other life experiences have been woven into a thorough analysis of the factors preceding his murders, including his lifelong tendency to pathological lying, which continued throughout his custody and trial to his execution.

The lay use of the term 'psychopath' should not allow the concept to be trivialised in the mind of the reader. Although not its sole cause, this inherent trait enables the more extreme behaviour of dangerous individuals such as Manuel. Many psychopathic individuals have superficial charm and also lack the 'emotional baggage' of more sensitive people, making the psychopath socially attractive in the short term. Having disarmed potential victims, they will proceed to entertain themselves by manipulating their prey to gain what they want, be that material, sexual or even murderous satisfaction. Being indifferent to the feelings of others while having an acute intellectual awareness of the effects of manipulation or intimidation gives psychopaths such as Manuel a predatory advantage over other criminals.

In fact, the notoriously pitiless and cold Manuel inspired Brian Cox in his portrayal of Hannibal Lecktor in the film *Manhunter*. In this book, the detailed account of Manuel's trial reveals something of the fictional character in him. Although he was finally unsuccessful in evading capture, Manuel's cunning and ability to manipulate the truth in court, accurately and revealingly detailed by the authors, point to a complex, intriguing character.

Manuel's is an important case history for detailed documentation. It is in society's interest that the factors that allow individuals such as him to cut a bloody path through a more obedient, rule-abiding population be made explicit. It is to the further credit of MacLeod and McLeod that this document tells a coherent history in an engaging way to enable the widest audience possible to learn from a very real crime case.

Dr David Holmes, Senior Lecturer in Psychology, Director of the Forensic Research Group, Department of Psychology and Social Change, Manchester Metropolitan University

PREFACE

In the early 1960s, as a priest new to the parish, young Father Gibbons made as many pastoral visits as he could to meet his congregation in the stark and rain-swept North Lanarkshire village of Birkenshaw. It was populated mainly by second- and third-generation Irish Catholic immigrant families living in local-authority housing, the men labouring in the collieries and steelworks. The most devout of his flock were middle-aged housewives, who vied with each other to show their religious devotion by offering generous hospitality to the young priest.

Bridget was no exception; she had placed him in the best chair in her front room and plied him with tea and home baking as she enquired as to his welfare and how he was settling in. As the young father made polite conversation, he gazed casually round a room that looked just the same as a dozen others he'd visited recently. His eyes alighted upon a glass-fronted display cabinet against one wall, which housed the treasured but never used crystal glasses, a bone-china tea set and several mementos. As he took all this in, his attention became fixed upon a framed photograph behind the crockery. His polite smile froze as he realised he was looking at an image of Bridget's dead son, Peter Thomas Anthony Manuel, the most prolific serial killer in Scottish history.

* * *

He was a spy in Russia, his father was sent to the electric chair, he knew the inside story of a huge bullion robbery, he helped the FBI, he saved a plane from crashing when the pilot was taken ill, he was a brilliant defence counsel. He did so many things, affected so many lives.

He was hanged before he reached his thirty-second birthday, convicted of seven murders (he would be found guilty of an eighth after his death) and almost certainly responsible for more. He was Peter Manuel. This is his story.

So many killings. Where did it all start? In Glasgow, New York, Motherwell, Coventry? And when? In 1939, when he first broke the law? Before that? In his family, in infancy, perhaps even in the womb? Was it already too late when he was sent to approved school, to borstal or to HM Prison Peterhead? And, above all, why?

Although Manuel was charged with nine murders and found guilty of eight, it is generally believed that all nine were certainly committed by him. Here they are: 2 January 1956, Anne Kneilands, 17, smashed about the head until she was dead (blood and brain matter splashed 8 ft away); 17 September 1956, Marion Watt, her sister Margaret Brown and Vivienne, the teenage Watt daughter, the first two shot through the head as they slept, Vivienne punched in the face, perhaps viciously toyed with and then shot through the head; 8 December 1957, Sydney Dunn shot through the head and his throat cut; 28 December 1957, Isabelle Cooke, 17 years old, strangled with her bra; finally, Peter Smart, his wife Doris and their young son Michael, shot through the head as they slept, early on the morning of New Year's Day 1958.

Five killed in twenty-five days, and the others before that: he was a busy little killer. And there may have been more murders. Did Manuel kill the London prostitute, the female office worker in Glasgow or the prostitute in Glasgow? And were there others still? Why was he able to go on killing for so long? Was it, as some of the police later claimed, because there was never enough evidence to bring a charge until the very end? Or was it incompetence or bad luck? As the killings continued, questions were asked, searches made, dark suspicions whispered, but Manuel was able to carry on. Clever Peter, cunning Peter, killing Peter. But why?

CHAPTER ONE

On Monday, 6 January 1958, Scotland's workforce trudged back to the daily grind after the New Year holiday. At 8 a.m., outside the offices of W. & J.R. Watson Ltd, Building and Civil Engineering Contractors, on London Road in Glasgow's East End, something was amiss. Mr Peter Smart, the works manager, who kept the office and safe keys, was not there to open up. As the staff arrived, wishing each other a happy New Year, they became concerned, for he was usually punctual.

A time-served joiner, by sheer hard work he had advanced to his current position. During the Second World War, he had broadened his skills, constructing airfields for the RAF, and later he'd worked in Alnwick, Northumberland, before moving north to Glasgow some five years before. He hailed from the Scottish Borders near Jedburgh, where his father had been a chauffeur in service. Several years before, Smart had bought a small plot of land in the ancient Lanarkshire town of Uddingston on the eastern outskirts of Glasgow. There he had constructed a snug family bungalow, where he, his wife Doris and their son Michael lived. As the house was being built, neighbours watched the endearing sight of Michael, then a toddler, with his little wheelbarrow, solemnly helping his father.

Outside the office, the badinage about hangovers gave way to a more serious tone when, at 8.45, the firm's secretary, Miss McDonald, received a call from the police to say that Mr Smart's car had been found abandoned in Florence Street in the Gorbals, Glasgow's notorious slum district. His colleagues began to worry: clearly something was far from right.

The New Year's celebrations had already been overshadowed by news reports about the sinister disappearance of 17-year-old Isabelle Cooke, who lived about two miles from the London Road office and not far from the Smarts' home. Early in the evening of 28 December, she had left home to catch a bus to meet her boyfriend and go dancing. She had vanished into the winter darkness. Later various items of her clothing were found scattered about the countryside. Police were scouring a wide area but by this point there was little hope that she would be found alive.

Two employees, Alex McBride and William Blackwood, drove over to the Smart house. Several full milk bottles on the doorstep and drawn curtains heightened their suspicions. Thoroughly alarmed, they went to the nearby police station, reported their fears and then went back to ask neighbours for any information. When they returned to the house, they found Sergeant Hogg and a constable waiting. Gloomy foreboding pervaded the group. Neighbours had gathered to stare at the silent house. Sergeant Hogg decided to take action and forced the back door. The two police officers, McBride and Blackwood entered the house. Inside, all was cold and quiet; the Christmas decorations and drooping mistletoe added to the air of melancholy. The sergeant entered the two [illegible]kened bedrooms and was confronted by terrible scenes of carnage. [illegible]ly shocked, he managed to collect himself and told the [illegible]agedy had occurred as he ushered them outside.

Within minutes, Superintendent Murdo Mackenzie, the senior officer at nearby Bellshill police station, was at the scene. He steeled himself to view the inert forms of Peter and Doris Smart in one bedroom and of young Michael in the other. All had been killed by a single shot to the head as they slumbered. Peter and Doris lay in a last embrace. He, being further from the killer, had been shot through the forehead, while she had been shot through the right temple. For both, death must have been instantaneous for there was no sign of any disturbance in posture, though blood had gushed from their wounds and noses. In the next room, Michael lay tucked up in his bed, his NHS glasses neatly folded on the bedside table.

A few weeks before Christmas, Michael had written a school essay in which he described his family and the places where they had lived. His concluding sentence was: 'I have lived a happy life.' He was 12 when he was killed.

The Scottish press quickly bestirred themselves from their patchy reminiscences of their recent festive excesses and surged forth to glean every snippet of information on what they knew would be a major story. The afternoon and evening editions across Scotland were emblazoned with lurid and sensational headlines. The infant medium of television came into play and soon viewers were shown black-and-white images of the murder house and of police activity. In the days that followed, detectives found themselves, not for the first time in recent years, playing a game of hide and seek with the press while engaged in a deadly war of wits with their prime suspect.

The murders of the Smarts and the disappearance of Isabelle Cooke caused panic in the local community. Few people ventured out after dark. There was a sudden demand for guard dogs and, as supplies of door and window locks sold out, harried husbands removed bathroom locks to put on bedroom doors. Vigilante groups were quickly formed and patrolled the streets at night, while the police searched an increasingly wide area in the hope of finding the missing girl or clues to her fate.

Viewing the three bodies, Superintendent Mackenzie was immediately struck by the similarity of this atrocity to three murders that had been committed some fifteen months previously in Burnside, a few miles away. There three women – two middle-aged sisters, Mrs Marion Watt and Mrs Margaret Brown, and Mrs Watt's vivacious teenage daughter, Vivienne – had been shot through the head as they lay in bed. To Mackenzie, it seemed almost certain that whoever had killed the Watts had also murdered the Smarts.

The Watt murders were a source of scandal and embarrassment to the Lanarkshire police. Shortly after the bodies had been discovered, they had arrested the husband, William Watt. He was charged with the three murders, held in prison for over two months and then released without explanation. Although many people still believed he was guilty, officially the murders were an unsolved crime and nobody else had been charged.

The Watt murders were not the only unsolved ones in Lanarkshire. Isabelle Cooke's disappearance recalled the events of two years before when seventeen-year-old Anne Kneilands had been brutally murdered just after New Year 1956 in East Kilbride, less than five miles away. The Glasgow police also had two unsolved murders on their hands. In 1956, Anne Steele, a middle-aged spinster, had been beaten to death with a poker in her own home and Ellen 'English Nell' Petrie, a 50-year-old widow, stabbed to death in a city-centre back street. At the end of January 1957, a group of local businessmen had offered a reward of £900 to anyone who produced evidence that solved the Kneilands or Steele case. Nobody did.

In Northumbria, the Durham police had another recent murder to solve. Just a month previously, a taxi driver, Sydney Dunn, had been found shot dead and with his throat cut near the moorland village of Edmundbyers. He had been dragged into the heather some distance his taxi, which had been smashed up.

murders and the disappearance of Isabelle Cooke within the area policed by the Lanarkshire force, the body that had so far failed to solve the Kneilands and Watt killings. Significantly, there had been two key changes at the top of the force within the last few days: on 28 December, the chief constable, Thomas Renfrew, had retired and with him the most senior detective, James Hendry. The new chief constable, John Wilson, already burdened with the search for Cooke and now faced with a triple murder inquiry, quickly sought assistance from the far more experienced and expert Glasgow force.

As a result, Detective Superintendent Alex 'Father' Brown and Detective Inspector Tom Goodall of the Glasgow CID joined Superintendent Murdo Mackenzie, Chief Inspector William Muncie and Detective Inspector Robert McNeil from Lanarkshire County Police. This formidable group was convinced that they knew the identity of the killer. He was a notorious local small-time criminal, Peter Manuel, who, since the beginning of the previous month, had been under police scrutiny. Now they set out to uncover the evidence needed to arrest him. Both sets of detectives were highly conscious that, over the years, he had played a complicated, almost mocking game with the local police. They were determined that he should not escape justice again.

CHAPTER TWO

The police succeeded and Manuel was hanged on a fine summer morning in July 1958. The story of how he came to the gallows is a long one, marked by deceit, violence and numerous encounters with the police.

It began among one of the poorest and most disadvantaged groups in Scotland: the miners of Lanarkshire. For decades, this grey, rain-soaked region to the south of the Clyde had been one of the centres of British heavy industry. The area's eighteenth- and nineteenth-century change from an agricultural economy to heavy industry was due to the abundance of coal and iron ore that lay beneath its fields. Most of the hugely profitable mines, steel mills and engineering works were on land owned by the Dukes of Hamilton, who became enormously wealthy.

In the nineteenth century, the Duke's agents recruited coalminers from Ireland, both from the Catholic community and from the Protestant minority, which was largely of Scottish origin. Other

Catholic Irish, driven by the Great Famine, also arrived in Scotland, seeking any employment they could find. Some ended up as miners. For centuries, coal mining in Scotland had been a dangerous and badly paid occupation. Miners had almost no rights and working conditions were appalling. The immigration into the west of Scotland of people from the two separate Irish communities brought with it bitter sectarian rivalry and hatred. In mining areas, there were villages exclusively occupied by one group or the other and this separation continued even within the mines themselves. It was out of this background of poverty, deprivation and prejudice that the Catholic Manuel family emerged.

Manuel's paternal grandfather, James, was a miner and the son of a miner. In 1884, he married Catherine Guy, who, like him, lived at Hamilton. They were wed in the Roman Catholic chapel. James's bride had been born in the USA, perhaps indicating an unsuccessful migration on the part of her family. By 1901, according to that year's census, they had three children, the family living 'in the hamlet of Hamilton Palace Colliery'. Their accommodation was a cramped terraced cottage, without running water and with a cesspit for sanitation. The eldest child, Catherine, aged 15, worked on the surface in the colliery, raking impurities from the coal as it passed along a conveyor belt. James, 13, was already a miner. The youngest child, 11-year-old Gertrude, was at school. In May that year, a second son, Samuel, was born. He was to become Peter's father.

Samuel would grow up fatherless. In December of 1901, James died after nine months suffering from fibroid phthisis, sometimes called galloping consumption. Miners inhaled coal and rock dust, and their lungs became infected and lost their elasticity. James was 38 when he died.

In 1923, Samuel, also a coalminer and still living in the same place, married Bridget Greenan from nearby Motherwell. Although both came from Catholic families, they chose to be married by declaration in front of two witnesses, an unusual form of marriage but one legal in Scotland. Their marriage was regularised on the same day by a sheriff court warrant. There was a reason why the couple chose this type of wedding: Bridget was pregnant.

It is possible that shame or criticism played a part in persuading Samuel to seek a better life in the USA. He left Bridget, heavily pregnant, and sailed to New York. She joined him once she had given birth, leaving her first child, James, in the care of her mother. On 15 March 1927, she gave birth to her second child at the Misericordia Hospital in Manhattan. He was christened with three saints' names: Peter Thomas Anthony.

The Crash of 1929 destroyed many hopes and work had to be sought wherever there was the slightest chance it could be found. It appears that the Manuel family moved to the Midwest, for a Peter Manuel, born in America in 1927, is recorded in the 1930 census as living in Michigan, one of the centres of the US car industry. Things cannot have gone well in the USA, because two years later the Manuels recrossed the Atlantic and returned to Lanarkshire, settling in Motherwell.

Their arrival in Scotland was a double dislocation for five-year-old Peter. Not only had he left the land where he was born but he also met for the first time his brother James. He was no longer the sole child; now he had an older, bigger brother, who was part of a society that was entirely alien to him. Now he had to fit into a different family and a different world. He began his schooling at Our Lady of Good Aid Primary School in Motherwell. It is possible that as an incomer with an alien accent, ignorant of local customs, he may have found school difficult. Years later, James would claim that Peter had been put with older and more advanced children and that as a result he could not keep up and was mocked by teachers and classmates.

In 1937, a third child, Theresa, was born and the Manuels moved again, this time to Coventry, an important centre of British car manufacturing. Here, Peter resumed his education at St Elizabeth's and St Helen's Roman Catholic School. Their stay in Coventry did not last long: the Manuels' house was destroyed by bombing in November 1940 and they returned once again to Motherwell and the support of their relatives. This time, however, Peter did not go with them. He was already confined for his criminal acts.

At his Coventry school, Manuel was often in trouble. On one occasion, his class teacher found an 'unspeakably filthy' drawing on her desk, which was traced back to Manuel. When she confronted him, she reported, 'he showed no sign of remorse'. This absence of remorse was to characterise his behaviour for the rest of his life and was an early sign of his psychopathic personality. Nevertheless, according to his family, he was bright enough to be awarded a place at the King Henry VIII School, a grammar school. As things turned out, he was unable to take it up.

Manuel's first recorded crime was committed when he was 11: he broke into the offertory box in the church next to the school and stole the contents. His break-ins and thefts continued. Towards the end of October 1939, he was bound over for 12 months for shopbreaking and larceny. Just over a month later, he was back in the same court charged with breaking and entering. He was sentenced to serve time in an approved school.

An official account of his character and background accompanied him. It first describes his home and family: his father earns £3 5s 0d a week as a labourer, his mother is a housewife; they rent a house for 19 shillings a week on a busy main street in a working-class area; it has three rooms downstairs, three upstairs and is kept clean and tidy.

What the document cannot describe is what it was like for a young boy to live in that house, to be a member of that family. We can only guess at that. One thing, however, is known: big brother James had already been in trouble with the law and had himself been sent to an approved school. Peter was following his example. What was it in that family that caused those two boys to go astray so early in life?

Before he was sent into his new environment, Manuel was given a medical. The official report of the juvenile court states that he was in good health. He did not suffer from fits or incontinence, his mental ability for his age was normal and indeed he showed no signs of any physical or mental abnormality. Again and again in the future, Manuel would undergo similar examinations to see if he suffered from any mental abnormality. All of them concluded that he was sane from a legal standpoint.

The rest of the document picks out traits that were to become more and more manifest as Manuel's criminal career developed. It gives us our first clear sight of the child who was to grow into Peter Manuel, the multiple murderer. It depicts a young boy whose character is already seriously flawed – or damaged. He is a liar, he is deceitful and he tries to incriminate others falsely in his crimes:

> The school report of the probationer is anything but satisfactory. Out of school he is said to be always in trouble. At school he is said to be cunning, and puts on an air of innocence, and is very deep. He is deceitful, difficult to believe, and appears to be the ringleader on most occasions. At one time he was constantly at the dirt track, and suspected of theft. He seems to go where he pleases. Once he stayed out all night after being chased by the police for the suspected theft of a £1 note from a pocket book at the dirt track. The headmistress's final note was that the lad should be away from his present environment. He has led younger boys into trouble, and he consorts with those suspected of theft. Probationer, after committing the offence for which he appeared at Court on October 20th, was arrested by the Station Police at 10.30 p.m. as he was trying to obtain a ticket to go to Glasgow. He asked when at Court for five other shopbreaking offences to be taken into consideration. He tried to incriminate other boys, but the police satisfied themselves that nobody else was

> implicated. He hid a certain amount of money, and a total of £5 1s 9d was not recovered. The parents were ordered to refund this amount. I am not at all surprised that the boy has appeared again at Court, and there is no doubt whatever that the magistrates adopted a correct attitude and committed him to an approved school.

Perhaps at the request of his parents, Manuel was sent eventually to St William's Approved School at Market Weighton, Yorkshire, run by the Catholic De La Salle order. Although the school had a good reputation at the time, in December 2004 a former principal, James Carragher, was sentenced to a long term of imprisonment following his conviction on several counts of buggery and sexual assualt. He had perpetrated the abuse at the school throughout the 1970s and '80s. In 2006, some 140 former inmates were reported to be suing for compensation for beatings and sexual assualts. It is not impossible that during his time at the school Manuel might have suffered physical or sexual abuse.

Almost as soon as he had arrived at approved school, Manuel ran away. He became a persistent, even relentless escaper from the various approved schools to which he was sent and while he was on the run he would commit crime after crime until he was recaptured. His record from those days notes: 'Frequently absconded and charged with housebreaking offences.' However, the writer adds: 'While actually with us was well-behaved and appeared happy and contented.' There were always two sides to Manuel: the almost uncontrollable criminal and the person who could seem normal, even charming. He was presentable and, if not actually good-looking, he had a sort of dark attractiveness, his black hair carefully greased and combed back in a sweeping wave from his forehead.

What he did during those escapes was frightening, even in the early years. On one occasion in 1941 – he was then 14 – he broke into a house just a few yards from his approved school and stole a handbag. The woman of the house came upon him as he was leaving her bedroom; he was carrying an axe. As a result, she suffered a nervous breakdown.

In June 1942, he again absconded from his approved school and carried out three break-ins. During one of these, a woman asleep in her bed awoke to find him striking her about the head. She suffered concussion and a haemorrhage and spent some days in hospital. Recaptured, he pleaded guilty to assaulting the woman but would not or could not explain why he had attacked her. Assaults to the heads of victims continued to be a characteristic of Manuel's attacks. In his final years, he would bludgeon one victim's skull and shoot others through the head.

Manuel's crimes continued. On 16 September 1942, he appeared in court at Hull on two charges of housebreaking and one of absconding from an approved school. He was sentenced to serve a further six months there. A mere ten days later, he appeared at Beverley charged with the theft of a bicycle and housebreaking. On 4 November, having escaped again, he appeared at Market Weighton charged with housebreaking.

When he was 15, he escaped yet again and his next crime was even more serious. He grabbed the wife of one of the school's staff members, hit her round the head with a stick, dragged her 140 yards into a wood, removed most of her clothing and tried to rape her. Why he desisted is not known; perhaps he ejaculated prematurely. The woman suffered a broken nose and shoulder bone.

About this time, he committed another type of offence: according to a school report, he committed 'wanton damage of an unbelievable nature to the content of a room, including malicious cutting of bedding and clothing and destroying foodstuffs'. Often in the future, when he broke into houses, he would vandalise them, pouring food onto the floor, stubbing cigarettes out on the carpet and dirtying the bedding. He seemed determined to create messes in the most personal and private spaces of other people.

After the attempted rape, Manuel was sent to borstal at Hollesley Bay, near Woodbridge in Suffolk. In an idyllic setting, this converted country estate was Britain's only borstal farm. We know a considerable amount about the life of inmates there as the Irish writer Brendan Behan served time at Hollesley Bay after being caught on an IRA bombing mission. He completed his sentence a few months before Manuel arrived. In his novel *Borstal Boy*, he describes an institution run by ex-military staff who showed less aggression towards the inmates than the prison staff he had encountered. The governor is portrayed as an amiable, enlightened and well-intentioned man who took a serious interest in the welfare of the inmates and tried to protect them from bullying. Prisoners worked on the farm and maintained the buildings, learning skills that would be of some use on the outside. Manuel learned woodwork.

A borstal official noted another highly significant aspect of Manuel's character: 'He liked to hear himself talk.' He adds that Manuel is 'the world's worst liar and does not know it'. This is doubly ambiguous: does it mean he did not know his lies were unconvincing or that he was unaware that he was lying? Was he the 'world's worst' because his lies were so blatantly false or because they were so numerous? However we choose to interpret the remark, Manuel would remain a liar throughout his life, a liar on an exceptional scale, a liar of exceptional ability. A police officer who knew him well described him as 'an inveterate liar' and he went on lying almost to the moment he was hanged. He had one outstanding ability that helped him to do so: he was gifted with an extremely good memory. He could remember facts and weave them into his tales and he could also remember the lies he had spun previously so that he did not contradict himself.

As if to balance this negative judgement, or perhaps to highlight an underlying puzzle about him, the official who noted his lying also recorded: 'Nevertheless he has many likeable characteristics.' Others were to confirm that Manuel did have an ability to make some people like him. At times, he could even show a sort of charm, especially to women.

More escapes were followed by more crimes. On 27 July 1943, Manuel appeared before magistrates at Chatham on a charge of housebreaking and after a day in prison was returned to his borstal. Whether he was further punished for escaping cannot be established but it would be surprising if he had not been. In the 1940s, corporal punishment was a major disciplinary tool. Summary punishment in the form of slaps around the face and head was commonly administered by staff in approved schools and borstals. Formal punishments included flogging with a cane or with a scourge made of birch branches conforming to a statutory weight and length.

The borstal was, of course, an all-male community. In Behan's *Borstal Boy*, an IRA inmate warns:

> They [the prisoners] talk about things, aye and do things, that the lowest ruffian in Ireland, Catholic or Protestant, wouldn't put his tongue to the mention of, things that you could be born, grow up and die an old man in our country without ever hearing the mention of.

The things to which this puritanical IRA man alluded were almost certainly homosexual practices. In the society in which Manuel grew up, homosexuality was not only abhorrent in the sight of the church, the media and the general public but also a criminal offence. Indeed, the crime of buggery was considered so unspeakable that many people were unaware that such behaviour existed.

Researchers have found that in borstals and other prisons, as within English public schools, homosexual behaviour was not uncommon. Within such closed institutions male rape, that most under-reported of offences, was used as a method of subjugating the victim and as an expression of dominance and power. It is not impossible that in borstal Manuel became familiar with this variety of sexual activity and learned to associate sexual behaviour with violence and the exercise of power to an even greater degree than he had done before.

When he eventually emerged from borstal and returned to live with his family, it is possible that, if he had been involved in homosexual practices, he found himself confused about his sexuality. This is speculation. What was certainly the case was that the working-class Catholic world of miners and steelworkers he re-entered was a misogynistic, macho society. Males earned their living through their physical strength and tough young men won the respect of their peers by their fists. They boasted of their sexual conquests (with the emphasis on conquest) and flaunted their masculinity. Whatever Manuel's insecurities and inclinations, this was an environment likely only to exacerbate them.

CHAPTER THREE

Manuel was released in March 1945 into a world still at war. He was an American citizen and, his family would later say, he had already applied to join the US Armed Forces. Perhaps not surprisingly, this offer was not accepted. He was sent call-up papers for the British Army but the Ministry of Labour did not pursue the matter, possibly because of his criminal record, possibly because he told them of his US citizenship. Later that year, Manuel appeared in Blackpool, where he worked for a few months in the amusement arcades frequented by holidaymakers from the mills and factories of Lancashire. He ran what he described as a 'roulette' stall (probably a 'Wheel of Fortune', where participants won prizes if the pointer fixed on the wheel stopped at a particular position). It may be that he also used his talent for sketching to draw caricatures for small sums. Little is known about this time in Blackpool, a place to which he returned from time to time, although it was later claimed that he had carried a gun on the Golden Mile and it is recorded that he was questioned by police about an assault on an elderly night watchman. The man who gave him an alibi later thought that Manuel might have slipped out to commit the assault while he was asleep.

When he left Blackpool and returned to live with his family in their three-bedroom council house at 23 Rosepark Avenue, Viewpark. Viewpark and the neighbouring Birkenshaw were schemes to rehouse miners and steelworkers in more modern and hygienic surroundings. They marked a huge improvement, providing tenants with running water, gas and electricity. Once again, Manuel was among his parents' coreligionists, for most of the families in Viewpark were Catholic. No doubt his mother and father hoped that he would settle down, take a regular job and put his criminal activities behind him. But he quickly showed that the world of his parents, with its unrelenting labour and constant threat of utter poverty, was not for him. Shortly after his return, he plunged again into crime.

The underworld would be Manuel's chosen milieu for the rest of his life. Crime for him was not simply a matter of how he got his money but of how he saw himself. Over the years, through his crimes and his fantasies, he created in his mind a Peter Manuel who was different from and superior to those around him. That Peter Manuel could exist only in a world that was set apart from the day-to-day drudgery of mundane employment. When, from time to time, he was forced to take unskilled jobs, he regarded them as inconvenient aspects of a secondary existence, an existence he despised. From this point on, all that was vivid and exciting in his life occurred in the world of crime and criminals. That was where his true life was lived.

So, crime gave him his excitement and it gave him his living. To separate himself further from the dreary dullness of his family and his impoverished surroundings, he drew on his American birth: he cultivated a fake US accent, was an avid viewer of gangster movies and read eagerly about the careers of such figures as 'Baby Face' Nelson and Al Capone. Eventually, he began to talk about himself in the third person, not as 'me' but as 'Manuel'.

Once back in Lanarkshire, he began stealing by breaking and entering, using the skills and techniques he had been developing since he was 11 years old. Providing he was not caught, thieving was a good way to live: the hours were extremely short, he had to work for no one but himself and theft brought in more money than any honest employment could. In 1945, Manuel did work briefly as a labourer, for four different firms, but the longest he lasted in any one job was three weeks. Why should he bother? The wage for a week's labouring – at most £4 before tax – was a lot less than he could get in a few minutes by breaking into a house.

Some insight into his local depredations can be gained by describing his activity during one short period. On 24 May 1945, he broke into a house in Motherwell; on the 28th, he burgled another in the same area, then another on the night of the 30th; on the 31st, he broke into yet another. Householders and police were shocked by the sudden increase in crime in the area.

Most of these break-ins were committed close to where he lived; he was unconcernedly preying on members of his own community. He would slip out at night, walk to his victims' houses and return home under cover of darkness. He preferred to operate within a very small area; sometimes he raided houses a few doors away from each other in the same street. Over a short period, he broke into no fewer than seven houses in four interconnecting streets. Sometimes he went a little further to steal, travelling to nearby Uddingston and Mount Vernon, areas he was to revisit in the closing months of his life with far worse consequences.

One of his thefts took him to a place that was to become particularly significant. On 6 January 1946, he broke into 29 Sheepburn Road, Uddingston, and stole a gold watch, a gold bracelet watch, a gold chain, a bottle of whisky, a fountain pen, a torch and ten shillings. It was a typical theft, with nothing to distinguish it from any of his others. The link with Sheepburn Road continued. In 1948, he wrote from Peterhead prison to a woman who lived at No. 15. Finally, he returned to the street early on New Year's Day 1958 – and killed the Smarts.

These thefts straddled the closing months of the war and the first year of the peace. It was a time of great hardship, austerity and shortages. Almost everything was rationed and supplies were short. Few luxuries were being produced, as wartime and immediate post-war production was concentrated on essentials. As a result, there was a strong black market for expensive pre-war items such as gold or silver cigarette cases, lighters and even fountain pens – all things that were easy to conceal and transport. Alcohol was also in desperately short supply and bottles of wine or spirits could easily be turned into cash.

Most of Manuel's break-ins produced a mixed bag. Another typical haul, taken in 1945, comprised a purse, three fountain pens, a cigarette lighter, three books of clothing coupons, a gold ring, a gold pendant and £2 15s. Manuel was always happy to find the highly saleable pieces of paper upon which people depended: petrol coupons, National Savings Certificates, identity cards and clothing coupons. From a house in Motherwell, for example, he stole: 'one watch, one ring, two wallets, two purses, one key, one pair of socks, two identity cards, one book of clothing coupons, one fountain pen, one badge and £8 0s 0d of money.' Besides the high-value things such as rings and watches, some of the items he stole were almost pathetic: one pair of socks, two towels, one pair of spectacles.

Did his family suspect nothing? Did they not know he was out at night? How did he explain away the money he had? Did they have no doubts about his activities and his explanations? It seems his family were unwilling to consider the matter too carefully or question him too closely. His mother would later say that when she asked him where he was when he stayed out all night, he told her he stayed with friends.

Manuel's resumption of trade as a housebreaker came to an abrupt halt when, in the early afternoon of a spring day in 1946, he sauntered out of a bungalow in Mount Vernon and was apprehended by DC William Muncie. Earlier in the day, Muncie and other officers had investigated a break-in at the bungalow. By pure chance, he had returned just as Manuel was leaving. Later, Muncie discovered that, while they were searching for evidence, Manuel had been concealed in the roof space. He had fitted his hiding place out with bedding. As the householder was away on holiday, Manuel may have been bedded down there for more than one night. He had coolly waited for the police to depart before making his escape, comfortable and secure in his hiding place, perhaps even amused and excited at being so close and yet completely invisible.

Needless to say, when he was apprehended he tried to lie his way out of trouble. He claimed he had only been acting as a lookout and named another man, who, he told Muncie, was still inside the bungalow. That proved to be false. Lying and trying to incriminate others: there had been no change in his behaviour since the age of 12.

During his time at approved school, he had done something similar to concealing himself in the roof space: he had hidden within the school, leading staff to believe he had run away. Manuel cherished the ability to become invisible. Over the years, night and the near invisibility that darkness confers were his allies. All of his crimes were committed at night and he specialised in moving about in dark byways and unfamiliar routes, cutting along railway lines, across back gardens and through woods. Being unobserved, being nearly invisible, gave him a sense of power, a feeling of being cleverer than those around him, able to observe them but be unseen.

Two more things are noteworthy about the arrest. First, Manuel had left peculiar traces of his presence in the house: tins of fruit had been opened and their contents scattered on the carpet, an act of wilful vandalism similar to that which he had committed when in detention. Second, when he was apprehended, Manuel was immaculately dressed and his hair well groomed. All his life, even as he prepared to go to the scaffold, he strove to appear smart.

Manuel was charged with housebreaking and his father Samuel, now a local councillor with some political influence, appeared with him in court and gave assurances of his future good behaviour. On the strength of these undertakings, he was allowed to find bail. The family somehow scraped together the £60 needed.

At this point, Samuel had to answer a standard set of questions for the authorities to help them decide what should happen to Peter. His answers give us an insight into Manuel's personality and behaviour and his relationship with his father. One question asks about Peter's educational level. Samuel, in his painstakingly careful handwriting, answers: 'Can't state seems intelligent.' (We reproduce Samuel's answers exactly as he wrote them.) He adds that Peter 'Claims he got Communist tuition at Borstal and would not attend Church since leaving Borstal might be a bit atheistic.' It is a fair guess his father disliked this, since the other members of the Manuel family were regular churchgoers. All except Peter attended Mass on the day he killed his final three victims.

'Was he obedient at home, and did he keep regular hours?'

'Very obedient until 11 years old and then got into trouble and sentenced to approved School.'

'What is the character of his companions, and how does he spend his leisure time?'

'One of his companions seemed to be a Fence and seemed to be getting rid of stolen property for him, we only discovered this after his arrest his other two companions seemed to be alright, he was very fond of Pictures [films] this seemed to be his only form of recreation.'

'Has he any knowledge of a trade? If so, what?'

'Good knowledge of wood turning very clever at wood Work and Cobbling, knowledge of french polishing. Seems very clever as an artist can let you have his book of drawings if you wish.'

Manuel was always keen on drawing and painting; art was one of his favourite activities during his years of detention. He even sketched when he was on trial for his life. The woodwork training he had received stayed with him in one way: ever afterwards, in court documents and in the press, he would be described as a woodworker or a woodturner, although it is doubtful whether he ever touched a chisel after he left borstal, except as an aid to breaking into houses.

The next question asks about Peter's employment. Samuel answers that his son had held four labouring jobs since the end of March 1945. 'If unemployed, how long has he been idle?' continues the questionnaire, and it is at this point that the hard-working Samuel's feelings become more apparent. He replies, 'Was idle most of the time he only worked on the average of three weeks at a time tells awful lies, that's the reason we don't know why he left his jobs, he usually said paid off, been idle since Dec 1945.'

'Has he ever suffered from any serious illness – physical or mental? If so, state nature of same.' Here, in his father's answer, there is a tantalising hint that might, if only we knew more, help to explain Peter's behaviour: 'Suffers from heavy nose bleeds since 3 years old had Tonsils removed at age 7 years this did not help him, last June had a nose bleed at Blackpool and took mental Black out, Very nervous and has violent temper.' 'Took mental Black out . . . has violent temper.' What does it mean?

'Can you give any other information which might be useful in dealing with his case?'

'Has Vivid Imagination. Always seems tired and sleeps to much. Seems to brilliant for his age.'

All this shows that in 1946 Samuel had few illusions about Peter's behaviour. His tone, in so far as it can be sensed from his brief answers, is one of worry and doubt about his son, perhaps tinged with anger at what he had done and apprehension about what he might do next. This is his son, a boy who may be too brilliant for his age, who sleeps too much, who is a terrible liar, an idler, who recently blacked out, a boy who has been in trouble since the age of eleven. What is to be done with him?

That is exactly the final question the document asks: 'Are you prepared to give him a home and supervision when he is again at liberty?' Samuel's answer, for good or ill, is a simple 'Yes'.

CHAPTER FOUR

Theft by breaking and entering was not the only crime Manuel committed following his return to Scotland. In the spring of 1946, there was a series of sexually motivated attacks in the vicinity of Uddingston. The first victim, a young mother, was attacked on 3 March as she walked along an isolated path in nearby Mount Vernon with her three-year-old child. Her attacker was surprised at the ferocity of her resistance. Though forced to the ground, she screamed and shouted as loudly as she could. The attacker made off but when her screams continued he returned to kick her about the body until she fell back to the ground. He then disappeared into the darkness. DC Muncie searched the scene and found several strands of long, dark and well-oiled hair. He also found a cap that had been reduced in size by a couple of stitches in the rim. Muncie, suspecting Manuel, went to his home but he was nowhere to be found. He did, however, discover a cap that had been altered in the same way.

On the evening of 7 March, at about 9.30 p.m., a young nurse was trudging home along Calder Road, Bellshill, a few miles to the east of Birkenshaw, returning from her duties at a nearby hospital, carrying a suitcase. She was attacked by a man who placed his hand across her mouth whilst trying to subdue her by punching her to the ground. Fortunately, she was able to dislodge his hand long enough to get out a loud scream, which drew the attention of a passing motorcyclist. He and another passer-by stopped to come to her aid and the attacker made off. She was able to provide a clear description of her assailant. This pointed to Peter Manuel.

On 8 March, it was dark by 9.30 p.m., when a housewife in her late 20s set out to walk the last mile home along a lonely road to the district of Fallside, a couple of miles from Viewpark. Soon, she felt that she was being followed, although she could see no one. Suddenly, she was set upon and forced to the ground, her cries stifled by a hand across her mouth. She tried to bite the hand but her head was dashed against the ground and she was told in no uncertain terms to be still and quiet. She pleaded with her attacker and offered him her purse, but he ignored her. He pulled her to her feet and, with one arm twisted behind her back, she was roughly shoved towards where a railway bridge straddled the road. As she pleaded with him, saying that she was unwell and had just got out of hospital (where she had been treated for TB), her attacker punched her and forced her forward onto the railway embankment. It was clear that this place had been particularly selected to avoid interruption. Having forced her to the ground, he ripped off her clothes and raped her. He then tied her scarf tightly round her eyes and ran off.

When the woman had related all this to the police, DC Muncie had little hesitation in identifying his suspect. Peter Manuel was arrested by Sergeant Murdo Mackenzie the next day. In an identification parade, he was picked out as the attacker of the nurse and of the young mother, who fainted at the sight of him. The victim of the rape did not identify him but there was other evidence. At the site were found strands of her clothing that had torn off on barbed wire, as well as fragments of her dentures, broken in the attack. Footprints were found leading to the scene that matched the heel of one of Manuel's shoes. Close examination of the fabric of his clothing produced particles that matched the dust on the embankment. There were also semen-stained items of clothing and other medical evidence.

The police needed to carry out various tests to support a charge of rape and so, at first, Manuel was charged only with the two sexual assaults. He was remanded in custody. On 25 June 1946, he appeared at Glasgow High Court where the Crown dropped the indecent assault charges and pursued the rape charge only. Manuel defended himself with some proficiency but the prosecution had little difficulty convincing the jury: they took only 15 minutes to find him guilty. He was sentenced to eight years in prison. He lodged an appeal, which he intended to conduct in person, but abandoned it just before the hearing.

While he had been in prison awaiting trial, he'd been charged by Muncie with 21 cases of breaking and entering. He was eventually charged in court with 18 and found guilty of 15. At his trial for those offences, he was sentenced to 12 months' imprisonment.

Manuel decided to appeal. On 19 October, he was transferred to HMP Edinburgh, commonly known as Saughton prison, from Barlinnie to await the hearing. It quickly became clear he was a troublesome prisoner. Already, in Barlinnie, he had incurred six disciplinary reports and at his new prison he was soon undergoing punishment for 'disobedience and insolence'. He was described as being 'very unsettled' and his behaviour was viewed with grave suspicion: 'He is an ex-borstal boy and has repeatedly tried to contact boys in the borstal section here.' Why he was trying to do this is not stated. There is a possible implication of homosexuality; perhaps, though, he was simply trying to impress younger prisoners with his greater criminal status. Either way, the authorities believed he needed to be watched very carefully. A 'reliable prisoner' told them that 'Manuel intended to escape from custody at the first opportunity'. In view of Manuel's own wish to be returned to Barlinnie to be nearer to his family, the governor at Saughton recommended that the transfer be effected. No doubt to his considerable relief, the recommendation was rapidly accepted and Manuel was sent back to the Glasgow prison.

Manuel still refused to accept that he was guilty of rape. We know that he was incensed about the physical evidence that convicted him. His ire was focused on Sergeant Mackenzie, who, he claimed, had framed him. He had good reasons to maintain this claim: first, it allowed his mother to believe that her boy was not a rapist; second, those convicted of sexual crimes, particularly the rape of a defenceless housewife, would be despised by fellow prisoners and liable to be beaten up.

Finally, after months in Barlinnie and Saughton, it was decided that Manuel, as a long-term prisoner, had to serve his sentence in Peterhead prison.

CHAPTER FIVE

Manuel arrived at HM Prison Peterhead in March 1947. This was the toughest prison in Scotland, housing many of its hardest criminals. Its officers had a reputation for beating up inmates; sources describe them forming a 'batter squad' to punish any prisoner who attacked one of their number. It was Scotland's Alcatraz, a place from where few escaped and those who did soon learned just how bleak, cold and inhospitable the Buchan countryside could be.

Most Peterhead prisoners were seasoned criminals who had spent many years behind bars and were tough, sullen towards authority and wary of newcomers. Within the prison community, there was a hierarchy of status: the most respected were the safe-crackers, men who specialised in opening bank and office safes with skill and the application of gelignite in sufficient quantities; those incarcerated for sexual offences were at the other end of the scale, despised by prisoners and staff alike.

Most inmates had to work in the nearby quarries, daily facing hard labour. Peterhead winters were bitterly cold, summers often almost as bleak. As far as Manuel was concerned, there were further disadvantages: he was a long way from his family and he was a convicted sex offender.

Things started badly. His first letter, to his mother, was immediately suppressed by the prison authorities. It starts almost jokingly: '[Peterhead is] some place, all you can see, is the sea.' He tells his mother he is allowed to receive books and magazines, though not newspapers. He asks for a toothbrush and toothpaste, as 'it is a long time since I cleaned my teeth'. He hopes that his father and his sister Theresa 'are keeping fine' but makes no mention of his brother James. His father, he mentions, had intended to do something about his case but he now thinks it is best to leave things as they are.

So far, so good. These are the sorts of things any prisoner might write in a letter home. Suddenly, though, the mood becomes much darker:

> You see I am prepared to do the eight years because I will have the satisfaction of giving McKenzie [*sic*] the little article he was looking for. You tell me I am best to do my time and forget him but unfortunately for Mr McKenzie I am not made like you, I know from your point of view that sounds all right. But it is me who is doing the sentence. I am watching the best years of my life roll away and I can tell you that after doing a year, it's no picnic, that is why I say it is no good giving advice my mind is made up. McKenzie is going to get it. But from what you have told me he has been on to you as well. [Presumably he was trying to bring other crimes home to Manuel.] Well next time you see him, remind him that he has a wife and kids too and 5 years and 3 months, to make the best of it but mind and stress the 'wife and kids' bit, he will understand.

And then he ends as any dutiful son might: 'Well I think that's all for now, So cheerio, Your Loving Son, Peter.'

It is obvious why the letter was suppressed. The straightforward threat to harm, possibly to murder, Mackenzie and his family is chilling. It reveals Manuel's conviction that anyone who harmed him deserved to suffer greatly. Years later, threatened with violence, he is reported to have responded with, 'Nobody does that to Manuel.'

During all these years, inside prison and out, he was creating for himself a separate personality: Manuel the exceptional being, someone with links to the US underworld, powerful, important, clever and, eventually, beyond the grasp of the law. Manuel believed he was special and that anyone who harmed or threatened him therefore deserved retribution. Normal rules of conduct did not – could not – apply in his exceptional case: 'I am not made like you.'

Prison set up a dichotomy in Manuel's perception of himself with which he struggled to cope. On the one hand, in his own eyes, Peter Manuel was an exceptional creature of great gifts and ability; on the other hand, he was prisoner 4379, forced to serve eight years and subject to all the indignities and controls of the penal system. At times, the conflict between the two would cause Manuel to erupt in outbreaks of violence.

There was a further problem: he was once again immersed in an all-male society. It is reasonable to think that sexual frustration was added to all his other frustrations. Some, perhaps all, of his previous heterosexual experiences had been violent ones. Now, locked away at night, did he fantasise on this link between sex and violence? Did he recall with excitement raping his victim? Was this what led eventually to another attempted rape and the deaths of three adolescent girls? We can only speculate.

Manuel was soon in trouble. Prisoners were sent to work at Stirlinghill Quarry, which was connected to the prison by a closed narrow-gauge railway. For obvious reasons, explosives were not used at the quarry. Instead, a prisoner would dangle from a rope down the face of the quarry and swing a hammer against the rock face to dislodge large stones to be broken up below. Towards the end of April, Manuel took exception to one of the guards, who, at the line-up to board the little train, had ordered him to undertake this task. His view was that the guard didn't know what he was doing and so he would not obey. Clearly words were exchanged and Manuel's hair-trigger temper got him into serious trouble. He made to punch the guard, who, with his colleagues, immediately set upon Manuel and beat him to the ground. There are in his prison file a number of letters from other prisoners complaining to the governor that Manuel had been subjected to excessive violence. (Perhaps by this time he had been accepted by his fellow prisoners, at least to some degree.) However, disobeying and insulting a guard was a breach of discipline and he cannot have been surprised to have been punished.

The records of Manuel's time in Peterhead include many examples of his recalcitrant attitude towards the prison authorities and his uncontrollable temper. There is no doubt he was an exceedingly troublesome prisoner. Successive governors and prison officers (and he would encounter again some of the latter when he was being tried for his life) regarded him with irritation, dislike and suspicion. He was never satisfied with the way he was treated and made numerous formal requests for things to be altered to suit him: he wants to listen to the radio broadcast of a football international, to have the small cell window left open to increase ventilation, the light to be left on till later in the evening, to have his worn-out boots replaced. The food is not always to his satisfaction: 'complains about getting no meat', 'complains about rations (bacon)', 'Breakfast too late and cold', the records note. The latter complaint gets a dusty answer: 'Own fault. Hurry up with slops.' In other words, Manuel must be quicker to empty out the urine and faeces collected overnight in the bucket in his cell.

There are more serious matters. He complains that a prison officer who threatened him has not been punished; he is told the man has been reprimanded. He complains about being kept in his cell and that a search of it was 'not a fair search'; the official response is: 'No complaint, search legitimate.' At this point, he asks, 'How long am I to remain in cells?' A prison officer responds: 'I have no idea.' Manuel writes to his parents about this but the authorities suppress his letter. During one eight-day period, Manuel bombards the governor with no fewer than six petitions. Sometimes, it seems, he had a legitimate grievance. When he complains that one of the officers called him a shitehouse, the officer concerned denies it, claiming that he might have said that someone was 'in the shitehouse' (meaning the lavatory was occupied). The response is hardly convincing.

Manuel wrote regularly to his family and received letters in return. Mostly, he wrote to his mother but he also sent letters to his brother James, who was serving time in prisons at Manchester, Durham and Edinburgh.

In March 1948 the prison authorities suppressed another letter. It has a certain grim humour (and Manuel could be amusing when it suited him). He apologises to his parents for the delay in replying to their last letter and goes on to explain:

> I have been in a spot of trouble, so I was tossed in the cooler . . . I can assure you I will benefit from the experience, if you believe the old adage honesty is the best policy you have got to alter it in here. You see one of the warders was going his paces, when it came to my turn, I informed him with all sincerity and from the bottom of my heart that if he didn't go away I would kick him in the teeth. Now in so saying this I was saying the truth. I was accordingly punished, now if I had went against the intention in my mind and told a lie, and said I won't kick you in the teeth, I would not have been

> punished, so the moral is, if you are going to belt anybody, don't let them know.

His letter concludes with enquiries about his sister's progress in learning shorthand. He himself is up to 'exercise 27 in Pitmans', he says, and 'that's one thing I can certainly say about this place, you've got oceans of time to study, I am learning Russian from one of the boys'. Was this true or was it another of his lying boasts?

At Peterhead, Manuel was regularly punished for breaking the rules. During 1948, he received eight such punishments, in the following year four. From time to time, he was involved in serious outbreaks of violence. On 10 April 1950, a Sunday morning, he was told to help gather in the breakfast crockery. He complained that he had already done his turn. When the guard insisted, Manuel lost his temper and threw a tray over the railing and down three floors, where it crashed to the ground. He then picked up a tea urn and smashed up a glass-windowed archway, shattering some 30 panes of glass. Punishment followed: he was given 14 days' special diet (a sort of oat gruel), 14 days' solitary confinement, 28 days of no exercise and no contact with other prisoners and 28 days without tobacco or payment. He also lost 84 days of remission. There followed a torrent of letters of complaint from Manuel, each annotated by prison staff with a comment on his uncooperative and sullen nature.

On 6 March 1951, he was again being punished, for resisting a search of his cell. On this occasion, he lost the privilege of being sent to Barlinnie to allow his parents an annual visit. Again, he complained in violent terms. In one of his diatribes, he reminded the authorities that he was an American and, as a jibe, suggested: 'It is a pity you don't deport me!' In May, he assaulted two prison officers and as he was 'being escorted to cells, he struggled and other inmates demonstrated'. In February of the following year, he was involved in an attempted mutiny.

During quieter times, he continued to draw. Throughout his time at Peterhead, he had sketchbooks and painting materials sent in and was allowed to keep the books in his cell. A year or so before his discharge, he asked to take a course in commercial art but this was not allowed. Much to his chagrin, he was told that, after testing, 'you were not good enough' for the course. This must have been an enormous blow to his ego.

As he said in one of his letters to his mother, being in jail provided 'oceans of time to study'. Besides his claim to be learning Russian, he acquired an Italian grammar and joined a discussion group. He was allowed to get books from the county library as well as having them sent in by his family; at one point, he complained about the quality of the library books. He enquired about boxing classes, joined the PT class, played football and took part in a Christmas concert.

Despite all these opportunities, there was in his behaviour a constant undertow of rebellion and contempt for authority. In another suppressed letter, written in August 1950, after mentioning the weather and enquiring about an uncle and aunt, he says, 'We have a new Governor, maybe now the place will get some improvements, the last guy was hopeless as a Governor, but after dutifully doing his time he was in due course liberated.' Whatever ironic humour there is in this remark, it clearly did not please the authorities.

In March 1951, yet another letter was suppressed. Writing to his father, he claimed he had been in solitary confinement for several weeks but that nobody would tell him why or when he would be released. On previous occasions, he admits, 'I broke certain rules and as can only be expected I was punished.' This time, however, 'I asked the Governor how long [I was to be held] and he said he had not the slightest idea . . . but it would be a very long time . . . one officer said I was down here for a year.' He says that he has written to the Secretary of State for Scotland asking to be told the reason for his solitary confinement and he now asks his father to do the same and to ask their local MP to look into the matter.

There was, apparently, an additional reason for his unhappiness. On the day he wrote this letter, he claimed, he was due to be transferred to Barlinnie and was looking forward to his family visiting him there. 'You better tell Granny and all at Forgewood I will not be getting down to see them, as I am stuck here on the orders of somebody in the department.' A brief annotation gives a prison official's view of the veracity of this claim: 'When did you apply to go to Barl.? liar.'

Manuel made one significant alliance in Peterhead: he met and befriended Charles Tallis, who was to play a large part in his life. Convicted of housebreaking, Tallis had arrived at Peterhead in the winter of 1949. He soon came to enjoy Manuel's company, especially when Manuel gave him some of his tobacco ration, although, according to Tallis, he spent most of his prison earnings on chewing gum, hair oil and toothpaste. The gum may have been part of Manuel's wish to be an American. Certainly, according to an anonymous newspaper article, possibly by Tallis, 'He talked a great deal about the American underworld. He had a mania for gangster stories, could recite the lives of Capone, Dillinger and Baby Face Nelson.'

By October 1951, Manuel was approaching the end of his sentence, yet he was still causing trouble. After so many breaches of discipline, and the punishments that inevitably followed, the prison authorities finally decided he needed his head examined. They arranged for him to be seen by a registrar at the Aberdeen Royal Infirmary's psychiatric clinic. They did this 'because he was not responding to prison discipline. He has been segregated since February of this year, when he was involved in an attempted mutiny – which he does not deny.'

As so often with Manuel, two versions of the story emerge. The first is the one Manuel told the psychiatrist. He broke prison rules, he said, because he had been disappointed. He had wanted to learn a trade in Peterhead but his application had been turned down by the governor. When a new governor had been appointed, his hopes had risen. Here we get an insight into Manuel's enquiring mind: he had 'carefully read up in a magazine' the new man's record at Perth prison. But the new governor also refused to let him learn a trade. After this, Manuel claimed that 'he did not care what happened, although, since segregated, he had taken pains not to behave in such a way that he would lose more remission'. It was, it seemed, all the fault of others: he had wanted to improve himself but this entirely reasonable ambition had been frustrated.

None of this impressed the examining doctor, who gave a very different interpretation of events. His summary of Manuel's character is totally damning:

> His record from the age of 12 makes it clear he is an aggressive psychopath. He has had all the benefits of the Juvenile Court treatment and Borstal treatment and it is doubtful whether, even at the beginning of his sentence, any constructive work could have been done with him. There is nothing I can suggest now.

He adds, almost as an afterthought, 'He is likely to be of better than average intelligence.'

'There is nothing I can suggest now.' The words are horrific for they accept there is no way Manuel can be reformed. Here is a criminal, probably more intelligent than most, who has been an aggressive psychopath from his early years and who cannot be changed. It is a frightening diagnosis. It was to be proved entirely correct within a few years.

Manuel resented being examined in this way and demanded to know why he had been sent. He was always deeply hostile to any suggestion that he might be mad or in any way mentally abnormal. Maybe he had a deep secret fear that this was actually the case or perhaps, what is more likely, his vanity did not allow him to think it possible.

The diagnosis of Manuel as an aggressive psychopath is important. It makes sense of many of the things that he had done up to that point and it predicts many things he would do afterwards. Since his first detention, he had shown many of the key characteristics of a psychopath: a willingness, even a compulsion, to lie; a total lack of empathy with other people; a desire to manipulate and deceive them; and a conviction that he possessed special abilities. Like many psychopaths, he was clever and he could be charming and amusing when he wanted, but he was also prone to sudden outbreaks of violence.

Psychopathy is a personality disorder. It appears that it is caused by a constellation of many factors, possibly including a genetic predisposition characterised by actual structural differences in parts of the brain, particularly in the limbic system. Other factors may include abuse or other childhood trauma of such severity that the mind immures itself by constructing a personality so self-absorbed, narcissistic and grandiose in outlook that it is incapable of normal emotion. The absence of feelings of love and an inability to feel for and empathise with others leads to a lack of remorse or any feelings of guilt. This in turn leads to the psychopath being intractable. He does not learn from imprisonment or other punishment and attempts to reform him are of no avail.

The psychopath may have a deep-seated contempt for and rage against his fellows and is capable of extreme sadism. He seeks to exert power over others in order to bolster his magnificent self-image. He is easily roused to temper and violence. He is incapable of seeing other people as being of value and despises them.

Psychopaths can appear superficially charming and attractive but they are habitual liars and manipulate others, entrapping and compromising them unscrupulously. Indeed, many psychologists are reluctant to work with psychopaths as they dissemble and fake improvement for their own ends, viewing cooperation as a method of extricating themselves from prison or other consequences of their actions. To a psychopath, immediate pleasure, dominance and power are all that matter.

But perhaps the last word on Manuel's behaviour at Peterhead should go to Chief Officer Mackenzie, who saw him in much simpler terms: 'One of the worst types we have in Peterhead. His police and prison record proves that it is utterly impossible to manage this man other than when he is locked up on his own.'

CHAPTER SIX

Peter Manuel was released from prison in October 1952 and returned to live with his family. Samuel was still a local councillor and was well thought of. Bridget had found solace in religious devotion and had become a pillar of the church. Theresa had left school and was training as a nurse. They had moved to another council housing scheme, at Birkenshaw. Here, several hundred yards from Viewpark, the family was closer to the largely Protestant and middle-class town of Uddingston, whose younger inhabitants viewed their Catholic working-class neighbours with contempt, referring to them as 'Birkies'. From time to time, skirmishes would ensue when a party from one side entered the other's territory.

When he was released, Manuel went to see Superintendent James Hendry of the Lanarkshire police. He was burning with anger because he continued to believe he had been framed for rape by Murdo Mackenzie, who would remain his hated enemy until the end of his life.

Manuel asked Hendry to investigate Mackenzie and what he claimed was his wrongful conviction. In return, he offered information to help solve two murders: those of a Maltese girl, probably a prostitute, in Soho and of a 31-year-old woman who had been killed in Stirlingshire in 1949 during a payroll theft. He told Hendry that a fellow prisoner in Peterhead had confessed to him and given him the details of the latter crime. He named the man but refused to give more information. From this point on, again and again, Manuel would tell the authorities that he had special knowledge, that he knew important secrets, that he and he alone could help them solve major crimes.

All his adult life, Manuel hungered for attention and stories like these were one way he could get it. Telling them gave him a sense of power, of being special. His claims to such knowledge allowed him to manipulate those credulous enough to believe him and, not infrequently, to mislead the despised and hated police and waste their time. By seizing on matters of great concern to the police or, occasionally, the security services, he could make himself the centre of attention, make people listen to him, make them run around – he became powerful.

Hendry paid no attention to Manuel's protestations of innocence and he found his claims to inside knowledge about these crimes too vague and insubstantial to be credible. He noted a characteristic that others also remarked on: Manuel's unwillingness to look people in the eye. However, Hendry also saw that Manuel had been changed by his years in Peterhead. He had educated himself. His vocabulary had expanded, he had become much more articulate and he had studied law. In one of his letters from Peterhead, Manuel had written, 'I will need to be able to quote fluently law and procedure.' Convinced of the injustice of his conviction, he wanted books on 'perjury, false arrest and conviction on prejudiced evidence'. His new legal knowledge did not help him with Hendry but eventually it would be used at the most crucial point in his life.

Manuel began to work for the Gas Board, where his father was a long-term employee, and then for the local council, emptying dustbins – a far cry from the glamorous world of high crime and gangsterism that he dreamed about. Householders remember him wearing a red beret; perhaps he was pretending that he had been a paratrooper. Eventually, the council sacked him. It was probably through the recommendation of his father that he found work as a railway freight clerk, managing the delivery of packages for the recently nationalised British Railways. Manuel kept this job for much longer than most. He must have given the impression that he was behaving well, although a fellow crook would later claim that he and Peter used to steal from railway wagons. After about 18 months, he was dismissed. He claimed it was because someone had tampered with a safe and he had been wrongly blamed. Others said he was sacked when his prison record became known to his employers. Next, his father helped him get another job as a labourer for the Gas Board.

It may be that Manuel had other plans. Though this is a blank period in his criminal record, he had not relinquished his criminal ambitions. Aiming to enter the higher levels of organised crime in Glasgow, he drank in the Gorbals pubs that were recruiting grounds for planned criminal enterprises. He would swagger in dressed like a gangster, using an American drawl, and give sinister sideways glances around the bar. He was reputed in gangland to be adept at sneaking up from behind with a cosh and was sometimes hired as a thug. There are several accounts dating from this period of his having mugged people at night. In Birkenshaw, he was referred to by the children as 'Mr Twitchy Eyes', as he never looked anyone straight in the eye and was always watching what was going on to either side. Canon Gibbons recalls stories of local girls coming across him late at night and being offered safe escort home.

Not long after Peter's release, the Manuel household was shaken by yet another court case. In 1953, Samuel was prosecuted for breach of the peace, a catch-all crime then beloved of the Scottish police.

Samuel had been caught as a Peeping Tom and fined one pound. He was forced to resign from his position on the district council.

Meanwhile, Peter Manuel's attempts to break into the criminal big time continued. In one of his books, 'Mad' Frankie Fraser, a senior figure in the London underworld, mentions that Peter Manuel offered his services as a hit man to gangs in the capital but was not taken seriously because, in Fraser's words, 'He couldn't keep his yap shut.' In September 1954, a London prostitute known as 'Red' Helen Carlin was found strangled in Pimlico. It was later suggested that she might have been a victim of Manuel.

In December, Manuel drew attention to himself in a most bizarre fashion when he went to see the US Consul in Glasgow in connection with his American citizenship and told one of his far-fetched stories. At the meeting, he revealed that he had information about an important security matter. The American authorities were interested, so interested that they flew him to a US airbase near London to be interviewed by an FBI officer. The interrogator quickly realised he had no information but by then Manuel had had a day out and received the attention he craved. It is not known if the US authorities flew him back. One suspects he had to make his own way home.

When he returned to Lanarkshire, Hendry and Muncie saw him and he told them another elaborate story, an account of a bullion robbery that had recently occurred in London. He narrated his part in transporting the gold. Despite the great detail he provided and his unhesitating narrative, they soon proved what they had already concluded: it was all fantasy, yet another fabrication.

Manuel also began to phone police officers anonymously and offer information about major crimes, sometimes giving himself a leading role in them. In 1955, he arranged to meet Detective Bob Kerr of Glasgow police in a restaurant to give information about a bank robbery in the heart of Glasgow's shipbuilding area. When Manuel solemnly informed him that the culprit was a Frenchman called Dante, Kerr burst out laughing and strode out, leaving a furious

Manuel to pay the bill. His imagination for names was limited: he gave the name of another foreign crook as Ferrari.

Manuel's fantastic narratives were not reserved for authority figures. He would also spin elaborate tales to his workmates and family. In one story, he recounted how, flying into Glasgow, the pilot of his plane was taken ill (or, in another version, became terror-struck) and Manuel made his way forward and landed the plane safely. He also told a story of how he had been flown to the USA to help unmask a spy and had been involved in a ferocious gunfight there. Each of these tales, like all his lies, contained just enough hard fact and plausible detail to allow it to teeter on the very edge of credibility.

These fantasies were not just tales to impress the gullible and increase his standing in their eyes. They were an essential aspect of his life; they allowed him to feel he was living the life he imagined for himself. His stories and his central roles in them helped him to reassure himself that he was much more than an unsuccessful petty thief and convicted rapist. They gave him a far more dramatic and important part in the world, one he thought appropriate to his true status.

Whenever he began one of his thrilling tales, his workmates would settle back and prepare themselves to listen to a good yarn. There was nothing particularly harmful in this. What was dangerous was the fact that his family never challenged his tales although they knew that they were fabrications. Perhaps they were afraid that he would fly into one of his rages; perhaps they had simply grown tired of all his lies and given up bothering about them. His mother said of one of his stories, 'We knew this was nonsense but we never let on we disbelieved him.'

Because of his stories, Manuel continued to be seen by the police as a fantasist, always seeking, as it were, a walk-on part in every public drama. Anything he said was almost automatically discounted as an invention. In time, this would protect him against deeper scrutiny. Within the police, there were those who believed the only way

Manuel would ever be involved in a major crime was in his fervid imagination.

In the autumn of 1954, there was a significant change in Manuel's life. He embarked upon a relationship with Miss Anna O'Hara, a bus conductress from Carluke, a mining town some distance to the south of his home. His behaviour towards her was chaste; there was little physical contact save for the occasional kiss. He behaved in a gallant and considerate way, presenting her with boxes of chocolates and treating her to trips to the cinema. Was it an attempt to transform himself at the prompting of his family?

Soon after they started going out together, Miss O'Hara received a typed letter informing her that the man she was dating was not the person she thought he was. It claimed he was the natural son of a notorious American gangster who had been executed in the electric chair and that the Manuels were not his real parents. It also stated that Manuel was a secret agent for the intelligence services and had been on a mission to the Soviet Union. When Miss O'Hara showed this strange letter to Manuel, he merely said that he knew the man who had sent it. There can be little doubt that Manuel wrote the letter both as a piece of self-aggrandisement and, perhaps, in an attempt to sabotage the relationship. He may have been anxious about the fact that he would eventually be expected to enter into a normal sexual relationship.

After a while, the two became engaged. His family was pleased but Mrs Manuel made it clear that she would not agree to meet his fiancée's family until he had told her about his criminal past. Her family had already expressed serious reservations as the relationship deepened and they began to hear rumours that he had been in prison. In May 1955, the engagement was broken off. It is not clear how far this was Manuel's decision and how far it was his fiancée's. Perhaps he realised that he could not lead a married life and continue to be a criminal. Unwed, he could shelter within his tolerant, apparently unquestioning family; living with a wife from an honest and respectable home, he would be exposed.

CHAPTER SEVEN

Manuel was by now well known to the local police. They kept a wary eye out for him and he was almost automatically suspected in cases of breaking and entering; it is also likely that he was considered as a suspect when assaults on women were investigated. The next crime they attempted to bring home to him was a serious sexual assault. The crime took place a few hundred yards from Manuel's home. The victim was 29-year-old Mary McLauchlan.

There can be no doubt that Manuel was guilty as charged. However, by his own efforts, he escaped punishment. The way he did so would have the gravest implications for the remaining two years of his life. If at this point he had been convicted or judged mentally ill, it is virtually certain that at least nine people would not have been murdered.

On Saturday, 30 July 1955, after a dance, Mary McLauchlan was walking home along a lane at about 11.30 p.m. Suddenly, she was attacked from behind and forced to the ground. She saw her attacker had a knife. He put one gloved hand over her mouth to stifle any cries. He threatened to cut her throat if she cried out and he forced her over a fence into a field. In her terror, she managed to scream once and although people nearby, including two policemen, searched for whoever had cried out, they failed to find anyone and eventually gave up looking. After she screamed, the threat to harm her was repeated. Next, she was forced across two fields. When she pleaded with her attacker, he hit her in the mouth. He forced the terrified woman to lie down and lay down next to her. They stayed there in silence for about an hour until all sounds of the search ended.

At this point Manuel – and there is absolutely no doubt her assailant was Manuel – told her he was going to kill her, cut off her head and bury it. He forced kisses on her and groped her sexual parts. She begged him to stop and told him she had two children. This was not true but she hoped it would make him spare her.

Suddenly, Manuel's demeanour changed. She later told the police he seemed to become calmer, more relaxed. In silence, they sat side by side until she asked him if she could go home. He refused this brave request but began to talk to her, claiming, 'I'm drunk. I don't know what I am doing. I just felt I had to murder somebody.' He then told her a typical Manuel tale, a story composed of scraps of truth woven into a larger fabric of fantasy. He had, he said, been due to be married on Saturday (that is, the day before; it was Sunday by now) but on Friday his bus conductress fiancée had broken off their engagement. He had felt he wanted to murder someone, had even thought of drowning himself in the Clyde but then remembered he could swim. He had then seen Mary McLauchlan, who, he said, resembled his ex-fiancée and decided to attack her.

After this supposed justification for his assault he asked his terrified victim if she knew him. Fortunately, she was able to say truthfully that she did not. If she had answered that she did, it is possible he would have killed her. He also asked her where she worked and she told him. Here was another moment of great danger: he said it was obvious they must use the same bus to travel to work. The implication that he was aware she might be able to identify him was frightening but again the danger passed. In any case, he told her, he'd not be on the bus on Monday. He asked her name and she gave a false one. He lit a cigarette and, by the flare of the match, she saw him clearly for the first time and recognised him as someone she had indeed seen on the bus, travelling with an older man who was almost certainly his father.

Manuel now seemed completely calm. Suddenly, he flung the knife away. McLauchlan repeated her question: could she go home now? Yes, he said, and then, astonishingly, offered to go with her to the police, saying that she'd want to report him. She sensed she would put herself in great danger if she agreed. She assured him she had no intention of reporting what had happened. Then they walked together towards their homes; she reached hers at three. Six hours later, she went to the police and told her story.

Why had Manuel suddenly changed from ferocious attacker, threatening to cut off his victim's head, to someone willing to talk more or less calmly and then walk home with her? John Bingham, in his 1973 book *The Hunting Down of Peter Manuel*, argues, using information from Muncie and the evidence of stains on Manuel's underwear, that Manuel had reached a sexual climax and, that achieved, became calm. The pattern suggested is one of placing women in great fear and through their terror obtaining sexual release.

The police investigation almost inevitably involved Inspector Muncie, whose career had periodically intersected with Manuel's since 1945 and would continue to do so until he was hanged. The police put a plain-clothes officer on the bus on the Monday morning and when Miss McLauchlan got on she quickly identified Manuel's father. Through this, Peter was arrested. The investigating officers acted quickly and took possession of several items of Manuel's clothing, including a pair of trousers stained with what was thought to be his victim's blood, probably from the finger she tore on barbed wire when he had forced her over a fence. They also found the knife he had thrown away and took samples of the soil and vegetation from the area around the assault to try to match these with traces found on his clothing. They also seized Manuel's diary. What a valuable insight into his psychology that might have provided.

Two things are particularly striking about the case. First, that Manuel felt able, or was driven by forces he could not resist, to commit a sexual assault so near his home and on a young woman who lived a very short distance away from his own house. (Her home was in Third Street, his in Fourth Street.) Second, because the victim survived and was able to describe what he had done to her, her account throws terrible light on the killings of Anne Kneilands and Isabelle Cooke. The assault on Mary McLauchlan seems almost like a rehearsal for the murders of those teenage girls. There was one difference: he allowed Miss McLauchlan to live and she gave evidence against him. Perhaps he determined never to run that risk again.

Manuel was charged, remanded to Barlinnie and, on 17 October, tried at Airdrie Sheriff Court. It looked as if the police and prosecution had a very strong case and this feeling must have been strengthened when the alibi Manuel had put forward as a special defence at a hearing before his trial was proved to be false. Initially, he claimed he had spent the crucial hours with a Mrs Kitty McGrogan. However, the lady said that, while it was true that she had spent a night with Manuel, it had been a week before the assault on Miss McLauchlan. It may have been because of this blow that Manuel wrote to the procurator fiscal before his trial claiming that one of the Crown's witnesses had lied. Was the supposed liar Mrs McGrogan? Or was it perhaps her husband, who had stated he had been away from home the weekend before the assault but had been back when it had occurred and that therefore his wife could not have been with Manuel on the night in question? Whatever he intended by this comment, Manuel nonetheless withdrew his special defence.

Before the case was tried, Manuel was examined by Dr Anderson, the medical officer at Barlinnie, who reported his findings to the procurator fiscal. Anderson was fully aware of Manuel's background and long criminal record. As for his mental state, he declared:

> He is properly oriented and he is not feeble-minded. His conversation is quite intelligent and he discussed himself and his activities quite freely. His sister told me that she believed him to suffer from delusions of persecution and feels that the world is against him. I can find no confirmation of this as he does not appear to me to suffer from hallucinations or delusions. By his own account he is happy in his present employment [as a Gas Board labourer] and his relationships with his family, workmates and friends are satisfactory. He appears to me to understand the nature of his charge and to understand the gravity of his position. As a result of my examination I can elicit no evidence to suggest that this man is insane. I am of the opinion that he is at present sane and fit to plead.

Dr Anderson ended his report with the solemn traditional formula: 'I hereby certify on soul and conscience that to the best of my knowledge and belief this is a true report.'

Manuel's mental state was to be scrutinised again and again with the same result: the examining doctors all declared he was sane according to the law and fit to be tried. Although there is little doubt that Manuel was a psychopath, this personality disorder was not as well understood at that time as it is today – nor was it considered a reason why a murderer should not be hanged. Three years later, Dr Anderson would watch Manuel drop from the gallows.

Manuel, certified sane, had therefore to be tried on the evidence. He took the highly significant step of deciding to defend himself. Hoping to impress the jury, he called his mother as a witness (perhaps a character witness) on his behalf. His performance in the Airdrie court demonstrated his quick intelligence and the amount of law he had picked up. Defending himself gave him a distinct advantage over the prosecution: he was allowed much more latitude than a professional lawyer. He used it to the full. As he chose not to go into the witness box, he did not have to swear to tell the truth nor could he be cross-examined. From the well of the court he told another of his concocted tales, garnishing his elaborate lies with just enough apparent truths to make them seem possible.

His story was this: for some time, Mary McLauchlan and he had been courting but they had quarrelled. He had met her around midday on the day she claimed he had assaulted her. They had words and he struck her and cut her lip. Then they had made up their quarrel and went together into a field where he had set snares for rabbits. She had torn her leg on some barbed wire, hence the blood on his trousers. He had lost his knife when throwing it at a dog that was in danger of being struck by a train on the nearby railway line. He had been unable to find and retrieve it. Her story was untrue, motivated by resentment and hatred.

The jurors were uncertain who to believe. Perhaps the seven female members of the jury of thirteen were impressed by his smiles and fluency, even by his dark looks and careful grooming. (Manuel certainly believed this to be the case, boasting to a friend, 'You have got to concentrate on the women when you give evidence to the jury. You have to sell yourself.' It is true that he had the superficial charm often found in psychopaths, and later he would receive several offers of matrimony while on remand on murder charges in 1958.) The jury clearly inclined towards the prosecution's account but not strongly enough to convict Manuel. Eventually, they brought in a not proven verdict. Bingham writes that as a result, until Manuel was finally hanged, poor Mary McLauchlan was regarded with dislike and suspicion by some of her neighbours. Manuel's father showed his hostility to her in a more direct way: he spat at her at the bus stop.

And Manuel? This time, he had escaped but he must have realised that leaving his victims alive meant they could testify against him. That would not happen again. However, he could delight in knowing that he defended himself successfully in open court. Moreover, he believed this was in part because he had been able to charm the women in the jury.

Meanwhile, as they looked on his latest victim with suspicion and uncertainty, his neighbours regarded him in the same way.

CHAPTER EIGHT

In the mid-1950s, East Kilbride was a quiet little rural community to the south of Glasgow and roughly seven miles from Manuel's home in Birkenshaw. This small country village, having been designated Scotland's first new town, was in the throes of becoming a major dormitory town, part of the new Glasgow that was emerging from the cleared slums of the city centre. By 1955, 400 new houses had already been built. The Gas Board had gangs digging pipelines to bring domestic gas supplies to the new housing estate in neighbouring Calderwood. In one gang was Peter Manuel, working with his father. The labourers had a small hut, which housed their equipment and provided much-needed shelter against foul weather.

In a time before television became widespread, the weekly entertainment highlight in rural areas was the local dance, usually in the village hall. On Friday and Saturday nights, the young would set forth in their finery to get together, appraise each other and meet any newcomers looking to widen their social contacts and hoping for romance.

Anne Kneilands was a tall, pretty, athletic 17-year-old, who lived with her family in the converted stables of the old Calderwood Estate and worked in a garment factory. Her family was Catholic and she had been educated at St Joseph's School in nearby Blantyre. She was a popular member of the group of youngsters who regularly attended the local weekend dances.

On Friday, 30 December 1955, she had been to a dance with her sister Alice. There they had met a couple of young men and after a convivial evening Anne had made a date with Andrew Murnin, a smart-looking soldier on leave, wearing his paratrooper's uniform. They arranged to meet at 6 p.m. on the following Monday, 2 January, at Capelrig Farm bus terminus, a little distance from her home. From here, a bus ran the one and a half miles to the town centre. Murnin's leave was celebrated in some style, for he was drinking almost continuously. The next day, he had no recollection of the arrangement he had made to meet Anne.

On that cold dark evening, Anne waited in vain for him at the end of the unlit farm road. The 6.14 bus came and went. At 6.20 p.m., feeling the cold and getting angry, she went some hundred yards up the road to the farmhouse and called upon the Simpsons, with whom she was on very friendly terms. She was consoled by Mrs Simpson and after a quarter-hour chat she got on the 6.44 bus heading towards East Kilbride. The bus conductress, Molly Peacock, clearly remembered taking her fare for the three-minute journey because she sat alone and was clearly put out. The bus stop at East Kilbride was just across the road from the Willow Café, a hangout of the local youths. Perhaps she had hoped that Murnin had misunderstood the arrangement and would be waiting for her there. At 7.10 p.m., the bus driver believed he saw her in a group of about a dozen others waiting to get on the bus back up to Capelrig. Having just been stood up, it seems she had decided to return home.

This was to be the last time she was seen alive. When she failed to come home, her parents initially thought that she had spent the night with friends; Anne was, after all, 17 years old and could be relied upon to be sensible. This was a time when few houses had telephones and when friends could drop in on each other unannounced and be received with impromptu hospitality. If the weather was bad and the bus service had ended, it was not uncommon to spend the night at a friend's house rather than face the 'long Scots miles'. When Anne did not return in the morning, however, Mr and Mrs Kneilands were very worried and the police were informed.

Later that day, George Gribbon, a 49-year-old labourer in poor health, was taking a walk across the local golf course. As he made his way into a small stand of pine trees just beside the fifth tee, he saw a woman's body lying face down amongst the tree roots. It was apparent that the body had been dragged there by the ankles, for the skirt had ridden up over the knees and the tweed coat was also disarranged, its collar drawn up over the ears. It was the body of Anne Kneilands.

Gribbon was close enough to glimpse the catastrophic injuries to the top of her head. The extent of the wound removed any doubt about whether she was dead. He rushed over to a gang of labourers working nearby and, in a state of agitation, told them of his find. They took this to be some sort of prank and dismissed his request for help. He then made his way to a farmhouse, from where he phoned the police. Meanwhile, some of the labourers had had second thoughts and gone to the site.

The police arrived quickly and began their investigations. A search of the surrounding area yielded clear evidence of what had happened. Anne's shoes were found separately, one embedded in the wall of a very wide ditch and the other some seventy feet from her body. A clear trail of footprints showed that she had fled for her life across fields, ditches and over or through barbed-wire fences. A local man, William Marshall, recalled that some 36 hours before he had heard what sounded like someone crying out. Near the body was the site of the killing, where, on the ground near a tree stump, there was a large amount of blood and what the pathologist, Professor Andrew Allison, was to describe as 'human debris': fragments of bone, hair and tissue. Kneilands had not been raped, although one newspaper reported that there were stains of ejaculate on her clothing. Her hands showed scratches and bruises and her clothes were torn, probably by her desperate flight through barbed wire. Her navy-blue cotton knickers were missing. The cause of death was the crater-shaped injury to the top of her head. She had sustained repeated blows to the head and the vault of her skull had been destroyed.

The Lanarkshire police habitually used the services of pathologists Professor Allison and Dr Imrie, who worked for the Glasgow city police. Professor Allison was a retired professor from the by then defunct St Mungo's College of Medicine. He was a highly experienced forensic pathologist, well into his 70s. Manuel had already crossed his path: he had been one of the expert witnesses in the 1946 rape case.

The head of Lanarkshire CID, Chief Superintendent James Hendry, launched a major murder investigation and every available officer was sent on door-to-door enquiries to put together a picture of the victim's last hours. Andrew Murnin was immediately traced and grilled as to his movements on Monday. Almost all the young men in the district were called in and questioned about their whereabouts on that day. Manuel was among them but he was freed without any charge. It was later claimed that his father had given him an alibi.

Then, on 4 January, one of the enquiring officers, PC Marr, visited a gang of Gas Board workmen to gather evidence. He noticed that one of the men had scratches on his face. It was Peter Manuel. He claimed that he'd got them in a fight in Glasgow at New Year. Others also saw these scratches and the evidence was recorded by the police but the matter went no further. Later, after Manuel was hanged, Hendry would state that he had not become aware that Manuel was working in the area until 11 January, at which point he decided that he was 'a strong suspect'.

Nevertheless, suspicion still hung around Manuel. In the Scottish *Daily Express* of 14 January, it was reported that he and the gang foreman had shown the police a sawn-off pickaxe handle found beneath the hut. According to the article, Manuel had said that detectives had questioned him for four hours but 'said it was only routine questioning'. A reporter told Manuel that Hendry suspected that he was Kneilands' killer and, as a result, he allowed his photograph to be published next to a story about the murder. Anyone who thought they had seen him in the area at the time was invited to come forward. Nobody did. Manuel regarded this as proof of his denials. Very probably he felt it also proved his ability to run rings around the police and to kill with impunity.

The trail of Anne Kneilands' killer grew cold but over in Glasgow there was soon another murder. Miss Anne Steele lived in a top-floor flat at 33 Aberfoyle Street in the Dennistoun area of eastern Glasgow. She worked as a bookkeeper and neighbours described her as a smartly dressed middle-aged spinster. At about 8 p.m. on 11 January 1956, downstairs neighbours heard a crashing noise that caused them sufficient alarm to run to her door. They found it locked and summoned the police. Once they gained entry, they found the dead body of Miss Steele. She had sustained head injuries. On a windowsill was the bloodstained poker from her fireplace, clearly the murder weapon. The bathroom window was open; the killer had escaped by climbing some 60 ft down a drainpipe. The police issued a description of a young man who was seen walking away from the direction of the flat at about this time, adding that they believed this person might have had bloodstains on his clothes or scratches on his face. Nobody was ever arrested for the crime. As the snow had started to fall, Anne Steele's attacker had walked away into obscurity. After Manuel's death, one of the detectives who brought him to justice said that he believed Manuel might have been responsible for Steele's death. Since there was no evidence, however, he had been unable to question him about it.

In midsummer, there was another murder. On 15 June 1956, a prostitute, 'English Nell', or Ellen Petrie, was found stabbed to death in a back street in the city centre of Glasgow. She had apparently bled to death from a knife wound to the thigh. Earlier, she had been seen in the company of a dark-haired young man. There was no arrest in the case.

On 12 September, Mr and Mrs Henry Platt and their son Geoffrey left their house in Bothwell, a small town less than a mile from the Manuel home in Birkenshaw, for a holiday in the Lake District. Three days later, police received a report of a break-in at the house. Inside, they were met by a scene that bore a certain signature. The intruder had heated up soup from a tin and poured some on the floor. He had also opened a tin of pears, drunk the juice and tipped the contents onto the sitting room carpet. Upstairs in one of the bedrooms was a jug containing some of the soup. There were muddy boot marks on the bedcover where someone had lain down, as well as blackened holes, which were taken to be cigarette burns, in the quilt and blanket. A seven- or eight-inch-long slit had been made in the mattress, probably with a pair of scissors that was found lying near the bed.

When the Platts returned and checked what had been stolen, they listed a very special electric razor among items missing. It was an experimental prototype produced in a batch of 50 at the Philips electrical factory in Hamilton. Mr Platt had bought it for Geoffrey from a Philips worker. The thief had also stolen cash and a considerable number of items but had left others heaped up in one of the downstairs rooms. Whoever had carried out the break-in had a certain degree of skill, for there were no fingerprints and nor had he attracted any attention. He must also have had considerable sangfroid to put his feet up in the midst of a break-in.

The next crimes occurred less than a week later. Burnside lies to the south of the River Clyde, on an area of high ground on the outskirts of Glasgow. In the mid-'50s the district was being transformed into a middle-class suburb with hundreds of single-storey bungalows. No. 5 Fennsbank Avenue, Burnside, was just another one of these bungalows. In 1954, it became home to the Watt family.

William Watt was an entrepreneur who owned the Deanholm Bakeries, a chain of several shops in the Glasgow area. His wife, Marion, was 45 years old and had been in poor health for several years. As a child, she'd developed rheumatic heart disease, which had damaged her heart valves. In 1955, she had undergone a valvectomy. The surgery had improved her mobility but she was still not fully fit and relied upon a home help to run the house. The Watts had a 16-year-old daughter, Vivienne. She and Deanna Valente, 17, who lived next door, were undertaking a commercial and secretarial course at Skerry's College in the city. Vivienne spent much of her time with Deanna, her best friend and confidante.

On 9 September, William Watt left home for a well-deserved fishing holiday. He had been working hard to get a new bakery outlet up and running and was suffering from sciatica. He and the family's pet black Labrador, Queenie, had gone to a small country hotel 90 miles away at Cairnbaan in the scenic highlands of Argyllshire. The hotel was situated at the far end of a notoriously steep and protracted hill, a spot known to Scots motorists as 'the Rest and Be Thankful'. Watt took with him a shotgun to shoot rabbits. He hoped to unwind, spending his days fly-fishing for the elusive brown trout in the area's many mountain streams and lochans. His evenings were to be spent relaxing in the hotel bar in the company of the owners, Mr and Mrs Leitch, who had become personal friends.

Mrs Watt had invited her sister, Mrs Margaret Brown, to stay while William was away. Margaret lived with her husband George, who ran a small dry-cleaning business in Stenhousemuir, some 25 miles away. The Watt bungalow had only two bedrooms so the two sisters would be sharing the matrimonial double bed. Vivienne had a room to herself next door.

On Sunday, 16 September, Vivienne and Deanna boarded a tram at about 6.30 p.m. to go to Glasgow. They wandered around the city centre, window-shopping and talking, and had a meal in a café before buying cakes from one of Watt's bakeries. When they returned home a couple of hours later, they went into Vivienne's bedroom to listen to music and chat. Between ten and ten-thirty, Vivienne was called to the phone to speak to her father. She returned and reported grumpily, 'I'm mad because Father didn't give me money this week but he's promised to double it when he gets back.'

About an hour later, Deanna went home. As she dozed off to sleep, she could still hear the strains of the Top 20 playing on Vivienne's radio. A passing neighbour, Frank Gilfillan, later reported that he had heard music coming from the Watt house in the early hours of the next morning and mentioned that this was not unusual.

At 8.45 on Monday morning, Helen Collison, the home help, arrived at No. 5. She was the wife of a miner and lived several miles away in Chryston. She was a loyal and trusted helper who had worked with the Watts when they had lived in Muirhead, before the move to Burnside in mid-July 1954. She would later describe Mrs Watt as a semi-invalid who would frequently stay in bed until the afternoon. The usual arrangement for Mrs Collison was that Vivienne left the back door unlocked when she left for college. That day, it was locked. Mrs Collison walked round the house, rapping on the windows as she went. When she got to the front door, she was alarmed to notice that a glass panel had been smashed. Prudently, she sought the assistance of the postman, Peter Collier, who had arrived on his morning round. As Mrs Valente watched in concern, he put his hand through the broken glass, opened the Yale lock and led the way into the house.

In one bedroom lay the two sisters, both clearly dead, rivulets of blood draining from their noses and mouths and staining the white pillows. They lay side by side, both with clearly visible gunshot wounds to the head. The bedclothes had been drawn up to their chins. They appeared to have been killed as they slept and to have had no inkling of their fate. In the other bedroom was the pathetic figure of Vivienne, again with the quilt drawn up to her chin. She too had been shot through the head but her room showed clear signs of a struggle. The floor was strewn with items of clothing and some of the furniture was upset. On the carpet was a stubbed-out cigarette end. As if to complete the horror of the scene, Mrs Collison and the postman heard three or four loud snorts from the inert Vivienne. These were her death throes.

Mrs Valente, on hearing the shocking news, took fright and ran screaming into her house. Peter Collier had the presence of mind to instruct Mrs Collison not to touch anything and to phone the police, who arrived promptly.

Mrs Watt and her sister had been shot where they lay through the right side of the head. Mrs Brown had also been shot in the face, just below the right eye. The killer must almost have touched them with the barrel of the gun, for there were powder burns on their skin. If the muzzle of a firearm is pressed against the skin, expanding gases enter the wound and cause the skin to split in a cruciform wound; such an injury was to be seen on Mrs Watt's face. For both women, death had been instantaneous. After death, their night attire had been disarranged, perhaps to expose their genitalia; Mrs Watt's nightdress had been rucked up, exposing her pubis, and Mrs Brown's pyjamas had been torn from waist to crotch. There was no sign of sexual interference but it is possible that the killer had indulged himself in voyeurism or handled the women's sexual organs and breasts. Examination by Allison and Imrie suggested that the two women had been killed at about 6 a.m., although it could have been anything up to two hours earlier.

Vivienne's death had been more drawn-out. She had a bruise on her chin, probably caused by a punch. There was bruising to the pubic area, which may have been caused by ripping off her pyjamas and pants or by rough handling. Her bra, which she apparently wore while sleeping, had been torn off and her right arm was twisted behind her back. She too had been shot through the left temple at almost contact range and there was powder blackening around the wound. She had not been raped but it seemed there was a possibility that she had been tormented and tortured by her attacker before being shot.

The police had barely arrived before the press reached the house. Not only did most reporters have friends among the police who were willing to tip them off but many had also discovered that their television sets could readily be tuned in to the police radio frequencies to monitor what was going on. The local newspaper editor swiftly got to work on a splash edition about the discovery of the murders.

At this point, William Watt took a central role in the drama, a position he was to hold until July 1958. Watt is the most controversial figure to emerge from this tragedy. There were aspects of his character and behaviour that engendered opposing opinions of him. To some, he was a pathetic victim of outrageous misfortune and police incompetence; to others, he was a scheming villain who was fortunate not to be convicted of murder.

Watt had been enjoying his holiday, although in the first week the fishing was poor. On Sunday, he had ignored the locally strict Sabbath observance and spent the morning fishing. He was not alone in his neglect of the Lord's Day, for he was able to enlist the aid of a local mechanic to try to sort an intermittent fault with his car's headlights. He returned to dine at the hotel and then went to visit his friends the Bruces in Lochgilphead a couple of miles away. The Leitches had introduced Watt to the Bruce family, the owners of a fishing beat where he wished to try his luck. Earlier in his holiday, they had provided him with a bed after inviting him to join them on an early-morning fishing expedition. At 10 p.m., Watt returned to the hotel, from where he phoned his wife and daughter; he went to the bar for a few drinks and then drank with the Leitches in their private room until about 12.45 a.m., when he went to bed. As he wanted to wake at 5.30 to fish, Mrs Leitch supplied him with an alarm clock. The next morning when she went downstairs at 8.30, she learned that Watt was out, presumably fishing.

At 11.20 a.m., Mrs Leitch took a phone call from someone claiming to be a business acquaintance of Watt. When the caller had to ask what Watt's first name was, she became suspicious and hung up. This was an enterprising member of the press. Ten minutes later, John Watt, William's brother, phoned and told her about the deaths. She immediately dispatched a taxi driver to summon Watt back, saying that there was an urgent call for him. Shortly after this, Watt phoned to ask what it was all about. Mrs Leitch insisted that he return immediately.

When Watt arrived, he found Mrs Leitch in a state of tearful near-hysteria. As she blurted out amid sobs the name 'Marion', he thought she was talking about her own daughter of that name. When he finally understood it was his wife she was referring to, he phoned his brother. John had already left for the Watt house and it was Watt's secretary who confirmed the dreadful news. He then phoned his house. The call was taken by a police superintendent who told him again what had happened.

Watt, still wearing his fishing clothes, made ready to rush back to Glasgow. Mr Bruce, who had by now come to the hotel to support Watt, insisted on going with him to keep him company and to calm him down, as the road to Glasgow was narrow and winding and required attentive driving. After about three miles, Watt realised the drive was beyond him, so they went to the local police station and explained the situation. A police driver was provided. At Alexandria, several miles from the north-westerly boundary of Glasgow, they were met by DS William Mitchell and PC Copland of the Lanarkshire force. They had been sent to escort Watt the rest of the way. Exactly what occurred during this part of the drive would become a matter of profound dispute but Mitchell's view of the bereaved man's demeanour would play a large part in determining the police's attitude towards him. Watt was taken first to Rutherglen police station. Later, he was escorted to the city mortuary to identify the remains of his family.

His brother-in-law, George Brown, had also been contacted by the press before the story broke. He had been phoned by a reporter from the Glasgow evening paper the *Daily Record* who asked him several questions about his family and marriage that caused him sufficient offence to make him hang up. Throughout the day, this reporter persisted in his efforts to elicit background details from Brown, who was unaware that his wife was dead until early afternoon.

At Fennsbank Avenue, a full-scale murder inquiry was under way. Fingerprint experts had checked all surfaces and the police photographer had recorded the scenes of death. Professor Allison had carried out a preliminary examination in the house before allowing the bodies to be removed.

Whilst all this was going on, up the street a lesser but highly significant discovery was made. The two unmarried Martin sisters lived at No. 18. They had set off the previous Saturday on an early train to holiday in Wester Ross, leaving a key with their neighbour. At 2.20 p.m. on Monday, a sharp-eyed Mrs Agnes Brown noticed from across the street that one of the glass panels of the front door had been smashed in. She immediately informed the police just down the road. Constable Steele was sent to investigate and gained entry by releasing the Yale lock through the broken panel, just as the postman had done at the Watts'. He saw that there had been a break-in and summoned the CID.

They found familiar features. A tin of tomato soup had been opened and poured on the floor of the sitting room, a tin of spaghetti emptied out and orange peel and pips scattered around in the front room and the bedrooms. The rooms had been ransacked, drawers opened and their contents poured on the floor. At one end of the settee there were muddy boot marks where someone had reclined and smoked a cigarette, stubbing it out on the carpet. One of the beds was disturbed, indicating that someone had lain there.

Had the intruder watched the street from this room and noticed two lively young girls walking back to No. 5? Curiously, the burglar had emptied every drawer and laid out the contents on the floor but had taken only two old-fashioned gold rings set with stones, leaving more valuable items behind. A small amount of money and four nylon stockings, ideal for putting over the hands to prevent the wearer leaving fingerprints, were also missing.

The story of the three women murdered in their beds made headline news nationally and it triggered near panic across the west of Scotland. There was great pressure on the Lanarkshire force to make an arrest. Manuel was quickly suspected, almost certainly because the police linked the Martin break-in with the murders a few doors away. Since creating messes in people's houses was characteristic of Manuel, they suspected him of the crime at the Martins and therefore of the Watt killings. As a result, a group of detectives arrived at the Manuel house at 4.30 a.m. on the Tuesday morning. Samuel was hostile and threatened to report them to his MP. They carried out a search but found nothing incriminating. In the next few weeks, they returned and carried out further unproductive searches, taking away items of Manuel's clothing and some of his shoes. Soon, though, they had a far more promising suspect.

In cases of domestic murder, family members are almost automatically considered as suspects and William Watt quickly came under suspicion. Police doubts about his innocence were strengthened when DS Mitchell reported that Watt had seemed far from shocked and distressed on the drive back to Glasgow. Eventually, at two identification parades, two witnesses came forward and identified Watt as a man they had seen driving south towards Glasgow on the night of the murders. One was a motorist who had been heading north along the side of Loch Lomond. He had seen the lights of an approaching car suddenly disappear. The car had stopped and as he drove past he saw the driver, whom he identified as Watt, lighting a cigarette before driving off. The other witness was the ferryman on the Renfrew Ferry, one of the routes across the Clyde that could be taken by anyone heading towards Burnside from the north. He claimed to identify Watt, his car and the black Labrador.

Watt was questioned several times and when he attended the funeral of his wife and daughter he was accompanied by CID officers.

The funeral was dramatic: he almost toppled into the grave as the coffins were lowered into it. Two days later, he was arrested and charged with the murders of his wife, daughter and sister-in-law by Superintendent Hendry in the presence of Chief Constable Thomas Renfrew, an indication of how seriously the murders were regarded. On 27 September, Watt was committed to Barlinnie prison.

Having made the arrest, the police assiduously went about searching for more evidence against him. The police may have had other suspicions about Watt. One retired officer remembers a rumour that he had bought stolen flour for his bakery business and it appears that he had had some irregular dealings in the 1940s in Jersey and had been a business partner of the proprietress of the Moulin Rouge pub in the Gorbals. They set out to prove that it would have been possible for Watt to have been in the hotel on the Sunday night yet still have been able to slip out unnoticed, drive to Burnside, murder three people and return. DS Mitchell and PC Copland drove the route south in just over two hours.

Finding himself in Barlinnie, William Watt did the most sensible thing he could and instructed the best criminal solicitor in Glasgow. Laurence Dowdall was a superlative courtroom practitioner. He coupled a brilliant legal mind with a considerable talent for forensic oratory, tempered by a wry sense of humour that went down very well with juries.

On 2 October, less than a week after Watt had been remanded in custody to Barlinnie, Peter Manuel appeared at Hamilton Sheriff Court. On 23 March 1956, he and an accomplice had broken into the canteen of Blantyreferme Colliery, one of the many coalmines that peppered the Clyde Valley, less than half a mile from Manuel's home. They stole 4,800 cigarettes, a cash box containing £11 16s 6d and a further 7s 6d. The police, however, had received a tip-off and were waiting. They arrested the other man at the scene but Manuel fled, leaving a scrap of clothing on a barbed-wire fence. He was subsequently arrested but, surprisingly, given his record, allowed bail.

In July, a 999 call informed police that two men were acting suspiciously at the rear of a house. When the police arrived, both men jumped from a high wall to escape. One landed badly and broke a bone in his foot; the other fled. The injured man, Joe Brannan, refused to name his accomplice: Manuel. By his loyalty and adherence to the gangland code of silence, he gained Manuel's trust. Once he was released from jail, towards the end of 1957, he was to play an important role in Manuel's life and crimes.

In his trial for the colliery break-in, Manuel, as before, defended himself and, as before, lodged a special defence of alibi and called his mother as a witness to support him. Another of his witnesses was meant to be his fellow criminal Charles Tallis. Tallis, however, reneged, perhaps deterred by the prospect of being sent down for perjury. Or perhaps he suspected, from Manuel's frequent revisiting of this topic in conversation, that it was Manuel who had killed the Watts and prudently decided to have nothing further to do with him. Manuel, forced to withdraw his special defence, was sentenced to 18 months' imprisonment. It appears that he left court seething with fury at Tallis and determined to be avenged for this betrayal.

CHAPTER NINE

Manuel and Watt were now locked up in the same jail, Watt awaiting trial for murder, Manuel sentenced to 18 months. They never met inside prison, though later Watt thought Manuel might have been one of the prisoners who shouted abuse at him from behind their cell doors: 'Watt, why didn't you shoot your dog, too?'

Manuel, of course, had been an early suspect in the Watt murders. His house had been visited within 24 hours of the bodies being discovered; his clothing and shoes had been examined and the house searched for a gun. But nothing incriminating was found in that or later searches and soon senior police officers became convinced that Watt was the murderer. It may be that Manuel feared Tallis was about to betray him to the police, having already shown his perfidy by not providing an alibi. Now, from his cell in Barlinnie, Manuel acted. If he had not done what he did, he might never have been hanged.

It started with a brief letter. On 8 October 1956, Manuel wrote to Laurence Dowdall. Manuel wanted Dowdall to represent him. He wished to lodge an appeal and, while the appeal was pending, to be released on bail. His letter ended: 'I have some information for you concerning a recently acquired client of yours who has been described as "an all-round athlete".'

Dowdall went to Barlinnie and advised Manuel about the appeal process. Later, he would tell the police, 'I then asked him what was the other business about which he wanted to see me and he answered, "It's about Watt."' Manuel said Watt was not guilty because 'I know the man who did it'. This, of course, was of immense importance. If he could name the real killer, Dowdall immediately asked him, why did he not tell the police? Manuel made it clear exactly what he thought of the police. Dowdall drily reported, 'In a few choice and terse sentences, [he] explained to me what he thought about the police and about the Lanarkshire police and about Inspector Hendry in particular.' In this at least Manuel and Watt must surely have been of one mind.

Dowdall showed scepticism. He told Manuel that, although this was the first time they had met, he had heard about him and that he 'knew he had a reputation for being a bit of a romancer'. Perhaps his doubt stimulated Manuel to add details to his story. He claimed he had special knowledge of what had happened. The day before the Watt killings, he said, he had been invited to rob a house in Burnside by a man who showed him a Webley Mk IV revolver. Manuel claimed that he had refused to participate in the robbery but it was still carried out and murder resulted. After the killings, the man with the gun had come to see him. He was afflicted by 'the horrors' and asked Manuel to dispose of the weapon.

All this was potentially of great significance to Watt, so Dowdall tried to learn more. To support his story, Manuel drew a picture of the revolver; he pointed out that a ring below the gun's butt that would have been used to attach a lanyard was missing. It had been broken off by the man who had used the gun at the Watt house. This sort of precise detail was impressive.

Manuel fleshed out his story, telling Dowdall that this unnamed man had told him that he had broken into two houses in Fennsbank Avenue. In the second, he had shot two women and then a girl had run out of her room. He had knocked her unconscious by striking her on the chin. 'He carried her then to the room and tied her hands and started to ransack the house but apparently the girl regained consciousness and he had to shoot her.' The man had stolen two rings from the other house and given them to Manuel, who described them in detail to Dowdall.

The solicitor knew that if this astonishing account was not just another of Manuel's attention-seeking fantasies, it could be of great importance in solving the Burnside murders. Once again, he expressed doubt and 'told him that while I might appreciate his pulling the leg of the police if he didn't like them, there didn't seem to me to be much future in telling me stories that were not true'. It was a clever ploy, stressing the separation between himself and the police and encouraging Manuel to tell him what he would not tell them. To counter Dowdall's continuing scepticism, Manuel went on to describe in detail the inside of the Watt house. Dowdall said that he would check this information.

He got in touch with Hendry and the police allowed him to see the interior of the Watt house: 'When I examined the house I certainly was astonished to note that Manuel's description was accurate.' The next day, he returned to Barlinnie. He was determined not only to establish what Manuel knew but also, if possible, to find out how he had come by his detailed knowledge. Anything he could learn might help his client.

Dowdall pointed out that some newspapers had printed plans of the murder house. He suggested to Manuel that he could have got his information from the papers. He now knew the best way to get him to say more was to express doubt. And say more Manuel did. He now claimed his informant, 'the man', had told him that the second woman had been shot twice. 'He shot the woman but apparently she was not killed and he fired another shot, one he described as about the side of the face, and the other about her forehead.'

This was the first time Dowdall had heard that one of the victims had been shot twice. As far as he knew, nothing to this effect had been revealed by the police. He went away, made discreet enquiries and found out that two shots had indeed been used to kill Mrs Brown. Her wounds were positioned as Manuel had described them.

Back he went to the prison. He told Manuel that his information was accurate but he still doubted it had been obtained in the way Manuel had claimed. He could not believe that anyone who had committed such a terrible crime would then describe to another person the interior furnishings of a house where he had murdered three people. 'And I said that led me inevitably to the conclusion that Manuel must have been there in that house on some occasion. Manuel denied it.'

Whatever Manuel may have felt about Dowdall's response, he still wanted him to help him get bail. He offered a further inducement to spur on the lawyer's efforts. If Dowdall did get him bailed, he said, he could recover the Webley used to kill the Watts. He had dumped it in the Clyde but knew how to get it out again. The two stolen rings, he said, were irrecoverable: he had put them down a street drain. Once again, Dowdall urged Manuel to tell the police what he knew; once again, he got a sharp refusal. Manuel also made it plain that, if he was questioned, he would deny ever saying anything about the Watt murders. Of course, there were no witnesses to their conversations.

Meanwhile, Dowdall prepared for a possible High Court trial and on 17 October he briefed Harald Leslie, QC, as Watt's leading counsel.

On 26 October, Dowdall received another letter. It opened in the same guarded, slightly cryptic manner as the first; it also contained a mysterious threat:

> Tonight I received a visit from a friend of mine who gave me some very disturbing news. While I am unable to state the nature of the news, I can assure you that it may alter the whole complexion of the proposals I put to you. In fact, if you are not able to obtain bail by next Friday there will be no chance of my participating in any way on your behalf regarding the matter we discussed.

After some reference to the bail process Manuel continued: 'I advise you to concentrate on this to the exclusion of all else, because if you get bail, I will be able to act immediately.' Finally he says, 'I think it is time you got some idea of what you have on your hands.' Whatever Dowdall may have felt about the tone of this letter, he applied for bail on Manuel's behalf. He was unsuccessful.

Perhaps some in the police were beginning to have doubts about whether they had the right man in Watt. Hendry questioned Manuel on 3 November and on the 14th Robert MacDonald, the Glasgow procurator fiscal, and Hendry visited the prison again. Around that time, Bridget and Samuel were asked to see MacDonald and were questioned about their son.

Dowdall now did two things that had momentous consequences. First, he saw his client Watt in Barlinnie and told him about his meetings with Manuel and the man's ability to describe the interior of the house. He urged Watt to find out all he could about Manuel from other prisoners. Second, he went to see Detective Chief Inspector Bob Kerr of the Glasgow police. Kerr had been involved in the Watt investigations and Dowdall knew him well. He told him what Manuel had said about the case. Kerr promised to act at once. He got in touch with the Lanarkshire police, and newspapers soon reported that they were digging up the ground around Manuel's home. The police had carried out what Manuel described in a letter as 'a big swoop' on his house on 22 November, 'when a small army of officers descended on the place and there were no holds barred'. However, nothing was found that might serve to implicate Manuel.

There were other stories in the papers, not all of them accurate, but they suggested reporters knew Manuel was still under active suspicion. Late in November, one paper reported that 'a young man' had been visited in Barlinnie by police investigating the Kneilands case. The deputy governor informed his superiors that the paper had got it wrong: the police had again been questioning Manuel about the Watt murders and the break-in at the Martins', not about Anne Kneilands.

Manuel was infuriated to learn that the police had been searching his family home. With typical assertive vanity he complained to the Crown Office about this latest police action, during which 'they removed all my clothing, and some of my father's. They have not returned these articles.' He added that they had also taken away personal belongings he had had in Barlinnie. 'The Governor of the Prison informed me that they had done so, but nothing else.'

What he says next is surprising because, if true, it indicates that at this date Hendry still considered that Manuel might have been guilty of four murders, even though Watt was still in prison charged with three of the killings in question. Manuel says his parents had 'informed me that Supt Hendry produced a warrant alleging that I had killed a girl called Anne Kneilands in East Kilbride last year and also alleging that I had killed Mrs Watt, her daughter and Mrs Brown at No. 5 Fennsbank Ave., Burnside'. Manuel, of course, was quick to deny any involvement in these crimes: 'I wish to state emphatically that I did not kill any of these unfortunate people.' If the warrant did not in fact mention Kneilands, then this is another example of Manuel drawing attention to himself and his crimes.

He demanded that the official to whom he was writing compel Hendry to announce that the police's actions had 'no bearing on any murder case whatever'. First the demand, then the threat: 'In the event that this request is refused I shall have to fix Hendry myself.' The fixing, he warned, would be done by releasing four documents he had drafted that would be damaging to Hendry. One would go to his MP, one to 'a friend of mine on the staff of the *Daily Express*', one to a solicitor and one 'to a Mr Brown'. A mysterious Mr Brown will reappear later in the case.

'I am not going to have my family treated like dirt by Hendry,' continues Manuel. 'This man has made some colossal blunders of late, but the biggest blunder he made was a report he made concerning myself which he used last year in this very prison to have me medically examined.' His complaint refers to the assessment of Manuel's mental state prepared by the Barlinnie medical officer in August 1955 while he was awaiting trial for the indecent assault on Mary McLauchlan. Exactly what Hendry had said in his report is not clear but it must have implied Manuel was in some way mentally impaired or ill. Manuel was infuriated that anyone might consider him unbalanced.

Manuel ends his letter of complaint by saying: 'Because he [Hendry] placed me in a position where I am unable to offer him the very information he needs. [*sic*]' Here, once again, he is holding out bait, implying that he has evidence that will enable the police to solve a crime. Needless to say, the idea that he might help Hendry was laughable.

At this point, the situation in regard to the Watt murders was confused. Watt had been charged but now Manuel was claiming Watt was innocent and that he knew who the murderer was. At least some of the police believed Watt was guilty. The Lanarkshire police had initially suspected Manuel and they had recently reinvestigated him. It is unclear, however, how far they now regarded him as a serious suspect. Had Hendry really produced a warrant alleging that Manuel had committed four murders or was that just another of his lies? Unfortunately, the content of the warrant cannot now be established. Were the police checking Dowdall's information only because they might be criticised if they did not? Was the search of the Manuel house, at best, a sort of fishing expedition, carried out just in case it turned up something damaging? And when it failed to do so, did that harden opinion against Watt?

It is almost certain there were different views within the Lanarkshire force. Later, Muncie maintained he had always suspected Manuel. However, Hendry was in charge and, from the records we have, it is fairly clear that he was still not able to see Manuel as a killer. A couple of weeks later, he was to indicate to Watt that he thought Manuel was a lying self-publicist but not a murderer.

But things were beginning to shift, at least in Glasgow. The Glasgow police, though the case was outside their jurisdiction, began to draw their own conclusions, conclusions that directly opposed those of some of their Lanarkshire colleagues. Kerr was the key to this change; we can track its evolution from his various reports to the procurator fiscal. The first tells how Dowdall had come to see him on 8 November and recounted what he had heard from Manuel. Kerr had passed on this information to Hendry. Yet he immediately makes it clear that he personally gave the information little credence: 'I may say I placed little reliance in the story concerning Manuel because I have known him for years and consider him a man of very low mentality but possessed of the most vivid imagination I have ever known.'

Kerr had good reason to regard anything Manuel said as likely to be a fantasy. Manuel had told him lies on more than one occasion. After one major bank robbery in Glasgow, Kerr had been telephoned with a tip-off. The anonymous caller named several criminals who, he said, had carried out the raid. Among the names he gave was Manuel's. Kerr thought the voice was familiar. It sounded like Manuel. He investigated and Manuel eventually admitted he had made the call. He had wanted to be thought a major criminal, someone suspected by the police in a notorious case. It was later reported in one newspaper article that he did not dare tell other crooks that he had been involved in the actual raid. Instead, he just hinted that he had driven the getaway car.

There were plenty of others who still had doubts about Manuel's guilt and Watt's innocence. In his report to the procurator fiscal, Kerr hints that Dowdall himself may have been unsure about Watt. When the lawyer and the policeman had met, besides repeating Manuel's account of the murders, Dowdall had also told Kerr of a rumour about Watt. It was said that at his previous house he had got into a dispute with another man over their dogs. 'On one occasion Watt had in his possession a revolver and threatened that if ever the other man's dog interfered with his one again he would shoot it dead.' If Watt had indeed owned a revolver, then Dowdall clearly felt the police should be told about it. Perhaps this story pointed to Watt's guilt, perhaps it had little significance or perhaps it was a baseless rumour. Dowdall, it seems, was leaving it to the police to decide what to do about it.

The Crown Office's response to Manuel's petition about the police search shows that they did not regard him as someone who might have murdered three or four people. To them, he was just a troublesome liar with an annoying tendency to claim he was involved in major crimes and who, by doing so, more or less forced the police to investigate him. In noting Manuel's complaint, the responding official wrote:

> The police conduct in connection with the affairs of Manuel is well known to this office and we have no fault to find in their activity most of which was, in any event, carried out on the instructions of the procurator fiscal. Manuel is a romantic and loves to have his nose in every investigation of consequence. If he would talk less about things which do not concern him the police would have no reason to search his house to ascertain the state of his knowledge. Accordingly we do not intend to take any action on this letter.

Yet again, Manuel was being protected by his well-deserved reputation as an attention-seeking liar.

Inside Barlinnie, Manuel's lies continued. He must have known Dowdall would pass on his story to the police. In typical fashion, he attempted to elaborate the tale and muddy the waters. In early November, he asked to see his hated enemy Superintendent Hendry.

He told Hendry that messages from Watt had been passed to him through the prison grapevine. Watt wanted him to tell Dowdall that he, Manuel, had sold a .38 revolver to a man who had used it to murder the Watts. He also told Hendry that he had owned a Luger and two .38 revolvers at the time of his last trial.

Meanwhile, Dowdall was developing Watt's defence. In his own Bentley, he drove the route between the Cairnbaan Hotel and Watt's house to see how long it took. He found that it could not be done in the time the police claimed. He also uncovered witnesses who told him that Watt's car had had frost on it on the Monday morning. If it had been used for a long journey during the night, there would have been none. These factors, and growing suspicions about Manuel, now shifted the balance in Watt's favour. Early in December, the procurator fiscal decided that the evidence against him was not strong enough to present in court and ordered his release.

Yet the situation remained highly unsatisfactory. If there was not enough evidence against Watt, the recent checks on Manuel had proved fruitless. The investigations seemed to have run into the sand. Nearly a year had passed since Anne Kneilands had been battered to death; two and a half months had passed since the three women had been shot in the Burnside bungalow. Thus far, the Lanarkshire police had been unable to gather adequate evidence to have anyone tried for these four extraordinarily high-profile murders. The murders remained unsolved; the public remained frightened. Some officers in Glasgow referred derisively to the Lanarkshire force as 'hand-knitted'.

CHAPTER TEN

Watt was freed from prison on 3 December. He had spent 67 days in jail. His return to freedom proved bitter. He came out to find that few people believed in his innocence. Old friends shunned him, business associates avoided seeing him when he called and, from overheard remarks, he soon learned that people who had never met him believed he had killed his family. The stink of guilt seemed to hang all around him.

Even today, there are those who still believe he only escaped the noose because of a lack of proof or because the police were willing to overlook his part in the crimes in order to destroy Manuel. Whatever the courts decide, suspicion, doubt, puzzlement and a belief that all is not as it is said to be can combine to condemn a man. Such was the case, at least to some extent, with William Watt.

In a paradoxical way, however, one good thing did come out of the weeks he'd endured in Barlinnie: he had got to know a lot of Glasgow crooks. When he was first jailed, other prisoners shouted insults and abuse after him. Eventually, however, some of them came to believe he was innocent. They began to pass him scraps from Barlinnie's rich soup of gossip. Among other things, he was told that there had been a plan to blow open the safe at his old house because it was believed to hold a large sum. The plan had been abandoned when the explosives expert failed to turn up, and soon afterwards Watt moved to Burnside. Stories of a safe, gelignite and a planned raid would turn up again when Manuel stood trial for murder.

Other shreds of information about the murders began to reach him. One day, he later said, he was passed a note from a fellow prisoner 'saying a man called Manuel had talked about the Burnside murders and had spoken to both Hendry and the procurator fiscal MacDonald – but never both together'. It was also said in Barlinnie that Manuel had been in Burnside on the night of the murders. Another rumour told that a crook called Charles Tallis had been involved. By the time Watt left prison, he had been given several strong hints, some from crooks, some from Manuel himself via Dowdall, that Manuel knew far more about the murders than he ought to have done.

Manuel, of course, was still serving his sentence in Barlinnie and he was in trouble. Soon after he had complained about his treatment by Hendry, he became involved in a fight with a fellow prisoner. As was usual, he was quick to protest against what he saw as the injustice of the punishment he got for this affair. Manuel gave his version of the fight in his petition. At recreation time, he claimed, he was approached by a prisoner named David Chisholm:

> [Chisholm] was in communication with an untried prisoner named Charles Tallis. This prisoner Tallis lives with Chisholm's sister. Tallis informed Chisholm that I had made a statement against Tallis to a Mr Robert MacDonald concerning an incident Mr MacDonald was investigating in the capacity of procurator fiscal. I informed Chisholm that

> such information as he gathered from Tallis was completely false. He immediately punched me in the eye.

Manuel then retaliated. The fight and the cause of the bad blood behind it are significant: Manuel would later accuse Tallis of being the man who murdered the Watts.

Once in the outside world, Watt set himself to rebuild his bakery business, which had faltered while he was inside, to prove his innocence and to try to find his family's killer. He had absolutely no faith in the Lanarkshire police, so he decided to investigate for himself. He had a certain amount of relevant experience. He had been with the railway police before the war; during it, he had been a special constable, working in the East End, and he had done some plain-clothes work. At one point, he had worked under Sergeant Alex Brown, who was now second in command of the Glasgow CID.

He began to frequent pubs and drinking clubs used by members of the Glasgow underworld to try to find out more about the murders and the enigmatic position of Peter Manuel in relation to them. Most of these places were near the centre of Glasgow or in the East End, areas he already knew well, so to a large extent he was operating on home territory, perhaps meeting people he had known by sight or reputation for years. In his encounters, he tried to get criminals to talk to him, trawling their conversation for any piece of information that might help his quest. As he became better known in the underworld, he found himself being invited to drinking parties after closing time. He went along in the hope of finding anything that could lead to the killer. He particularly wanted to discover more about the gun used in the killings and, if possible, to trace it. Watt's apparently eager mixing with well-known crooks was noted by the police and the newspaper reporters who still hovered around him looking for a story. It did nothing to weaken the commonly held view that he was guilty.

One day, Watt said later, he got an anonymous phone call arranging a meeting with a housebreaker, one of the criminals he'd met in Barlinnie. He was told that one of Manuel's associates had been shown by him two rings. Manuel had claimed he had got these from Burnside, i.e. the Martins'. This associate was in fact Charles Tallis, the man who had been mentioned in Barlinnie as possibly playing a part in the murders. Watt was also told that Manuel had two guns at the time of the murders.

Other informants came up to Watt in the street and in pubs, and increasingly Manuel was mentioned. It seemed he had been boasting in jail, claiming that he knew who had committed the Burnside murders and that Watt was under some kind of obligation to him. It began to look as if a large part of the criminal population of Barlinnie and Glasgow believed Manuel could be the murderer Watt was seeking.

It was suggested that Watt should talk to another well-known Glasgow criminal, 'Scout' O'Neil. O'Neil was rumoured to have helped Manuel get a gun shortly before the killings. Watt managed to meet O'Neil and later said he spent three weeks trying to get him to talk about this gun. Eventually, O'Neil admitted that he had been involved in providing Manuel with a firearm, although he refused to tell the police about it.

At this point, Watt enlisted the help of the Reverend Russell Anderson, a local minister who also worked as a chaplain in Barlinnie. Anderson, visiting Watt in jail, grew convinced of his innocence and had become a great supporter. After Watt was released, they saw each other almost every day. It was Anderson who finally persuaded O'Neil to talk to the police.

Watt then took him to see Superintendent Hendry. Hendry insisted on speaking privately with O'Neil. Watt was left outside the door, so he did not know what transpired between the two men. Later, two things emerged. First, that O'Neil had lied to Hendry about the exact circumstances in which Manuel had come by the gun. It was to take Detective Superintendent Alex Brown from the Glasgow force finally to get the truth from him. Second, Hendry claimed he had known all about O'Neil and the gun well before

Watt brought the man in – that was why Watt was excluded from the meeting.

Watt's investigation into guns also led him to take an acquaintance who had a .38 revolver to the police. The police tested the gun and found it was not the one used to kill his family.

Meanwhile, Kerr had been reconsidering what he knew about Watt, Manuel and the murders. He still regarded Manuel as a great liar – how could he not? – but Manuel's apparent knowledge of the killings was puzzling. While Kerr was mulling this over, he too was garnering information from his contacts in the underworld and from other policemen. Dowdall's story, plus longer-term doubts about Manuel, with his extensive criminal record, had finally begun to shift his suspicion from Watt to the younger man. At some point in December 1956, he came to the conclusion that Watt was innocent.

Watt had heard a lot about Kerr from his underworld acquaintances and had formed the impression that the detective was greatly feared and respected. In January 1957, he took a crucial step: he decided to speak directly to Kerr. He phoned Govan police station and asked if the officer was willing to see him. Kerr, aware of the delicacy of the situation, first cleared the meeting with the procurator fiscal. He then went to one of Watt's offices, where he and the baker spent almost three hours talking together. What he learned there, added to what he already knew, convinced him that Watt was completely innocent.

Kerr was quick to report to the procurator fiscal. He had, he wrote, found that the baker was bitter towards the police, and especially those of the Lanarkshire force, but that he had also found him frank and spontaneous in his answers. 'He . . . is convinced that one of two men, Charles Tallis and Peter Manuel, or both, are in some way involved in the murders of his wife, daughter and sister-in-law.' Next comes the key sentence: 'The interview in general further satisfied me within myself that Watt was, as I have lately maintained, innocent of the charge of murdering his family.'

There was more. 'As you are already aware, I am absolutely satisfied that it was Peter Manuel who murdered Anne Kneilands – of that I am convinced.' So, by January 1957, one of Glasgow's most senior detectives had become convinced that Manuel had killed Anne Kneilands. And now that Manuel was linked with the Burnside murders, Kerr found himself 'deeply concerned about the situation . . . [I] have come to the conclusion that he, and not Watt or Charles Tallis, is most likely to be the murderer of Watt's family.'

Kerr went on to tell the procurator fiscal that he believed Watt had been completely misjudged by the police and the public. He continued: 'I now find myself equally concerned and worried about Manuel, who for the time being is safely confined to prison.' The police, he believed, had made a grave error over Watt and they must not repeat it with Manuel. 'I would, however, sincerely suggest that great care and consideration should be given to him so that he, like Watt, will not be misjudged and by such escape from the condemnation he may rightly deserve at this time.'

Watt, for his part, had been completely overwhelmed by the way Kerr had treated him when they had met for their talk. He was almost speechless with emotion at the end of their meeting. He had expected scepticism, even hostility, but here was a very senior detective who did not think he was guilty of murder. Later, he told the press that Kerr had assured him he *knew* he had not killed his family. Kerr had added, however, that nothing could be done about it for some time. Watt decided that this meant that the police would have to wait until Manuel was released from jail. But perhaps Kerr was simply indicating that the police would have to do more work to gather evidence against Manuel. Whatever the meaning of Kerr's phrase, it is clear that there was now strong suspicion at a high level in the Glasgow force that Manuel was a killer.

Apparently, it was still otherwise in Lanarkshire. Kerr arranged for Watt to meet Superintendent Hendry and another officer from that force, and Watt reported his suspicions about Manuel and gave them all the information he had gathered. Watt would later tell the *Weekly News*:

> I went over every single thing I had heard about [Manuel]. When I finished, the senior of the two detectives stood up. His words fell on me like a sheet of cold water: 'You can forget about Manuel. If anyone knows Manuel, I do. If anyone knows how Manuel thinks, I do.'

Despite the mounting evidence and the recent investigations of Manuel, Hendry apparently refused to accept the possibility of his guilt. Other officers in the force might believe otherwise but Hendry was adamant. He, of course, was the officer who had arrested Watt and charged him with murdering his daughter, wife and wife's sister. It must have been very difficult for him to accept that he could have been wrong.

All this happened towards the end of 1956 and in the following January. Weeks then months passed and there was no public indication that the police were making any progress in solving the Watt murders or the Kneilands killing. The end of November 1957, the time set for Manuel's release from Barlinnie, drew near. Now Watt began to pick up new stories about him. It seemed Manuel was boasting that he had something on Watt that would provide him with a meal ticket once he was free.

It was at this point that Manuel sent another of his letters to Dowdall. This soon set in train one of the most bizarre episodes in the whole tangled affair, an episode that still poses unanswerable questions.

CHAPTER ELEVEN

On 27 November 1957, Manuel wrote to Dowdall, addressing him as 'Dear Lawrence [*sic*]' and telling him that he was to be released on Saturday, 30 November. 'I would like you to phone my house on Saturday morning at 9 a.m. sharp,' he wrote, so they could arrange to meet that evening. 'The subject matter of the interview you can put down to unfinished business concerning a party who was, to my certain knowledge, doubly unfortunate.'

There certainly was a great deal of unfinished business to be dealt with and, despite the peremptory tone of the letter, Dowdall agreed that they should meet on the following Monday, 2 December. When they met, Manuel told Dowdall that he wanted to clear up the Watt murders and said more or less what he had already said in prison a year or so earlier. He also produced a small black-and-white photograph of a girl and told Dowdall it was Vivienne Watt. Dowdall later told the police, 'I could not say anything about it as I had not seen the girl.' Once again, he told Manuel he should go to the police. He got the usual negative response. Manuel did say, however, that he would like to meet Watt.

And so Dowdall arranged for Watt and Manuel to meet, although he could not be present himself. Oddly enough, exactly when this meeting had occurred was a matter of some disagreement. In the second half of January, Watt told the police it was sometime around mid-December. It is very strange that he was so uncertain about the date of a meeting that was of such crucial importance to him. Dowdall, relying on his diary, said it took place on either the second or third of the month and this dating is supported by Manuel in a statement he gave to the police.

Watt and Manuel met at 6 p.m. at the Whitehall Restaurant in the city centre. Here were two men, both suspected of the same three murders, facing each other across a table. The physical contrast alone must have been striking, the burly thick-necked Watt, 15 st. and 6 ft 2 in., looming over the lightly built, sharply dressed Manuel, less than 5 ft 6 in. in height and weighing less than 10 st. Watt was almost bald; Manuel's heavily greased hair was carefully combed back in waves. They were an odd pair in every sense – and one of them was a multiple murderer.

There are, as so often with Manuel, two totally contradictory accounts of what happened next: Watt's as he reported the events to the police a few weeks later and when he testified at Manuel's murder trial, and Manuel's, also given in court. The accounts differed on one vital point: according to Manuel, Watt confessed he had murdered his family.

The whole situation of the meeting was extraordinary, verging on the unbelievable. Watt gave an account of his first face-to-face encounter with Manuel in a statement to detectives from the Glasgow force shortly after Manuel was arrested. Two versions of his account have recently been discovered. One seems to be a rough draft based on shorthand notes made by a police stenographer at the time; the second is a longer and more detailed account, elaborating on the first, although differing in a few places.

Watt had met Manuel at the Whitehall Restaurant although, at Manuel's insistence, they did not stay there long. Just after Watt arrived, Manuel handed him a newspaper on which he had written that two men sitting nearby were journalists. Watt did not take this seriously: 'I threw the paper on the table.' Watt explained why he had agreed to the meeting: 'I told him I had come here thinking that he had something to tell me about the Burnside affair. I told him frankly that if he had anything to do with the Burnside murders, I would like to get hold of him and tear him to pieces. He said, "People don't do that to Manuel."'

Watt made it clear that Manuel had no hope of getting any money from him, perhaps in response to the story that Manuel had boasted in prison that Watt could be a source of income for him. Later, whenever he talked about his encounters with Manuel, Watt was always keen to emphasise that he never gave him any money.

Because Manuel had indicated that he was unwilling to stay in the restaurant because of 'the newspapermen', they went to a nearby pub. Here, Watt said, 'Manuel told me many things and also answered many questions. His attitude was that he knew all about the murders.' Manuel told him that three people, Charles Tallis, Martin Hart and Mrs Mary Bowes, had gone housebreaking in Burnside. They robbed a house several doors away from the Watts' and then went looking for the Valentes' house. They believed that the Valentes kept between five and ten thousand pounds in a safe in their house. They had spotted the Valente daughter in the Watt house and concluded that that was where she lived. They went away but came back later to rob what they assumed was the Valente house. Their plan was to shoot all the people there except for one, whom they would force to tell them where the safe key was kept. Thus, Manuel claimed, the Watt house had been raided in error.

Manuel went on to tell Watt that Tallis had shot the two women and then killed Vivienne. Hart and Bowes had fled when the shooting started. The gun used was one he, Manuel, had given to Tallis and

Tallis had returned it to him after the murders; five bullets were missing from those he had supplied. At that point, Tallis was in 'a terrible state'. He had also shown Manuel two rings he had stolen in the first break-in.

'I realised there was something very wrong,' Watt said, 'and asked him to give me details about the house and he could detail everything.' Not only was Manuel keen to show Watt how much he knew about the murders, information that he claimed Tallis had given him, but he also 'tried to impress on me that he was responsible for getting me liberated and was quite emphatic about that'. He also claimed he could clear Watt completely. As so often in the past, he was proclaiming himself to be the possessor of special, secret knowledge.

Watt expressed his concern that, even if what Manuel was telling him were true, it was difficult to see how the information could help him. If Tallis would not admit to the crimes and the police could not prove he had committed them, what then was to be done? Manuel's reply was chilling. 'He then said, quite coolly: "Tallis could commit suicide by shooting himself with the gun that shot your family and if he was found dead with that gun beside him, it would give the big legal brains something to get over."' Watt put the obvious interpretation on this: 'I was shocked at hearing this because it appeared to me that he had a plan to murder Tallis if it suited him.'

Manuel added that it was possible that proof against Tallis might be obtained. About a week before the murders, he claimed, the same three people had broken into an unoccupied house and spent some time there; they had a gun with them. Tallis had wanted to have intercourse with Mrs Bowes in a bedroom. She had refused, they had struggled and she had fired a shot. The bullet had grazed Tallis's side and gone into the mattress. Manuel thought it could still be found there or in the floor. The same gun, he said, had been used in the Watt murders.

Manuel told Watt he had dumped the gun in the Clyde. Watt asked how it could be retrieved. 'He replied that it had been dropped in the Clyde all right but in a way he could get it whenever he wanted it. He added at this time that he had two other guns anyway, a .38 and a .45.' This detail of Manuel claiming to have two other guns appears only in the longer version of Watt's statement.

Manuel and Watt continued to sit in the pub and Manuel apparently told Watt more about the murders, interspersing his talk with outbursts of hatred for the Lanarkshire police. Next came a strange episode, a key part of which is recorded only in the first, shorter draft of Watt's statement to the police. 'He mentioned that money had been taken from my house although it had been said none had been taken. He also said there was no safe in my house. I asked him if he had been in the kitchenette and he said he had looked but there was no safe. He did not appear to have been in the kitchenette, where my safe is actually situated.' If this statement is taken at face value, it means that Manuel admitted having been in Watt's house and looking for a safe there. However, for some reason, the account was changed in Watt's final, longer statement, where he simply says: 'He maintained that money had been taken from my home although it had been said that none was taken, and he said there was no safe in my house.' As we shall see, the matter of the safe came up again at Manuel's trial.

One can only speculate about the puzzling matter of the money. Had money actually been taken during the raid? If so, what money was it? Is the explanation that Watt, like many businessmen, kept a considerable amount of cash at his house? But if Manuel had stolen money from Watt's house, what had he done with it? There is no evidence that he suddenly became flush with cash about this time and police searches of his house found nothing. Moreover, in court, Watt stated that all his money was tied up in his bakery business and he did not keep large amounts of cash in the house. On the other hand, it will be recalled that he had been told in Barlinnie that there was a plan to raid the safe in his previous house, so it must have been believed then that he held a considerable sum in cash at home. The matter remains obscure.

Next Manuel told Watt his daughter was not a virgin. This was an extraordinary thing to say and it is odd that Watt does not comment on it or mention taking Manuel to task over it. Manuel then showed him the small photograph of the young girl that he had already shown to Dowdall. 'He said, "Is that your daughter?" I told him it was not and he tore up the photograph.' That was Watt's testimony just after mid-January. By the time he appeared at Manuel's trial, it had been expanded and he said this: 'To my amazement – I said, "That is not my daughter," but I recognised the photograph. It was a photograph of Anne Kneilands which I had seen in the newspaper.' This version, of course, was far more damning of Manuel.

Watt and Manuel had been together for two hours. At this point, Watt drove them to find his brother John at one of his bakery premises. John was not available so they went to another pub, where they stayed till about eleven o'clock, and there John eventually joined them. While they were waiting for him, Watt introduced Manuel to the landlord's wife, who had a reputation as a spiritualist, telling her he was with someone who knew something about the murders. 'She said that she thought he was going to be good to me and that she had a feeling that he knew something that could help me. Manuel did not speak at all. He later asked me who she was and I told him she was a great spiritualist . . . he appeared taken aback and seemed worried.'

Once John had joined them, they all drove to his flat, where they met his wife. Manuel repeated what he had told Watt. They ate and drank together, 'And not all the time was spent in hard talking,' as Watt recalled. Then, at around 6 a.m., Watt drove Manuel to his home. They arranged to meet again at the Whitehall Restaurant that evening.

Thus Manuel and Watt, the first time they met, spent no less than eleven hours together, eating and drinking and talking, first in a restaurant, then in two pubs, and later at John Watt's flat, possibly talking some more in the car as Watt drove Manuel home. Eleven hours together: what on earth was being said, what was being thought, during all that time? How could Watt sit down and eat a meal with a man he suspected of killing his family? Unfortunately, there is no adequate record of what was said during most of that time. All we have to help us understand what went on are Watt's two statements and what he eventually said in court and later to the newspapers. None of these accounts can account for why things lasted so long. The explanation Watt himself gave was: 'My aim was to question him and try and see if the truth would be revealed as to how and by whom my family were murdered. I gave him drink to this aim. His aim, I think, was to impress me that he was the man who got me liberated, could clear me and knew all about the murders.'

Later that day, Watt phoned Dowdall and told him about the meeting. Not unnaturally, Dowdall was surprised it had gone on for so long. They agreed they would meet Manuel again that evening. When, at about six o'clock, Watt returned to the Whitehall Restaurant, Dowdall and Manuel were already there. Manuel went through his story again. He told Dowdall of how Tallis, Hart and Bowes had broken into an unoccupied house, about the scuffle on the bed and the fact that a shot had been fired into the mattress. He thought the bullet might still be there and, if so, could be recovered.

No doubt Dowdall passed all this information to the police. They began to look for someone who could get close to Manuel and report his activities to them. But a few days after his meeting with Dowdall and Watt, Manuel seemed to have disappeared from his usual Glasgow haunts.

CHAPTER TWELVE

The four weeks of December 1957 are of critical importance to this story, for during them Manuel certainly murdered four people, very probably five. His activities during this time, his final days of liberty, can be reconstructed from evidence given at his trial and information that emerged later. Not all of those who testified in court can be regarded as completely reliable, honest witnesses but the overall picture of events during this period can be drawn with a degree of confidence.

By early December, at least some members of the police were already convinced that he had murdered the Watts and Anne Kneilands, and they were beginning to keep an eye on him. Much of the information about Manuel in this period comes from Joe Brannan, who, at some point in the first week or so of December, was persuaded by the Lanarkshire police to get close to him and report daily, at around midnight, on what he did.

The first key event occurred near Newcastle. On 8 December

1957, the body of a taxi driver called Sydney Dunn was found on the moors near the village of Edmundbyers, about 18 miles from Newcastle. He had been shot through the head and his throat cut; he had not been robbed. His taxi was parked 140 yards away, parts of it smashed up. On 29 January 1958, Manuel was charged with Dunn's murder. He denied the charge. After he was executed, a coroner's jury decided Manuel had killed Dunn. Despite the verdict, there remain puzzling aspects to this murder. What was Manuel doing seeking work in Newcastle? Why should he wish to be driven to the village of Edmundbyers? How did he get back to Lanarkshire from the isolated village in time to sign on for National Assistance the next day? And, of course, there is the much greater question: if it was Manuel, *why* did he kill the taxi driver? The Dunn murder raises many questions and we will examine it in detail later.

We get a picture of Manuel's ordinary life in these weeks from the numerous enquiries the Glasgow police made following the Smart murders. As they set out to find more witnesses to his behaviour, they obtained a set of statements that show him in his usual role as a petty thief, selling stolen goods around the pubs of Glasgow and mixing with other crooks.

The first witness to provide information was James Curran, a 45-year-old unemployed labourer. At 6 p.m. on 6 or 7 December, he was walking down Renfield Street in Glasgow city centre with a friend. They were approached by a man who recognised Curran and knew his name. It was Manuel, who reminded Curran that they had met in prison some eight or ten years before, presumably, therefore, in Peterhead. The trio went for a drink. In the pub, Manuel produced various items of jewellery, including two wristwatches, a bracelet and a couple of rings, one of which was set with opals, and offered them for sale. Curran was certain they were stolen and declined the offer. Manuel approached a barmaid, Betty. She was tempted by the opal ring but settled for buying the bracelet for two pounds.

It was decided that Curran's friend's brother might be able to sell the rest of the jewellery at something like retail price, so they went in a taxi to his house. He took the items on a sale-or-return basis. It was agreed that they would meet next day in the town centre. The brother arrived as arranged and had not made a sale. The jewellery was returned to Manuel, who said he would sell it to a nearby bullion dealer but didn't.

Curran and Manuel next went to see a fence they both knew and Manuel sold the items for five pounds. The two then went to the Moulin Rouge, a pub in the Gorbals. There they drank until closing time, 2.30 p.m. They had been joined by two women, Mamie and an English girl. The Moulin Rouge was not noted for the refinement of its clientele and these were a pair of 'hairies'. (In Edwardian Glasgow, only disreputable women did not wear a hat, hence the appellation.) The party adjourned to Curran's home where, according to his friend's statement, 'We sat talking and drinking till about 5 p.m. [the magical hour when the pubs reopened] Manuel had bought a good deal of drink and he appeared to have plenty of money.'

Whilst they were at Curran's house, Manuel tried to interest him in a business proposition. 'The only thing he made clear was that he would take over one or two of my rooms and that a man and a woman would come to stay. He said I would receive a letter from a man about the business and whenever I got that I was to phone him and let him know. He then gave me a sort of luggage ticket with his phone number on it. The ticket had foreign writing on it and when I spoke about it he said something about two American men.' This sounds like one of Manuel's deliberately mystifying fantasies.

The police also took statements from Mamie, a 39-year-old widow, and her English friend. When we recently asked a former barman of the Moulin Rouge if he could remember any particular female regulars, he replied instantly, 'Big Mamie! She was a lady of the night.' He described her as a heavily built, busty dyed blonde. Her party trick was to pull up her jumper to liven things up. 'She had a wee friend, whose name I can't remember, but she was also on the game.'

These two ladies told the police they had been in the Moulin Rouge when Manuel, Curran and the other man introduced themselves and bought drinks. At Curran's house, 'We had a number of bottles of wine, etc., which the man Peter had bought.' Mamie told the police, 'I gathered that the man had been to London and other places in England but beyond that I did not get much out of him.'

Betty the barmaid also gave the police her version of events. According to her, a regular and his friend Curran had come in with a third man whom she didn't know. This stranger came over to offer her some jewellery he was selling 'on behalf of his mother'. She agreed to buy the bracelet for two pounds, which her husband gave her, 'as it was to be a gift from him to me for my birthday which was the following day'. The fact that this lady escaped prosecution for what was a classic case of reset (receiving stolen goods) gives us an idea of the latitude the police were allowing potential witnesses against Manuel as they investigated him for murder.

The events described by these witnesses were probably representative of Manuel's life while he was out of prison: stealing, drinking in rough pubs, mixing with other criminals and prostitutes, and selling what he had stolen for whatever he could get.

Peter Manuel's activities in December also shed light on a far more serious matter: how he got the gun with which the Smarts were murdered. Just before Christmas, Manuel called at the entrance to the Gordon Club in central Glasgow. This was a haunt of local criminals, incongruously situated above the Girl Guides headquarters. Manuel asked for Andrew Thomson, who worked there, and told him that he was to collect a parcel from his house. This item had been left there some years before by a former lodger, Tony Lowe. Samuel 'Dandy' McKay, who also worked at the club, and who had met Manuel in Peterhead, drove him and Thomson to the house in Florence Street in the Gorbals and the parcel was handed over. McKay would later claim that Manuel showed him that it contained a Beretta automatic pistol and ammunition. The Smarts were shot with a Beretta.

On Christmas Day, the Reverend Alexander Houston and his wife left their home in Mount Vernon to join friends for Christmas lunch. On their return, they found that their house had been broken into and several items stolen. These included a pair of gloves, a Brownie camera and the contents, about two pounds, of a foreign mission collection box and a single woollen sock. No fingerprints were found and police assumed the sock had served as a glove for the thief. Manuel would later be convicted of this break-in.

On the Friday after Christmas, Brannan, the police spy, met Manuel at the labour exchange in Bellshill and went with him first to Pacitti's Café and then on to the Windmill Tavern in Birkenshaw. According to Brannan, Manuel said he had recently carried out a break-in at a minister's house in Mount Vernon and had got some money and a camera.

On the evening of Saturday, 28 December, a pretty young woman, 17-year-old Isabelle Cooke, was preparing to spend the evening at a dance. She dressed in her finery and set off, carrying her dancing shoes, to catch a bus to meet her boyfriend Douglas Bryden in nearby Uddingston. She walked into the winter night and disappeared. Bryden waited forlornly as bus after bus arrived. In the small hours of the next day, her distraught parents searched for her but in vain. It later emerged that she had taken a short cut to the bus stop along the same path where Peter Manuel had some 11 years before brutally attacked a young mother walking with her child. Frantic with worry, Cooke's parents contacted the police the next morning. Later that day, they were horrified to be shown her vanity case. It and several buttons had been found at the mouth of a disused ventilation shaft. Worse was to follow. The next morning, her underskirt was found and later her panties, one of her walking shoes, a raincoat and a stole. Yet more items were found, virtually destroying her parents' hopes of seeing their daughter alive again. A vast police operation was set in train to find clues and, it was feared, her body.

New Year's Eve was pay day for Peter Smart and he was in holiday mood. He planned to take his wife and son to see his parents for a family gathering in Ancrum, near Jedburgh in the Borders, and was undecided whether to go on New Year's Day or, if the roads were bad, to wait until the 2nd before heading south. Alternatively, he thought he might go to Dumbarton and stay in a hotel run by a friend. He received his monthly pay cheque of £187 15s 11d and took it to the Parkhead branch of the Commercial Bank of Scotland, where he paid in his cheque and withdrew £35. He was issued new, consecutively numbered notes from a bundle of 500. These notes were predominantly blue in colour. He returned to his firm and used some of the money to pay off an advance he had received.

Hogmanay, that particularly Scottish festival, is a time for meeting and drinking. Smart had bought several bottles of whisky before Christmas. Now he called in at his local pub, The Noggin, and bought two more bottles. He later returned for a few drinks before going home at about ten to ten. He paid using some of the new banknotes.

Manuel, in contrast, was short of funds on 31 December. He had only 2s 2d in his savings account and he seems to have been without cash. He bought a packet of five Woodbine cigarettes, the cheapest brand, in the local corner shop. His brother James took him to the local off-licence to buy a bottle of wine for eight shillings. They returned home and soon afterwards his mother handed him five shillings to go out for a drink. He, James and their father set off to a pub called The Stag, where they had some drinks before James went elsewhere and Samuel and Peter went to the Royal Oak. There they were joined by Joe Brannan. It soon became clear that Peter Manuel's finances were parlous, for when it was his turn to buy a round, his father passed over a pound note to him. As he pocketed the change, Manuel said, 'That's a pound I owe you.'

At closing time, father and son returned home to a family gathering, where James joined them. Theresa, now a fully qualified nurse, was off duty and a cousin, Ron Faubert, an American serving with the US Army in Germany, was staying with them.

As the bells rang out, healths were toasted and all were in high spirits. Theresa had a friend, Mary McDonald, a nurse at the Southern General Hospital in Glasgow, who was on duty that night. After midnight, she received a phone call from Theresa wishing her a happy New Year. Clearly things were lively in the Manuel household, for as she sat in a darkened ward, Theresa and Ron chatted with her and Peter serenaded her by phone, singing several verses from 'Come Back to Sorrento'. At about 1.30 a.m., the night sister entered the ward and Mary had to cut off the call. A little later, she was on the phone again and this time Peter sang 'Here in my Heart'. Eventually, at 2.15 a.m., this telephone marathon ended. The Manuel party continued until about 4 a.m. before people began to drift off to bed. The exact time each person claimed to have retired would be of crucial importance. Mary McDonald later told a newspaper that Theresa had said she was the last to go to bed, at about four o'clock.

The little two-bedroom house was full. Theresa and her mother had one bedroom to themselves, whilst Samuel, James and Ron were in the other and Peter slept in a folding bed-chair downstairs. The two brothers claimed that they were the last to retire, staying awake in order to do the washing up and tidying. James, being short-sighted, later said he hadn't been able to read the time on the kitchen clock.

At about 5 a.m. on New Year's morning, as a taxi driver was travelling east along Sheepburn Drive, he encountered an Austin A30 being driven erratically. It was without lights. He signalled by flashing his own lights but was ignored by the driver. As the car passed him, he noticed from the quantity of exhaust that the engine had not been running for long. He later identified the car as Mr Smart's. Later, a similar car was noticed by a Mrs Graham parked in the car park of a firm called Ranco, about seven minutes' walk from the Manuel house. The car's presence was noticeable because, it being New Year's Day, the car park was nearly empty. Meanwhile at Sheepburn Road, it was noted that the curtains at the Smart house were closed, the garage doors open and the car gone.

Manuel was up and about early, buying Capstan cigarettes. The local shop owner remembered that, although it was New Year's Day, he was freshly shaved and neatly dressed. Around midday, Manuel set out to see his drinking crony Joe Brannan. He arrived at Brannan's house at 12.30 p.m., half an hour earlier than had been agreed. Brannan's original plan, he later claimed, had been to treat the moneyless Manuel to a New Year drink using money he had saved in a Christmas club fund at the Woodend Hotel. But instead, Brannan was confronted with a Manuel in funds, who presented his two children with two shillings each.

Manuel and Brannan then went to the Woodend Hotel, where they met James. Peter Manuel put on a display of prodigal spending that impressed not just Brannan but other hotel guests and staff, too. That afternoon session saw rounds of drinks paid for by Manuel, who clearly enjoyed showing off. At one point, he paid over a five-pound note, mistaking it for a one-pound note of a similar colour and size, and commended the barman for his honesty in giving the correct change. Brannan could not contain his curiosity and asked the source of the sudden riches. 'The Gordon Club,' came the answer. Manuel claimed he had gone in to see someone for 'a payment through the Watt business'. This display of wealth came to a close with the purchase of more drinks to take home. Manuel told Brannan that there was to be an engagement party later that day for his cousin, the daughter of his mother's brother Patrick Greenan.

The party got under way towards the end of the afternoon. Manuel seemed eager to show off how much money he had and impress people with his generosity. He arrived carrying a bottle of Johnnie Walker whisky and four or five packets of Capstan cigarettes, which he shared around. He handed out pound notes to relatives and, at about 8.30 p.m., he went back to the Woodend Hotel to buy more drink, spending the considerable sum of £8 17s 6d. According to Brannan, Manuel told him he had driven an A30 to and from the hotel to collect these supplies. Staff at the hotel would tell the police that he had paid with new pound notes. After the party was over, Manuel and a number of young people went to a local dance; he paid for all the tickets. This was the apotheosis of Peter Manuel, impressing the party with his ostentatious and lavish generosity. Less than a mile away, three dead bodies lay in a cold and silent house.

The next morning, at about 8.10 a.m., a local police constable, Robert Smith, hitched a lift from a passing motorist heading towards Glasgow in a grey A30. He was in uniform and on his way to assist in the search for Isabelle Cooke. The driver and he chatted about the weather and the driver said he was on his way to St Enoch Square Air Terminal to collect a young lady. At a later identification parade, Smith unhesitatingly recognised Manuel as the driver. It may be that he was the third person to be chauffeured by Manuel that morning, for, earlier, Francis Jack and Charles Scott, who had finished their night shift at Law Hospital at 7 a.m., had hitched a lift from the driver of a small car travelling from Wishaw to Carluke.

That day, 2 January, the postman noticed that the curtains of the window to the right of the door at the Smarts' house were drawn while those to the left had been opened. Later that afternoon, a refuse collector noticed that all the front curtains were closed again.

On the morning of Friday, 3 January, Brannan met Peter Manuel at the labour exchange to sign on. At Sheepburn Drive, it was noticed that all the Smarts' curtains were open. By 2 p.m., the curtains were all drawn. That evening, a light was on in the house. Meanwhile, Manuel and Brannan went on drinking in pubs and Manuel bought for them both.

In the early hours of Saturday, 4 January, Mr and Mrs John McMunn, who lived near Sheepburn Road, woke to the sight of a face at their bedroom door. The husband called out, 'Who is it?' and, to his wife, 'Where's the gun?' She responded, 'Here it is!' The figure dashed downstairs and escaped through a ground-floor window. Though the matter never came to court, Manuel was later identified as the intruder and a heel print found on a chair cover matched the diamond pattern of a pair of his shoes. The McMunns had been very lucky.

The next day, there were more changes in the curtains at the Smarts' house and a couple of small windows had been opened. Whoever had killed the Smarts was returning from time to time and spending time in the house with their decaying bodies.

The discovery of the Smart family murders on 6 January created uproar across the whole country. This was the most heinous crime imaginable. An innocent family had been foully murdered as they slept in their own beds. If this could happen in a sleepy Glasgow suburb, then no one was safe.

The next meeting of Manuel and Brannan was on Wednesday, 8 January, two days after the Smarts had been found. Manuel, with his usual insouciance, had gone to sign on at the labour exchange. He and Brannan later sat on the upper deck of a bus to watch the police scouring the area around the Calder River in an effort to find the body of Isabelle Cooke. Manuel, clearly delighted by the futile efforts of the hated police, crowed to Brannan, 'It's a red herring they are looking for.'

They next met up on the Friday to collect their dole. Manuel told Brannan that he had to go to Glasgow to collect some money and that he was going to go away. He suggested that Brannan join him in going to London. Matters had changed considerably the next day, the 11th, for when Brannan called on him, Peter Manuel's face was scarred down one side and his nose was 'busted'. He had clearly been in a fight. Had he gone to the Gordon Club in an attempt to extort money from Dandy McKay by threatening to link him in some way to the Smart murder gun? If so, he had clearly misjudged his man, for McKay was not the sort to succumb to blackmail. Manuel may have attempted to harm his fellow crooks at the Gordon Club in another way: Peter Smart's A30 had been abandoned in Florence Street, near the home of Andrew Thomson, from where Manuel had collected the gun. Was this intended as a hint to the police?

Manuel was becoming increasingly aware that police were circling closer and closer. McKay had told him the police had mentioned his name when they had been questioning others and had asked if he had been seen near Florence Street. Around the 12th, Manuel realised his house was being watched at night. Though he despised the police and considered them inept, he found their vigil demoralising. His sister would later report that he had to be restrained from rushing out of the house with a poker to set about one of his watchers.

Elsewhere, the painstaking work of detection was continuing. Officers had succeeded in tracing some of the brand-new banknotes that Smart had received the day before he died. The trail always led to the same source: Manuel. It was sufficient to allow the procurator fiscal to apply for a search warrant. For Manuel, the storm clouds were about to break.

CHAPTER THIRTEEN

At 6.45 a.m. on 14 January, a cold dark wintry morning, a group of police officers arrived at the Manuel home empowered by a warrant to search for money, banknotes and keys believed to be stolen from the Smart home. The line-up was formidable: Detective Superintendent Alex Brown, Detective Inspector Tom Goodall, Chief Inspector William Muncie, Detective Inspector Robert McNeil, Inspector Scott, Detective Sergeant Scott, a police woman sergeant and two other officers. Before they had left the police station, they had been given a strict instruction: only Brown and Goodall were to speak to the Manuels; everyone else was to remain silent. Brown was determined to give Peter no chance to browbeat the officers or involve them in arguments.

At Manuel's trial, the police gave their account of what happened at his house and what he said once he was in custody. The following account is based mainly on their testimony. It is only fair to say that the police version was challenged in court by Manuel and his family, who swore that many things reported by the police never happened. That crucial dispute will be dealt with when we come to the trial itself.

The search team met Samuel Manuel at the gate as he set out for work. Superintendent Brown introduced himself, produced the warrant and explained that the group were going to search his house. Samuel Manuel's attitude was hostile and defensive but he took them into the house, where they found Mrs Manuel and James up and dressed and Peter Manuel asleep on the bed-chair in the living room. Samuel Manuel demanded to read the warrant, which was allowed. He then made several very hostile remarks and threatened to complain to his MP.

Only after this was Peter Manuel roused from sleep. He too read the warrant and, for good measure, Brown read it aloud and cautioned Manuel, his father and mother. He made it clear that they were interested in finding evidence relating to the Smart murders only. Manuel became aggressive and used violent and threatening language; this played to the police's advantage. Brown told Peter Manuel to get dressed, as he was required to go with them to Bellshill police station for an identity parade. Manuel exclaimed, 'You can't take me. You haven't found anything yet.' He was told to wash, shave and get dressed. Brown stood by him as he did so. His mother made tea for him and the officers. This done, at 7.30 a.m. Peter Manuel was taken away. It was the last time he would see his home. As he left, he called to his parents to 'phone Jimmy Bell, the reporter, and get Dowdalls [*sic*]'.

The removal of Manuel from the scene was a tactical masterstroke: his parents were left unprotected by his bluster and legalistic mendacity, while he was prevented from controlling them. He was left in ignorance of what they might say or do. He had no idea what might happen in his absence.

Samuel Manuel was driven to his workplace, where he handed over keys needed by his colleagues and was taken straight back to Fourth Street. The search started in earnest. Soon a pair of men's gloves was found in an upstairs chest of drawers and Muncie discovered a camera. These proved to be items stolen from Reverend Houston's manse on Christmas Day. Samuel Manuel was asked to account for them. He stated that they belonged to him. By doing so, he laid himself open to a charge of theft by housebreaking or alternatively reset (receiving). He was charged and removed from the scene. Now that the two most turbulent protagonists had been taken out of the equation, the officers were able to continue their searches unimpeded. They discovered a National Assistance form on which was written: 'Mr McKay central 7118.' This, together with a bank book and all Peter Manuel's outer clothing, was removed for further examination.

Manuel was now taken from Bellshill to police headquarters at Hamilton. He was interviewed by Brown, Goodall and McNeil. Brown informed him that his father was now in Bellshill police station, having been charged with theft.

The account we have of how he reacted has expletives deleted and is couched in restrained terms, so we are robbed of the full fury of Manuel's reaction. (John Bingham's book tells us that there was much profanity, while Brown described 'sour comments'.) When he recovered, he said he wanted to talk about the money traced to him. Brown speedily reminded him he was under caution and that this was a robbery in which three people had been murdered. Manuel claimed Dandy McKay was the source of the banknotes. McKay was found and brought to the station. The two confronted each other. When he learned what had been stated by Manuel, McKay vehemently denounced the whole thing as a pack of lies and prophesied to Manuel, 'You'll swing for this!'

Identification parades were held. Witnesses identified Manuel as the man who had been spending new pound notes and who had been seen walking along the railway line on the night Cooke had been killed.

Manuel had now antagonised Dandy McKay and the view of many Glasgow criminals was that he had to go. The police enquiries that followed the Smart murders had caused many of them inconvenience and anxiety. McKay himself was so infuriated that he soon felt willing, perhaps having received certain assurances from the police, to impart all that he knew about Manuel's acquisition of the Beretta in mid-December.

Later that night, Muncie and McNeil charged Manuel with the Houston housebreaking and the Smart murders. His response to the first charge was, 'No, nothing.' He gave no reply to the second charge. His clothes were removed for examination and he was put in a cell. The next morning, he was taken to court, remanded in custody for four days and then taken back to police headquarters at 10.15 a.m. All officers were instructed to maintain a strict silence at all times. No one was to speak to him about anything whatsoever, not only in order to avoid unhelpful confrontations but also to unsettle the suspect.

McNeil returned to Bothwell police station to attend to the investigation, which was now gathering pace. The press, of course, were at the heels of every officer involved in the case. They were in a frenzy of anticipation, for the world now knew that a man was helping police with their enquiries into the Smart murders. In Dublin, Joe Beltrami, the future doyen of Glasgow criminal lawyers, was on honeymoon when he saw newspaper reports naming Peter Manuel as having been charged with several murders. He and many other Glaswegian solicitors knew the name all too well, for their clients in the criminal underworld despised Manuel as a loudmouth and a liability whose boasted knowledge of their activities sometimes carried to the ears of police snitches. As Mr Beltrami was later to put it, 'They regarded him as a disgrace to their profession.'

At 12.30 p.m., McNeil was informed that Manuel wanted to see him. About an hour later, the request was repeated. It was not until 2.50 p.m. that he and Detective Inspector Goodall talked to Manuel. He said he wished to speak 'about unsolved crimes in Lanarkshire'. On hearing this, McNeil again cautioned him and reminded him of the gravity of his position, advising him that he should avail himself of the services of a solicitor. After her son had been removed, Mrs Manuel had contacted Laurence Dowdall, who prudently declined to act for him, as he quite rightly anticipated that he would find himself in the witness box giving evidence against Manuel. (According to Manuel's mother, Dowdall gave Manuel some gratuitous advice, telling him that he ought to plead insanity, but she recorded that his response was as unrelenting as ever: 'Let's have no more of that nonsense!') Dowdall did, however, agree to act for Manuel's parents.

Even at this critical juncture, Manuel's huge self-esteem impelled him to handle matters without the advice of a solicitor. He asked McNeil about the charges facing his father and then said, 'Bring my father and mother here and I will see them in your presence, and after I have made a clean breast of it with them, you can take them away and then I will clear up everything for you and I will take you to where the girl Cooke is buried.'

Manuel was supplied with writing materials, after again being cautioned and offered the advice of a solicitor. He wrote:

> 15th January 1958
>
> To Detective Inspector McNeill [*sic*],
>
> I hereby promise to you personally that I am prepared to give information to you that will enable you to clear up a number of unsolved crimes which have occurred in the County of Lanarkshire in the past two years.
>
> This promise is given that I might release my father and my family from any obligations or loyalties they may feel on my behalf. I wish to see my parents, and make a clean breast with them first.
>
> The crimes I refer to above are crimes of Homicide. I further wish to stress that I volunteer this statement of my

> own free will, without duress or pressure of any description being brought to bear on me.
>
> (signed) Peter Manuel

Having written this, Manuel decided to go even further and, telling the police, 'This won't do, I'll write you another,' he then penned:

> 15th January 1958
>
> To Detective Inspector McNeil,
>
> I hereby freely and voluntarily give the following promise. I will lead information about the following specified crimes:
>
> 1. Anne Kneilands
> 2. The Watt murders
> 3. Isabelle Cooke
> 4. The Smart murders.
>
> On condition that my father is released and allowed to see me with my mother. The information I refer to concerns me, Peter Thomas Manuel, and my part in the above mentioned crimes. I will give complete and concise information on these crimes that will clear them up completely.
>
> (signed) Peter Manuel

McNeil knew that this in itself was insufficient to obtain a conviction. Also, knowing with whom he was dealing, he suspected a trap might be sprung at any time. He explained that it was not within his power to order the release of Manuel's father and that the matter would have to be referred to the procurator fiscal, who had remanded him in custody. He also cautioned Manuel again. At this point, according to McNeil, Manuel made a verbal confession about the Smart murders:

'I did it about six o'clock in the morning of New Year's Day. I got in the kitchen window. I went into a bedroom and got eighteen or twenty pounds in new notes and four or five ten-shillings notes in a wallet. It was in a jacket hanging on a chair in the man's room. I shot the man first and then the woman and then I shot the boy, but at first I thought it was a man in the bed.

'I then went to the living room and ate a handful of wee biscuits from a tray on a chiffonier and I got about eighteen shillings from a red purse in the woman's handbag. I took the man's keys and then took the car. The car key was on a bunch on a ring.

'I put it in the Ranco car park and took it to Florence Street the next day. I left it there about eight o'clock the next morning. I gave a policeman a lift on the way. He is a young fellow who lives at Powburn. But I never took these cigarettes I saw in the papers.

'I threw the gun in the Clyde and the keys in the Calder at the bridge. I think I threw the purse there too.'

The procurator fiscal was consulted and agreed that Manuel's mother and father should see him. They were brought to police headquarters and prepared for the momentous meeting. Soon they were ushered into the room where Peter was sitting surrounded by several police officers. According to the police, he had some difficulty in getting to the point but after telling them he had been 'fighting this thing alone all my life', he said: 'There is no future for me. I have done some terrible things. I killed the girl Kneilands at East Kilbride and I shot three women in the house in Burnside.' He then went on to say that he had murdered Isabelle Cooke and would take the police to where her body lay buried. He rounded it all off with a graphic description of the Smart family massacre.

When the meeting came to an end, Samuel Manuel was returned to his cell in Barlinnie to await his release, which could not happen until a liberation order had been granted by the procurator fiscal.

It was arranged that Peter would be taken to Barlinnie, checked in, as it were, and then immediately released on a temporary liberation order so that he could fulfil his promise to lead the police to where he had concealed Cooke's body, in a field near a brickworks in Baillieston.

There followed one of the most bizarre episodes in Scottish criminal history as he led them across country, through hedges and over ditches in pitch darkness. First, he pointed to a shallow excavation in the ground by the boundary hedge and explained, 'I dug that hole. I had her body here but I was disturbed by a man taking a short cut out of the brickworks and I had to take her away.' As he led them across a farm, they passed by the edge of the brickworks, where he removed from a pile of broken bricks a girl's dancing shoe and soon revealed the other under some ashes. He then went into the fields of Burntbroom Farm and there found his bearing from a tree and, counting his paces, reached a spot in the midst of a recently ploughed field, where he solemnly announced, 'I think she is in there. I think I am standing on her.'

There, about half a metre below the surface, they unearthed the remains of Isabelle Cooke. She was still clad in her woollen cardigan; her underskirt was bunched up around her waist. Below the waist, she was naked apart from her suspender belt. She had been asphyxiated. Her scarf had been forced into her mouth as a gag; her brassiere had been used as a garrotte and was deeply embedded around her throat. Strangulation is a particularly brutal act, allowing the killer to feel his victim slowly succumbing to death. There were bruises to Cooke's left eye and the left side of the face. She had been dealt a series of disabling blows by a right-handed person. A grim silence fell upon the officers as they rigged up screens and lighting, preparing to photograph and record the scene.

What was the motive for this killing? Cooke had been dragged off a suburban Glasgow street and into a country field. We know Manuel had removed some of her clothing, exposing her as she lay unable to defend herself, entirely within his power. Did this give him an immense, even orgasmic, pleasure? Did he store in his memory every detail of the thrill he felt as he dominated her and ended her life?

This was a crime about power and sexual domination. The killer of Isabelle Cooke had gained another experience to draw upon in his secret world, along with the abuse and destruction of Anne Kneilands, the tormented death of Vivienne Watt and those exhilarating moments when, gun in hand, he had held the power to destroy life as his oblivious victims lay slumbering before him.

At 4 a.m., the police called upon the Reverend Alexander Houston in nearby Mount Vernon to ask him to impart the heartbreaking news of the discovery of Isabelle Cooke's body to her parents. He immediately made his way to the Cooke house just round the corner.

The police had removed Manuel before Cooke's body was unearthed and they took him back to the police station. Inspector Cleland was called in from his home to take the suspect's third statement:

> 4.15 a.m.
> Thursday, 16th January, 1958
>
> I am at present in custody in County Police Headquarters, Hamilton, on a charge of murder. I have been informed that I am not obliged to say anything unless I wish to do so, but whatever I say will be taken down in writing and may be given in evidence. I have been informed that I am entitled to have the benefit of legal advice before making this statement. I wish to make a statement.
>
> Signed: Peter Manuel
> Date: 16.1.1958
> Witnessed: Matthew Cleland, Inspector
>
> I hereby confess that on the 1st day of January 1956, I was the person responsible for killing Annie Kneilands.
>
> On the 17th September, 1956 I was responsible for killing Mrs Marion Watt and her sister Mrs George Brown, also her daughter Vivienne.

On the 28th December 1957 I was responsible for killing Isabelle Cooke.

On January the first, 1958 I was responsible for killing Mr Peter Smart, his wife Doris, and their son.

I freely admit and acknowledge my guilt in the above mentioned crimes, and wish to write a statement concerning them.

On the first of January, 1956, I was in East Kilbride at about 7 p.m. in the evening. At about 7.30 p.m. I was walking towards the Cross when I met a girl. She spoke to me and addressed me as Tommy. I told her my name was not Tommy and she said she thought she knew me. We got talking and she told me she had to meet someone, but she did not think they were turning up for the meeting. After a while I asked her if she would like some tea or coffee. She assented and we went into the Willow Café. I do not remember how long we were there, but it was not long. When we came out, she said she was going home and I offered to see her home.

She said she lived miles away, and that I would probably get lost if I took her home. I insisted, and she said all right. We walked along the road up to Maxwellton Road. From there we went along a curving road that I cannot name. About half way along this road I pulled her into a field gate. She struggled and ran away, and I chased her across a field and over a ditch. When I caught up to her I dragged her into a wood. In the wood she started screaming and I hit her over the head with a piece of iron I picked up.

After I had killed her I ran down a country lane that brought me out at the General's Bridge, at the East Kilbride Road. I do not know where I flung the piece of iron. I then ran down to High Blantyre and along a road that brought me to Bardykes Road. I went along Bardykes Road and over the railway up to where I live. I got home about 10.15 p.m.

I went up to East Kilbride from Hamilton about 6.30 p.m. in the evening.

On the 16th September, 1956 I left the Woodend Hotel, Mossend, at 10 p.m. in the evening. I took two women in to Glasgow, one . . . I dropped from a taxi at 283 High Street, Glasgow. The other one . . . I took to Merchiston Street in North Carntyne. I left her there and took the taxi to Parkhead Cross. At the Cross I caught the bus to Birkenshaw. When I arrived home I met a man I knew and he took me in a car up to Burnside. He had another man and a woman with him, we broke into a house in Fennsbank Avenue, number 18. We were there some time and somebody went to bed. I do not remember much about this house. The car was left in a lane in a small wood bordering the East Kilbride Road.

After a while I went scouting about looking at other houses. I found a house that looked empty, and went back to No. 18. Somebody had brought the car around and put it in beside the house in front of the garage. I told them and they drove me up and I got out at the other house. The others did not like the look of it, so they went back to the other house at No. 18.

I broke into the house by breaking the front door panel, which was made of glass. I then went in and opened a bedroom door. There were two people in the bed. I went into the other room and there was a girl in the bed. She woke up, and sat up. I hit her on the chin and knocked her out. I tied her hands and went back to the other room. I shot the two people in this room, and then heard someone making a noise in the other room. I went back in and the girl had got loose. We struggled around for a while and then I flung her on the bed and shot her too. I then went back to No. 18 and found them all asleep. We then took the car and they dropped me at Birkenshaw, and then they went to Motherwell, at about 5 a.m. on the 17th September. I did not steal anything from the house at No. 5 Fennsbank Avenue. That same day I went into Glasgow and flung the gun in the Clyde at the Suspension Bridge. I got the gun in a public house in Glasgow called the Mercat Bar, which is at Glasgow Cross. I do not remember the date I got the gun. I got the gun as one of a pair I bought. The man who fixed it for me told me the two men who came into the pub were policemen. The other gun was taken by a man from Burnbank. I never found out what became of it.

On the 28th of December, 1957, I went to Mount Vernon about 7 p.m. Going by bus from Birkenshaw to Mount Vernon. I walked up a road leading to the railway bridge that runs from Bothwell to Shettleston.

Just over the bridge I met a girl walking, I grabbed her and dragged her into a field on the same side as Rylands Riding School. I took her along the field following the line in the Bothwell direction. I took her handbag and filled it with stones from the railway. Before going any further I flung it in a pond in the middle of a field. I then made her go with me along towards the dog track. When we got near the dog track she started to scream. I tore off her clothes and tied something round her neck and choked her. I then carried her up a lane into a field and dug a hole with a shovel. While I was digging a man passed along the lane on a bike. So I carried her again over a path beside a brickwork into another field. I dug a hole next to a part of the field that was ploughed and put her in it. I covered her up and went back the way I came. I went back to the road and got her shoes which had come off at the outset. I took these and her clothes and scattered them about. The clothes I flung in the River Calder at Broomhouse. The shoe I hid on the railway bank at the dog track. I went up the same path and came out at Baillieston. I walked along the Edinburgh Road and up Aitkenhead Road to Birkenshaw, getting there about 12.30 a.m.

The first hole I dug I left as it was.

On the morning of the first of January I left my home at about 5.30 a.m. I went down a park path to the foot of Lucy Brae. Crossing the road I went into Sheepburn Road and broke into a bungalow.

I went through the house and took a quantity of Bank notes from a wallet I found in a jacket in the front bedroom. There was about £20 to £25 in the wallet. I then shot the man in the bed, and next the woman. I went into the next room and shot the boy. I did not take anything from the house except money. I got the gun from a man in Glasgow in a club. The Gordon Club. I took a car from the garage and drove it up to the car park at Ranco Works. Later that day I took the gun into Glasgow and threw it in the Clyde at Glasgow Green.

The next day, Thursday the 2nd I saw the car was still in the car park, so drove it to Glasgow, about eight o'clock in the morning and left it in Florence Street, in the South Side. Then I caught a bus back home.

I got into the house through a window, and left by the back door.

(signed) Peter Manuel

Witnessed by me Donald MacLeod
Constable 137

Witnessed by me Samuel Mather
Constable 15

This statement completed at 6.15 a.m. on 16/1/58
Matthew Cleland, Inspector

The circumstances of the discovery of the body of Isabelle Cooke and the appearance of 'a man' in court charged with her murder as well as many others caused a sensation.

Numerous resources were now dedicated to bringing about a successful prosecution as the Crown Office set about the Herculean task of preparing for the trial. As police enquiries continued, statements had to be taken and recorded from more than 280 witnesses. The actual statements, or precognitions, were to be taken by the procurators fiscal of Glasgow, Hamilton and Airdrie in person. They would then be forwarded to the Crown Office in Edinburgh, where the Lord Advocate and Solicitor General would review them in minute detail before deciding on the charges to be brought. It is interesting to note that at no time did the Crown have to compel any witness.

More physical evidence had to be collected. Manuel took the police to the General's Bridge and there they recovered Smart's bunch of keys and several pieces of angle iron, one of which seemed to fit the wounds to Kneilands' skull. He also showed the police where he had dropped the two guns in the Clyde. David Bell, a diver employed by the Clyde Navigation Trust, searched the icy, polluted waters of the river for the weapons. Eventually, he was able to retrieve the Webley revolver used in the Watt murders. It was missing its lanyard ring, just like the one Manuel had drawn for Dowdall. Its barrel had been smashed against a hard object and the front part closed up, probably to prevent it being fired for purposes of comparison. Then Bell found the Beretta. The eager press was on hand to record his efforts and his success.

Both guns were passed to the City of Glasgow Police's firearms expert, Detective Sergeant George Sowter, who speedily cleaned them, opened up the Webley's barrel and test-fired them. The Beretta's loading mechanism was defective but, with some practice, Sowter found that he could fire and reload and fire again within six seconds. The markings on the bullets that killed the Watts and the Smarts were compared with sample bullets fired from these guns. The results showed a conclusive match; these were indeed the weapons used to kill six people – and perhaps, as we shall see, a cow.

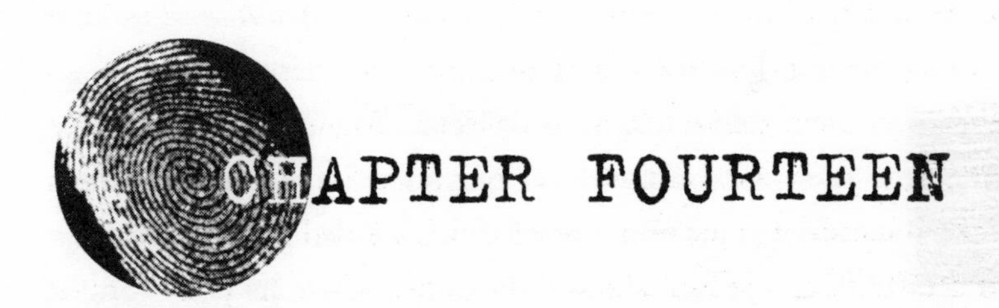

CHAPTER FOURTEEN

As the evidence against Manuel increased, so did the charges. He was interviewed by Durham police on 21 January. On the 29th, he was charged with the murder of Sydney Dunn. As that crime had been committed in England, he could not be tried for it until after he had faced the Scottish court. On 15 February, he was charged with nine murders: eight in Scotland and Dunn's.

His two solicitors – in Scottish legal terminology 'agents' – John Ferns and Ian Docherty, briefed Harald Leslie to be his leading counsel. It was an ancient tradition of the Scottish Bar that no one was allowed to stand in jeopardy of his life without the availability of the services of the best of the Faculty of Advocates. The Dean of Faculty would call upon QCs in turn to 'volunteer' to defend in the High Court where a person accused of a capital crime could not afford legal fees, and Manuel's case had fallen to Leslie. Because he had been briefed by Dowdall to defend Watt if his case ever came to trial, it was thought inappropriate that he should cross-examine his erstwhile client. That role, and others, would fall to William Grieve. They had as a junior Malcolm Morison, who would take notes, look up cases and examine witnesses of lesser importance.

Manuel was already planning his defence and making it clear he wanted it done his way. From the very start, he had doubts about his lawyers. He was sure he knew better than they did how to frame his defence. In early March he wrote, 'I am not at all satisfied with my agents [*sic*] lack of enthusiasm concerning line of defence. So much so that I may have to conduct my own defence.' He saw Leslie and Ferns a few days later and appeared less discontented with Ferns. Nevertheless, the idea of defending himself remained in his mind. It would be an extraordinary thing to do. Manuel, however, believed he was exceptional and had absolutely no doubt he would succeed.

To some extent, he had reason to feel confident about the idea. He knew all about court procedure; after all, he had been on trial often enough. By attentive observation, he had picked up lawyers' techniques and their patter, and he had studied Scots and English law in Peterhead. His superb memory would also help him. Most important of all, he had rejected his lawyer's advice to plead guilty in the Mary McLauchlan case. By defending himself, he had secured a not proven verdict in the face of almost overwhelming prosecution evidence. This triumph over the police had strengthened his already powerful self-belief.

And then there was his charm. He was always confident of that. He instructed his counsel not to object to women on the jury; he was sure they would respond favourably to him, just as he believed they had in the McLauchlan trial. 'They will know I am innocent,' he wrote, asserting blithely and with unconscious irony, 'I have a way with women.'

However avidly he imagined success, there were times when the grim reality of the situation could not be ignored. He was prisoner 450. When he wanted the records of his last two trials in order to prepare his defence, he was informed that it would cost one hundred and sixty pounds to get the trial transcripts; he complained, 'I have exactly two pence.'

He was preparing for the trial in other ways. Towards the end of March, a prison officer reported that Manuel had told him he was going to refuse all solid food 'until he goes to court so he will appear as pale as possible'. He soon gave up, for by early April his family was paying for food to be sent into Barlinnie, a privilege allowed to prisoners on remand. He received meat pies, bars of chocolate, biscuits and pints of milk. His mother told a reporter her son simply did not like prison food. Well, perhaps he'd had enough of it over the years. Manuel began to put on weight. Any chance of appearing pale and wan was past.

There are hints in his prison records for the period that he was planning alternative methods of strengthening his defence. He complained that visitors had been told they would 'be thrown out and the visit terminated' if they discussed why he had been arrested. He went on a two-day hunger strike and the authorities lifted this ban. Almost certainly, he wanted to discuss with his family and friends how they could help his case. During his trial some defence witnesses would commit perjury and Manuel must surely have had a hand in concocting their stories.

As he waited for the trial to start, Manuel had numerous visitors, family and friends, some convicted crooks, some not. One of the latter was Harry Benson, who would become a world-famous photographer. His first big exclusive had been a picture of the scene of Anne Kneilands' murder. Benson took Manuel cigarettes and books. Once he saw him suddenly lose his temper and strike one of the prison officers. He was told by the officers to forget what he had seen. Later, Manuel wrote to him and asked him to do the same. With Manuel, there was always a danger of sudden violence breaking out.

In return for Benson's gifts, Manuel wrote letters to him and his mother. Mrs Benson burnt hers without reading them, feeling they were contaminated. One of the letters to Benson, written on the eve of the trial, shows Manuel eager for it to start: 'Tomorrow sees things starting to roll. Not before time either.' There is a grim facetiousness in what he writes. One newspaper had claimed someone was selling bits of hair, supposedly his: 'It seems young birds are buying it. If I get slung they can have all the hair I have got gratis.' He has received a letter from a woman who wants to marry him: 'It seems that an acquittal will open up pleasant possibilities here. I might need a couple of stand-ins.'

The letter shows that, even so close to the beginning of the trial, Manuel was hardly worried by the prospect of appearing in court or the possibility that he might be hanged. Was there not something profoundly abnormal about his attitude?

Since his arrest, both the authorities and his defence had faced a crucial question: was he suffering from some serious mental defect or disability that might mean he was unfit to stand trial or, if tried and found guilty, unfit to be hanged? And if he was sane now, had he been insane when he'd committed murder? Had he known what he was doing or had he been acting under some uncontrollable impulse? Was it possible to establish which was the case? These were extremely difficult questions to answer. Manuel's life might depend on what the experts thought.

And so, almost as soon as he arrived in prison, he became involved in a series of medical and psychiatric examinations. On one hand, these were humiliating, something he was almost forced to undergo. He had always been opposed to the idea that his mental state should be medically scrutinised. On the other hand, they presented a splendid opportunity to talk about himself to avid listeners. Manuel always enjoyed a captive audience.

This, as we have seen, was not the first time that his mental condition had been examined. In October 1951, when he was in Peterhead, the Aberdeen psychiatrist had concluded damningly: 'His record from the age of 12 makes it clear he is an aggressive psychopath.' In August

1955, before the McLauchlan trial, the Barlinnie Medical Officer had decided he was fit to be tried: 'I can elicit no evidence to suggest that this man is insane. I am of the opinion that he is at present sane and fit to plead.'

This had been decided despite Manuel's own family having severe doubts about him. Theresa had told the medical officer that she believed her brother had 'a split mind' and that she had gone to the procurator fiscal at Hamilton to urge that Peter should be certified insane and locked up for his own safety and that of others. Samuel Manuel had written to his son suggesting he should agree to be examined by a psychiatrist. His response? 'No psychiatrist is going to look over me.' The clean bill of health from the Barlinnie medical officer and his subsequent success in defending himself must have increased Manuel's already near limitless self-belief.

But following his arrest in January 1958, he had to undergo a series of examinations. On 20 January, the forensic pathologists Professor Allison and Dr Imrie, who had both examined the murder victims, now appraised Manuel. The next day, a neurologist, Dr Angus MacNiven, made the first of six examinations; the last would take place a few days before Manuel went to the scaffold. MacNiven had already become involved in the case, for he had examined Watt just after he had been charged with murdering his family. (His report on Watt is not available.)

MacNiven spoke to Manuel's parents and to Theresa. According to his report, Samuel and Bridget told him that there was no history of mental illness in the family and claimed that they had never seen any signs of mental disorder in their son, despite what Samuel thought in the McLauchlan case. Slight but significant differences appear in how he and his wife regarded Peter. Samuel told MacNiven that Peter had been a very clever child, able to draw even before he went to school and 'a model boy in the house'. He described him as 'kind and generous' and said 'he would give away anything; he would give you the shirt off his back'. Though Samuel does not mention it, Peter had bought the family a television set and a record player. Perhaps it was not too hard to give away things got by stealing.

Bridget admitted to worries about Peter's behaviour. He had been a healthy baby, she told MacNiven, but, as he grew up, 'she never felt that she had his complete confidence'. She added that he never discussed his criminal behaviour and she complained that he 'took it all too light-heartedly' and had a 'hard core somewhere'.

According to his parents, Manuel read dictionaries and encyclopedias. Samuel claimed he was a good cook, and 'could provide "a really fancy tea"', baking cakes and preparing roasts. He had a typewriter, which he used a lot. (He wrote stories and sent them to publishers but they were all rejected. How one wishes to be able to read what he wrote.) He was never violent at home, his mother and father said.

These touching accounts of his amiable and helpful behaviour at Fourth Street are, of course, in total contrast to how he behaved in other peoples' homes: smashing his way in, thieving, leaving foul messes and, in later years, shooting the inhabitants as they slept.

The views of Theresa, 'a certified mental nurse' and, by all accounts, Peter's favourite in the family, were utterly different. She said she had long thought her brother was a psychopath as he was 'always indifferent to other peoples' opinions'. In 1953, he had threatened her with a bread knife during an argument. In 1955, as we have said, she had suggested to the procurator fiscal that he was insane. Two nights before his most recent arrest, when Manuel was aware that the police were watching their house, she had seen him 'in a state of frenzy'. He had taken a poker and said he was going outside to attack the policemen. Theresa also told MacNiven that two cousins on their mother's side were epileptic.

MacNiven's account brings out other characteristics of the accused. He says that Manuel has a remarkable memory and is able to produce 'a lucid and connected narrative . . . He never hesitates in his speech and he is never at a loss to remember a detail.' Strikingly, MacNiven notes that Manuel was 'composed and easy in his manner' during their interviews. 'He shows no anxiety or apprehension about his situation.' Perhaps this was because of another characteristic noted by MacNiven: Manuel, he wrote, was completely lacking in self-criticism and showed a strange detachment when talking about himself, as if he were describing someone else's actions. MacNiven noted that this quality meant that Manuel inspired no feeling of responsibility or concern in him. He had to remind himself that he was listening to a man who was about to be tried for eight murders, 'not merely listening to a reading from a work of fiction'.

Manuel made it clear to MacNiven that he believed his situation was the result of a police conspiracy. He claimed that the police wanted revenge because he had been acquitted in the McLauchlan case. 'They are out to destroy me and I am out to destroy them,' he said. MacNiven tentatively concludes that Manuel's attitude to the police 'may have been magnified and distorted to the degree that these ideas came to dominate his mind so that they may have the significance of a paranoid system in which the accused sees himself in the role of a master criminal engaged in a struggle with the police which he confidently expects to win'.

'A master criminal engaged in a struggle with the police.' It is a highly convincing description of how Manuel viewed himself. If he was sure he would be found innocent and, in the process, destroy his enemies, it would help explain his almost carefree attitude as he awaited trial.

Manuel denied to MacNiven that he had 'ever suffered from any gross form of mental illness' but he did claim two significant things had happened during adolescence. In 1943 or 1944 he had been hit by a fragment of flying bomb and been unconscious for six or seven hours. The shrapnel was surgically removed, leaving a small scar on his forehead. In about 1944, Manuel told MacNiven, while he was in borstal, he had received a severe electric shock from a concrete mixer. Three other borstal boys were killed in the same incident. He was unconscious for two days and his mind remained 'a blank' for the following three or four weeks.

Both stories are highly unlikely. If the wound and electrocution had actually occurred, they would almost certainly have been noted in his borstal record and his father would likely have mentioned them in his 1946 account of Manuel's health. MacNiven does not say whether he believed these stories. By telling them, Manuel was creating hugely dramatic incidents for his teenage years, years otherwise filled by humiliating detention, escape and recapture.

It might be thought that he was preparing a second line of defence by hinting at events that had left him mentally damaged and therefore not culpable of his crimes. We think this is unlikely: his massive egotism probably excluded any possibility that he could think of himself as mad.

Manuel also claimed three incidents of memory loss. The first, he said, was when driving a lorry in 1945. He told MacNiven he had consulted a neurologist in Blackpool called McFarlane or McIrlain. Three years later, he went to see a film with a girl and could not recall making an arrangement to meet her some days later. Eighteen months ago, he claimed, he had been boxing in Barlinnie on a Tuesday and did not remember anything until he found himself in Bible class the following Sunday.

So what is MacNiven's verdict? 'The accused is a very abnormal character and I am inclined to think that he comes within the category of psychopathic personality, but he lacks certain of the characteristics of this condition.' He also says that in his opinion Manuel 'showed no symptoms of mental disease'. Most striking was his untroubled state of mind: 'The accused is remarkably detached from what one might regard as the realities of the situation.' And MacNiven's answer to the most important question? 'My opinion is that the accused is sane and fit to plead.'

Other examinations were carried out by neurologist Dr John Gaylor. Two electroencephalograph tests produced, according to him, no indication that Manuel suffered from epilepsy. Gaylor had also heard the stories of memory lapses and therefore tried to trace the colleague who was supposed to have examined Manuel in 1945. His report says that he can find no record of a neurologist under the names given by Manuel, perhaps a hint that he doubts the story.

Hunter Gillies, another psychiatrist, saw Manuel no fewer than five times during February and March, and he also talked to his parents and Theresa. He too had examined Manuel before the McLauchlan trial. His opinion was the same: the man was fit to stand trial. He also noted that Manuel's 'memory for details is remarkably good and clear' and, like MacNiven, he found him unworried by his position: 'On every occasion when I saw him his mood was cheerful and confident.' Gillies writes: 'He told me he had a complete answer to the charges against him.'

Gillies had the gumption to check Manuel's claim of a memory lapse in 1948. He found the girl who had been with him at the cinema. She was a nurse at a mental hospital just outside Glasgow. She denied that any such incident had occurred. He concluded, 'There is thus no corroboration of his claim that he has suffered from attacks of loss of memory.'

Professor Ferguson Rodger of the University of Glasgow Department of Psychological Medicine examined Manuel in February. Speaking to him, Manuel claimed he had been framed for the rape in 1946 and said he had been unfairly dismissed from his job on the railways when someone had tampered with a safe and he got the blame. His 1956 conviction for the colliery canteen break-in was because the police had fabricated evidence against him. Like the others who examined him, Rodger was struck by the fact that Manuel was 'relaxed . . . even jovial' and claimed to have 'no doubt that he would vindicate himself without any trouble'. This detachment perhaps came from a lack of any sense of responsibility for his actions. Rodger records that: 'The explanation of his behaviour, he says, rests in the fact that he is a dishonest person and that some people are made that way.' He is just 'made that way', claims Manuel; it is really nothing to do with him.

To add to these formal reports, a unique and illuminating piece of evidence has surfaced recently: a tape recording of Manuel talking to Rodger. It is astonishing. Here is Manuel, multiple murderer, talking freely, even happily, about the evidence against him. He speaks almost without pause. An unstoppable flood of words gushes from him as he ignores Rodger's comments and questions. He is so eager to move from one subject to the next that the relentless narrative becomes hard to follow. He also admits things that he will deny on oath at the trial.

The 13-minute tape – some of which is indecipherable – begins as Manuel is giving an account of meeting Watt. Watt had apparently accused Manuel of having the gun used to kill his family. 'I'm the only one who knew where the gun came from other than the fellow that shot his wife and he didn't get it from me . . . So when he told me a gun that was a mistake in there.' At this point, Manuel says, they drove to the Fourth Street house and sat outside. Manuel claims he didn't drive Watt there; at his trial he will say he did. We give the next section of the tape in full as a sample of how Manuel talked:

> He [Watt] said I'll give you a boost, he tried to buy me, anyway I got hold of this Mary Bowes again I went and seen her and I told her, well I've been to see this newspaper reporter, *Daily Express*, I didn't actually I went and seen they two Gordon Rennie and Jimmy Gordon and I told them, I told them the whole case, I says, I'm going to do something about this, I want to be quite frank, I've seen him on the Monday night and he'd told me he heard rumours that Watt had paid someone £5,000 to shoot his wife, see. I said, I don't believe that for a minute. I don't believe it. As far as I know they pair went up to break into a house called Valente next door to Watt and they looked through the window

and the Valente girl was in that night and they saw her and thought that was the Valente house and they shot the people and they were going to keep one of them alive to open the safe, there was supposed to be a safe with money in it and then when they found they were in the wrong house they just shot the girl and left her there, made a blunder and left it at that. Well, after that [unclear] seen them, well, I can tell you quite candidly now he definitely knows who shot his wife and he knows where the gun come from and I said he could only have got it from the man who shot your wife so your story must be true, your information must be authentic. The man, there's no doubt about it, the man has paid someone to shoot his wife, see. Well, the other night I seen Mary Bowes, I says, listen you, you told me a tale about a guy called Martin Hart, he was supposed to be the guy who was with Big Charlie but I know he wasn't because I met him while I was in prison at my appeal and he knows nothing about it. However, this fellow Watt, he thinks it's Martin Hart, I know, and so does Dowdall. Somebody's trying to sell me a dummy, somebody's trying to get me to make a statement on a story somewhere that's gonnae come unstuck. Well, I said, I'm not having it, I'm not making a move until I know [unclear] in it. I've been [unclear] the newspaper and they've guaranteed to back me and any move I make regarding anything I wish to divulge about this case and I'm going to divulge you were up at the house with them. I say, I don't think it was you . . . but I know there was a woman up there with them. So she kinda broke down then and says, look, I'll give you all I know, leave me out of that, she says, and that statement I made about Tallis being at my house, that statement was lies, he came home with me that night and then he left at half past eleven, she says, I was at home alone.

The unstoppable narrative rushes on. It is clear Manuel is trying out stories to tell at his trial. He is asked by Rodger if he feels any enmity towards Tallis:

> Oh, no, no, no, I don't feel anything against him, he's played the game the way he's seen it. I mean, if I'd shot anybody and I thought I could do somebody else for it, I'd do it in a minute. But the point is these people accused me of shooting and in this case this fellow McNeil did that and he says I think Watt paid you £5,000 yourself to shoot these women and I says, in that case, Mr McNeil, I says, what am I doing breaking into houses and shooting people for 20 quid? It seems kinda stupid, it's no as if I've spent it, I've been in prison for 14 months, I'm just out, you say I've got 5,000 quid, why should I shoot someone for 20 quid? So he says it's nothing to do with that and I says it is [unclear] round me, I sees the way the wind is blowing. I had it from an authentic source I was going to be the joe [the fall guy] in this girl affair once they found her body.

He is supremely confident he is not in any danger. Rodger suggests, 'You're in what appears to be a very grave situation.' Manuel interrupts him: '. . . appears to be a very grave situation, I mean, if it was an authentic case, just say it was a case I knew nothing about, see, and I'd be on my head, of course.' Then he immediately goes on to talk about the Smart murders. He says he went to the house on the Thursday 'and I made the move I was making and I went out . . . yes, and I took the car, I thought that was a good move, take the car and dump it, it looks like somebody shot them and went away in the car.' At his trial, he will deny on oath that he took Smart's car and he will also deny something else he admits on the tape: that he gave a lift to the young police constable. He shows his usual malice, claiming that senior officers had to trick the constable into telling them about his lift by saying they were interested in a car that had been in an accident. With a laugh, he says the PC told McNeil, when he identified Manuel as the driver, 'he was very sorry'.

He says the police accused him of shooting the Smarts with a Beretta, saying he'd 'shot them with an automatic pistol like that: bang, bang, click'. He explains why this was not possible: 'The spring is broke, the only way to load it you can load it, put the safety catch on, pull back the carriage, the whole carriage [unclear] that ejects it over the thumb and it catches on the safety catch. You've got to put a bullet up the spout and then you let the spring back very carefully, 'cause you just put the safety off it, it goes off, then you can fire it. You cannae stand in somebody's house holding the gun like that [unclear] shoot a man [unclear] without waking somebody up. I mean if you're lying there with your wife if somebody fired a gun at his head [unclear] bound to wake up.' Suddenly, he reverts to the constable he gave a lift to and laughs, 'I don't think he'll be a policeman long.'

Rodger asks him about the charge of murdering Dunn. 'Oh, aye, I cannae make head nor tale of it. That's just a guy who turned up . . . so he questioned me.' He denies he was in Newcastle and says he has remembered where he was on the Saturday and Sunday concerned: with a man who came up for trial the next day. In any case, he claims, he has not been officially charged with Dunn's murder as he's not been in court: 'It's just a warrant and a caution sort of thing, you know.' The police are simply trying to get someone blamed for the killing, thinking: 'This mad fellow [himself], see, this guy's stuck here, he's gonnae get done for this murder, just as well charge him. If he does get done, that's my books clear. That's his idea.'

Manuel's lack of concern, his self-confidence, his apparent obliviousness to the extraordinary gravity of his situation, these qualities also concerned the man most responsible for him. The governor of Barlinnie feared there would be an eventual reaction, a reversal of his composed behaviour: 'We will suffer for this later,' he thought. For the moment, however, all seemed calm.

As the time of the trial approached, Manuel's defence team had to deal with a legal problem. In Scotland, once a prisoner is committed for trial, the trial must start within 110 days. This is to ensure that accused persons do not have to wait an excessive time to be tried. If the limit is exceeded, they go free. Early in April, Manuel's lawyers asked for more time to prepare his defence, as at that point no fewer than 280 prosecution witnesses had been listed to appear. They were given an extension to the 110-day limit. The trial would open on 12 May.

The indictment served on Manuel was a two-page document but in essence there were eight charges against him. These were: the capital murder of Anne Kneilands; breaking into the Platts', stealing from the house and damaging the mattress by firing into it; breaking into the Martins' and stealing; breaking into the Watts' and the capital murders of the three women; breaking into the Houstons' and stealing; the capital murder of Isabelle Cooke; the capital murders of the Smarts and theft from their house; and the theft of Smart's car.

Manuel submitted a special defence to two of the charges: he accused Charles Tallis and Mary Bowes of the break-in at the Martins', and, more sensationally, William Watt of killing his family.

The world did not yet learn of these special defences; that would have to wait for the first day of his trial. This was not because of any lack of interest on the part of the press. Manuel's arrest and forthcoming trial were enormous news and mass-circulation newspapers began a desperate battle to secure Manuel stories. They were ready to pay extravagantly to get them. Rival papers struggled to reach Manuel and his family and sign them up. Within a fortnight of their son's arrest, Samuel and Bridget had agreed to sell their story exclusively to the *Empire News*, a Sunday paper. His brother James signed up with the *Glasgow Herald*. His sister seems to have refused to have anything to do with the press but at least one of her nursing colleagues told, perhaps even sold, her version of life in the Manuel family. Reporters also approached prison officers and prisoners in contact with Manuel in Barlinnie. It is said that one newly released prisoner offered to reoffend so as to be returned to the jail, from where he would report on Manuel at visiting times – all for a good sum, of course.

Prison officials and the Scottish Home Department disapproved strongly of the publicity Manuel was getting and of the huge sums rumoured to be going to his family. A senior official wrote, 'I understand . . . that Kemsley Newspapers have come to some arrangement with the prisoner's family which they hope will enable them to publish what purports to be his autobiography, based on information given by the family.'

Officials had good reason to worry about the almost unprecedented level of press interest. In the febrile atmosphere now enveloping the case, they had to ensure that nothing appeared in the press that could prejudice the fairness of Manuel's trial. They held hurried discussions to establish what could be published and what power they had to control Manuel's contact with the media. They faced the additional complication that Scottish and English law differed on these matters and newspapers were produced on both sides of the border. Not all London editors were aware of the legal differences and indeed ignorance at one paper nearly caused a disaster the day before the trial started.

Meanwhile, not to be outdone by his parents' deal, Peter claimed that he had been offered a similar one. He told the prison authorities that his solicitor Docherty had offered him 'a considerable sum of money for his life story' on behalf of a Sunday paper. Manuel must have known this allegation would cause trouble for Docherty and possibly for Ferns, too. Why he said it is unclear: perhaps he was jealous of his parents' deal; perhaps he was trying to establish some sort of dominance over Docherty; perhaps it was just another example of his casual malice. Whatever his motive, the claim forced Ferns to assure the authorities that, although Docherty was a representative of the *Empire News*, he had visited Manuel only as a member of the defence team. Ferns also justified the family's contract with the paper by saying that their fee would help pay for counsel and associated legal costs. After this shaky start, relations between Manuel and

Docherty seem to have settled down and Docherty was a member of the defence team until the end.

Many papers did seek an exclusive inside story. On 11 February, a representative of the *Sunday Pictorial* wrote to Manuel telling him that, even though his parents were already contracted elsewhere, it would be possible for him to tell his own story and that any agreement he made would not conflict with his parents' contract. As well as the publicity he had always craved, he would receive money. 'The *Pictorial* is prepared to offer you £3,000, or a figure to be negotiated.' In 1955, £3,000 was a huge amount of money; it would buy a decent three-bedroom suburban house. Peter Smart's salary after tax was only about £2,300 a year and he was a fairly well-paid foreman in a building firm, able to build his own house. And, of course, £3,000 was just the opening bid; clearly, the paper would have gone higher.

This was not to be allowed. The prison authorities made sure that neither the letter nor any mention of it reached Manuel. 'Prisoners, whether untried or convicted, may not communicate, orally or in writing, material intended for publication,' the governor wrote. The authorities took this line in response to all efforts to get Manuel to tell his own story.

Nevertheless, the attempts kept coming. Nigel Morland, an enormously prolific author of fictional and factual books and articles on crime, wrote to the governor in the middle of March enclosing a letter he hoped would be passed to Manuel. The letter is a mixture of boasts and indirect flattery. Informing Manuel of his status as a leading crime writer, he tells the prisoner that he feels a 'responsible' book on his case would counterbalance the sensational material that is bound to surface. Morland wants to arrange a face-to-face talk with Manuel, writing that he feels sure it would be easier to create an accurate portrait of him after meeting him. No doubt Manuel would have been tempted if the letter had reached him.

However, the governor returned it and Manuel never learned of the proposed book. Morland went on to write a few brief pieces on the trial for Glasgow's *Evening Citizen*, published alongside the paper's daily trial report. Later, he published short accounts of Manuel and his crimes, not always totally accurate. The planned book never appeared.

All this media attention built up tremendous anticipation of the trial at Glasgow High Court. This was to be 'The Trial of the Century', according to one newspaper. By the first week in May, the immense task of preparing for it was complete. The witnesses were ready to appear, the technical reports prepared. Before long, all the physical evidence was taken to the court.

The judge was to be Lord Cameron, an immensely experienced lawyer who had served as Dean of the Faculty of Advocates and been elevated to the bench in 1955. This was his first murder trial. Advocate Depute Gordon Gillies was to lead for the Crown, supported by the relatively inexperienced but highly able Ranald Sutherland. Leslie, Grieve and Morison were to defend. All these lawyers would go on to have highly distinguished careers.

CHAPTER FIFTEEN

Monday, 12 May 1958, and the trial begins. Manuel is brought from Barlinnie in a small police van, his natty appearance in dark blazer and grey trousers somewhat marred by the handcuffs he is wearing. The case is heavily weighted against him: a conviction for only one capital murder will get him hanged. Yet, as he enters court, he shows the utter confidence he has exhibited since late January. He has no doubt that he can persuade the jury he is innocent. And, at last, he has the vast audience he has always wanted.

Public expectation has been growing daily since his arrest; now, it is almost feverish. Since eight o'clock the previous evening, people have been queuing for the sixty public seats; they include an eager neighbour of Mrs Bowes and a sixteen-year-old boy. Among the spectators inside will be a Nigerian law student and two grandmothers from North America. Local lawyers, civic dignitaries, even Celtic footballers have called in favours to be admitted to the trial. Newspaper, radio and television reporters cram into court or wait eagerly outside, hoping for any scrap on which to build a story.

The sheer number of witnesses and the vast amount of physical evidence marshalled by the Crown is almost overwhelming. No fewer than 295 witnesses are listed to appear, all but a handful on behalf of the prosecution. Most will not be called but, just in case, they are ready. Each has given a precognition. Ranald Sutherland, the junior prosecuting counsel, would later recall that what each witness said in court hardly diverged from his or her precognition. It is unclear whether some witnesses have been taken over their evidence; there will be times when a few witnesses, all convicted criminals, suggest to the lawyers what they are supposed to say next.

The list of productions (the items of physical evidence) is similarly long: 158 items. They range from detailed medical reports to items that would seem completely innocuous in a different context: *Radio Times*, newspaper, watch, currency notes. Other things are chilling: fifteen pieces of bone, piece of bone and brain matter, blood, two pieces of skull, angle iron. Police pertinacity in collecting evidence is illustrated by productions 204, 205 and 206 – tin of salmon, wrapper from salmon tin, tin opener – all removed from the Smarts' to support Manuel's confession that, after murdering them, he fed their cat.

The jury, reporters and those lucky members of the public who have managed to get in are immediately confronted by bloody evidence of murder. There are on display in the courtroom a bloodstained mattress and a chunk of tree, covered with blood, recovered from the site of Anne Kneilands' death. The murder guns are also on view and, within anonymous cardboard boxes, they will soon learn, there lie fragments of Kneilands' smashed skull.

Just as the case seems about to start, there is a delay. There has been a huge amount of publicity and one paper has gone too far. Leslie rises and draws the judge's attention to an article about the case in the previous day's *News of the World*. This 'is prominently associated with a photograph of the panel [the accused],' says Leslie. 'In my humble opinion, that is an impropriety.' Under Scots law, printing a picture of the accused in a forthcoming trial is not permitted because it may affect witnesses' identifications. Cameron says he will consider the matter. Later that day, he refers it to the Lord Advocate 'for such action as he thinks fit to take'. By the evening, the paper's editor, Reginald Cudlipp, has sent a grovelling apology, claiming he had been unaware of the difference between English and Scottish legal practice. The matter is closed. In fact, the small picture, which actually appears to be a sketch, not a photograph, bears only a vague resemblance to Manuel. It would be hard to identify him from it.

He sits in the dock between two constables (later in the trial, Superintendent Brown's young policeman son will be one of these guards). Nine men and six women are quickly selected as jurors; Manuel has instructed his counsel not to object to women, as he remains convinced he can charm them. Now comes the first sensation. The clerk of the court reads out the indictment and then the special defences, including the accusation that Watt murdered his family. There is a shocked silence, then a storm of whispering. Reporters sidle out to phone in the extraordinary news.

Each jury member is given a copy of the indictment and of the special defences, as well as a notebook and pen. Manuel also has a supply of these; he will write and sketch throughout the trial. In the dock, he leans forward and listens as Gillies rises. There is a sudden attentive silence. Gillies begins to set out the facts of each crime, moving from the earliest to the last.

The first witness is a police constable, who explains how he drew maps of the place where Anne Kneilands was murdered and made plans of the Smarts' house. This is all detailed, technical stuff, far from sensational but necessary.

Next comes Anne's father and now the horrors start. He tells how his daughter failed to return home on 3 January 1956, of his rapidly growing fears and how he alerted the police. Then he describes carrying out the dreadful task of identifying her body as well as items belonging to her. He is followed by his wife and Anne's sister Alice.

Both testify that Anne always wore pants, establishing that someone had removed the ones she was wearing.

Andrew Murnin, who failed to meet Anne, tells his story and Mrs Simpson recounts the girl's visit to her house on the night she was killed. Other witnesses tell of seeing Anne that night and help establish that the murder probably took place on the evening of 2 January. A man living near the scene tells how, between about 8.40 and 8.50 that evening, he heard two cries: 'Just a squeal cry, "Oh, oh,". . . just like someone hitting you and you crying, "Oh!"'

The horror increases as George Gribbon describes discovering the girl's body: 'Her head was split open, very badly split open.' The jury, press and public are given more facts about the terrible nature of the first death. A police officer testifies: 'The skull was very badly smashed, with brain material spattered around, and blood.' Others describe how it appeared that Anne had fled, losing her shoes as she ran across a wide ditch and scratching herself against barbed wire. A few questions by the defence fail to weaken the effect of this evidence, though one officer admits there is no proof that the scratches were made by barbed wire.

Now the prosecution begins to focus on Manuel himself in the days following the murder. They want to show that Kneilands scratched his face as she tried to defend herself. The first witness is PC James Marr. He saw Manuel at about four or five o'clock on the afternoon the body was found. Manuel was working close to the murder site. 'He had several scratches on his face . . . They appeared to be of recent origin.' Another constable states that when he was investigating an alleged theft of wellingtons from the Gas Board hut several days later, on 9 January, Manuel 'had scratches on both sides of his face and he had not shaved for, I would say, two or three days'. He thought the scratches 'would have been two or three days old'.

More damning evidence comes from the gang foreman, Richard Corrins. He says that Manuel's face was unmarked on the morning of Saturday, 31 December but by the following Wednesday morning

Manuel had 'cuts on his face'. He cannot describe them more precisely because 'it is that far gone'. Manuel said he had been in a fight. Corrins had said more. It seems he told the police that the same morning he had seen Manuel taking away a pair of bloodstained wellingtons from their hut. Perhaps he had been wearing them when he killed Anne Kneilands? Corrins' account of the scratches is supported by a Gas Board pipe layer, John Lennan, who says Manuel had scratches on his face on 4 January; significantly, he thinks they had been made by fingernails.

Some jurors may wonder at this point if so many people had seen scratches on Manuel's face, why the police did not investigate him more thoroughly. Some may also question why Kneilands' fingernails were not examined for traces of skin from her attacker. She had a habit of chewing them but if they were long enough to scratch her assailant, they were probably long enough to retain fragments of skin.

The evidence returns to more technical matters. A police photographer reports that he photographed the scene of Kneilands' murder and the Watt house. He also recorded the Watt post-mortems. Grisly facts intrude: at the post-mortem he had been given a bullet 'from the left side of the head of Mrs Watt' to take for examination. The jury members look at the copies of his photographs. The stark black-and-white images convey in sickening detail the brutal horror of the Kneilands and Watt murders.

The next charge relates to the break-in at the Platts'. This is a crucial link in the chain tying Manuel to murder. The prosecution case is that Manuel went there to steal but, for some unfathomable reason, fired a bullet into Mr and Mrs Platt's mattress. The bullet came from the gun used to kill the Watts. This link between the Platts, the Watts and Manuel is strengthened by the fact that the distinctive Philips electric razor was stolen from the Platts' and a razor of exactly the same type was recovered from Manuel's house after his arrest.

Mr Platt tells what happened. He, his wife and their son had left home on 12 September 1956 for a tour of the Lake District. They were called back by the police; their house had been entered and they had been robbed. There was strange damage: tinned soup had been scattered about in the kitchen and 'a tin of pears had been opened and that was scattered on the lounge carpet'. There were other puzzles: the contents of a deed box were 'scattered all over the floor and on the settee, as though it was in the process of being sorted, because the contents were arranged in little piles'. Yet Mrs Platt's engagement ring, his own signet ring, a gold watch chain and cufflinks, all objects presumably of considerable value, had not been taken. On the other hand, a lot of tools and scientific instruments belonging to one of his sons had been stolen, as well as two sets of commemorative Coronation money. It seemed a puzzling break-in.

Something very strange had also happened to their bed. There was 'a hole in a blanket and in a quilt and a large split in the mattress'. The bedcover was 'rather grubby – blackish'. The area of blackening was around one of the holes. Platt assumed the slit had been made by someone looking for money that might have been concealed inside the mattress. His story becomes even more curious at this point. His wife had mended the slit but about a year later her foot struck something in the mattress. It turned out to be a watch that they had believed stolen. The thief must have hidden it there. Then, just before Christmas 1957, Platt's wife showed him a bullet. It had fallen out of the mattress. It 'excited some small curiosity but we didn't pay particular attention to it other than to put it in the dresser drawer. Like most people, we were sceptical that anything could happen to us and we didn't really pay any vital attention to it.'

The key question is how had the bullet got there? Did he associate it with the damage he had seen to the bedclothes? 'Yes,' he replies, 'in a half-hearted sort of way, but it seemed so fantastic that a bullet would have been fired into the mattress that we put it out of our minds.'

In January 1958, things changed: 'We discovered the police were after a .38 revolver and then the penny dropped. We thought it was a .38 bullet and we checked it over and that was the size.' Platt took the bullet to the police on 25 January 1958, 11 days after Manuel had been arrested. It was a wonderfully useful discovery for them: gun, razor, the Watts and Manuel – all could now be tied together.

The defence tries to cast doubt on his account. How could Platt be so sure of the calibre of the bullet that had reappeared in this strange way? He answers that he has been an engineer for 30 years and '.38 is just over three-eighths of an inch and three-eighths was just about the size of the bullet'.

All this is fairly bizarre and perhaps some of the jury find it puzzling. Why had the police not linked the dark stains on the bed cover, which were almost certainly powder burns, with the holes in the bedding and the mattress? Did nobody consider that a firearm might have been involved simply because it was unlikely? But then, shooting into empty beds is hardly a feature of most break-ins.

If the prosecution can convince the jury that Manuel fired the gun, then they will have taken a major step. They will maintain that after the shot into the mattress at the Platts' – which now seems almost like a practice run by Manuel, the acting out of a fantasy of power and violence – he repeated his action, firing not into empty beds but occupied ones, killing first the Watts and then the Smarts.

Mr Platt provides another crucial piece of evidence for the prosecution case. He tells the court about his son's electric razor stolen from the house. He is shown the razor retrieved from Manuel's home. It is 'certainly the same model, the same colour and the plug was the same'. Geoffrey, his 19-year-old son, is even more positive: he says the razor shown is undoubtedly the one he owned. It has the same dent, the same break in the plug. He describes damage to an interior part and then opens the razor and points out the flaw exactly as he has described it. Evidence is given that his razor, bought for Mr Platt by a staff member at the Philips factory, was one of a special experimental batch of only fifty.

It is getting towards the end of the first day and now Miss Margaret Martin begins to tell the court about the break-in at the house she shares with her sister, a short distance from the Watts'. Once again, the jury hears of strange vandalism.

She and her sister returned from holiday on Monday, 17 September after the police told them of the break-in. Their house was 'a wild scene of confusion'. The sitting room carpet had been ruined: 'Someone had poured tomato soup over it and made a large stain.' A tin of spaghetti had been opened and someone had lain on her sister's bed: 'The clothes were tossed down and there were marks on the fresh linen.' This mess makes a link with the break-in at the Platts'.

Despite the disorder, little had been stolen. The most important items were two rings. She says she did not notice the rings were missing until three days later.

When Miss Martin has finished, the court rises and Manuel is returned to Barlinnie to be watched over by the shifts of warders who share his cell.

CHAPTER SIXTEEN

As the second day starts, the prosecution moves on to the Watt murders. Mrs Collison, the Watts' daily help, enters the witness box. She describes how she tried to get into the house, how Deanna and Mrs Valente joined her and how the postman put his hand through the broken pane in the front door and released the lock. She tells how, once inside, it was hard to see what had happened to Vivienne as she was 'smothered up with clothes', while Mrs Watt and her sister lay under bedding that seemed neatly folded down 'as if the bed was newly made'. Her testimony must surely strengthen the jury's sense of the brutality of the killing: three people shot where they should have been most safe. She also testifies that the Watts got on well and had gone abroad on holiday together in the year before the murders.

The defence needs to suggest Watt had a motive for killing his wife, so William Grieve tries to weaken her evidence that they were an affectionate couple. Eventually, she admits that she did not see them together very often, as generally Watt was out when she was there.

Manuel's team also need to establish that Watt had reason to kill the women while Manuel had none. Harald Leslie hints that insurance money may have been a motive for murder. Mrs Collison tells the court that after the murder Watt had wanted to get insurance books from a locked cabinet. She told him the keys were in a jug in the kitchenette. For the moment, this is enough; the defence can raise the matter again when Watt is questioned. Towards the end of her evidence, Mrs Collison makes a startling remark. Watt, she says, did not think the crime was a robbery as very little had been taken but, 'he said, well, if it was who he thought it was, he knew them.' This brings an entirely new possibility into the case: Watt knew the killer.

Next, Deanna Valente describes the afternoon and evening she spent with Vivienne the day before the murders. She paints a picture of two carefree girls enjoying their freedom. When she went back to her own house, she was kept awake for a while by the sounds of the Top 20 coming from the Watts' radio. Poignantly, she adds that she had never seen Mrs Watt looking so well. 'She looked very happy.' Because a cigarette butt was found by Vivienne's bed, the prosecution gets her to confirm that neither she nor Vivienne smoked that evening.

Her mother tells the court that there was never any money kept in her house. Gillies wants to establish this to counter Manuel's claim that there was a plot to raid the Valentes' house because it was believed to contain between five and ten thousand pounds.

Dr Arthur Nelson, who had been called to the house to certify death, states: 'The two women were lying sort of partly on their left sides, very peaceably. They looked as if they were asleep, in fact. They hadn't moved.' His testimony adds another touch of horror to the case the prosecution is building.

It is important for the Crown to establish as precisely as possible the time of the murders. A witness, out walking his dog, says he heard music coming from the Watt house at about half past midnight. A supervisor at the local telephone exchange states that they were phoned from the Watts' at 1.26 a.m. on Monday to book a wake-up call for 7 a.m. In previous months, there had been several requests from the house for these calls. Nobody answered the first call or two subsequent ones. This establishes that the murders took place after 1.26 a.m. and before 7 a.m.

Following the previous day's accounts of the curious damage at the Platts' and Martins', Superintendent Andrew McClure tells the court that the only disorder at the Watt house was in the two bedrooms. He had found a cigarette end and a burn mark on the carpet beside Vivienne's bed. Significantly, there were no cigarettes in the house. The implication is that it was the killer who left the stub behind. He tells the court that Vivienne's body showed signs of a struggle, that Mrs Watt's nightdress had been pulled up and that Mrs Brown's pyjama trousers were 'torn from the waist to the crutch'.

So far, the evidence has come from policemen or ordinary people unwittingly caught up in the crimes. Now, they are followed into the witness box by two Glasgow crooks.

The first is James Tinney O'Neil, 44, a scar-faced habitual criminal known to the police and his associates as 'Scout'. His evidence is vital in linking Manuel to one of the guns. In 1956, he says, he met Manuel twice. The second time, Manuel asked him to 'get a gun for a hold-up in Liverpool'. The supplier was to be a Peter 'Dick' Hamilton, another convicted criminal. O'Neil testifies that he saw Hamilton later that evening and they arranged that he should return with Manuel the next day. They all met in the street and Hamilton and Manuel went into the common hallway of a block of flats while O'Neil waited outside. At first, he says he does not know if Manuel got the gun. Then he tells the court that when Manuel reappeared he made a gesture that he assumed meant he had. When pressed, O'Neil tells the court that this happened about nine days before the Watt murders.

Leslie tries to weaken this testimony and O'Neil responds with a slipperiness presumably polished by the many times he has faced interrogations by police and lawyers. Has he always told the same story about the gun, he is asked. He answers yes.

'Were you in the habit of getting guns for people?'

This gets the fine reply, 'I don't think so.'

Not surprisingly, Leslie asks, 'Will you answer the question yes or no?'

O'Neil gives the brilliantly ambiguous response, 'No.'

He gives an equally smooth, even mocking, response to Leslie's next question: 'Do you still say you have always told a consistent story about these matters?'

'That is my story here.'

It is a bravura performance, worthy of O'Neil's status as a Glasgow hard man.

Despite the witness's evasiveness and his freely admitted links to the underworld, which could potentially discredit him in the eyes of the jury, the prosecution has gone some way to establishing that shortly before the Watt murders Manuel had obtained a gun to carry out a robbery, albeit one supposed to be taking place in Liverpool.

Dick Hamilton, the supplier of the gun, is the next criminal to give evidence. His story is slightly different from O'Neil's. He says he'd seen O'Neil and Manuel drinking together in Meldrum's Bar 'just before the Watt murders' at about five o'clock on a Saturday night. 'Well, they were kind of drunk, I wanted out of their company,' he remembers. One of them – he cannot recall which – spoke to him about a gun. The next day, they all met. He maintains the encounter was entirely accidental. He took them to his house and went with Manuel into the kitchen, where he handed over the gun and seven or eight bullets. He'd originally got the gun from 'an RAF fellow' called Henry Campbell. He'd paid five pounds and sold it to Manuel for the same sum. Manuel had told him he was going to send the gun to London.

He denies there was any discussion of the price of the gun.

'Weren't you interested in what price you would get for it?'

'No, no.'

'Why did you accept the five pounds?'

'Would you not have taken it?' is his cheeky reply to Leslie.

The judge tries to pin Hamilton down: 'You are being asked questions about how you came to hand over a weapon which, according to you, was to be used for a criminal enterprise. Kindly answer the questions.'

'Well, he was looking for the gun and I had it and I gave it to him. That is all.'

Gillies asks, 'How did you come to get five pounds?'

'Well, he just gave it me.'

The prosecution's aim is to link this gun to the one used in the Watt murders and later recovered, with Manuel's guidance, from the River Clyde. Hamilton is now shown the gun recovered from the river. He says he is not sure if it is the weapon he sold to Manuel, although it is like it. This one has no lanyard ring; his did. It will be recalled that Manuel had drawn a revolver with the ring missing for Dowdall. Hamilton does not think the gun he sold to Manuel bore a maker's name.

Grieve cross-examines him, trying to show that he and O'Neil are untrustworthy. He gets Hamilton to admit that O'Neil has previously asked him for a gun for his own protection, saying he was 'in just a wee bit of trouble'. He refused this request, he claims virtuously. He explains that he bought the gun from the RAF man because: 'I was in a bit of trouble myself.' He now thinks he paid two or three pounds for it. It must seem clear to the court that he and O'Neil are crooks. Whether or not that invalidates their evidence is for the jury to decide.

Twenty-five-year-old Henry Campbell, who sold Hamilton the gun, is next. He is working as a storeman – an interesting job for a self-confessed thief. He admits that in about 1952, when serving in the RAF, he stole the gun and a quantity of ammunition from an officer's quarters. On weekend leave in Glasgow – and he made it a long weekend by overstaying a fortnight – he sold the gun and about ten rounds of ammunition to Hamilton; he thinks he got thirty shillings. The gun he stole was like the one he is now shown, although it had its lanyard ring.

The next witness provides even more startling evidence linking Manuel and the gun. He is Joseph Liddell, a labourer. In 1956, he met Manuel in the felicitously named Crook Inn. They chatted about the time they both worked for the county council. As they spoke, Manuel pulled a gun from his waistband. 'It was very startling. It startled me,' says Liddell. Manuel told him he'd been helping to clear out a house belonging to two old ladies. He had seen a holster hanging on a wall. It contained the gun and he promptly stole it. (Perhaps Manuel based this story on an incident in his past: in 1945, he had broken into a house, found a firearm and taken it.)

The prosecution asks Liddell when this meeting occurred: 'It was in the evening,' he replies accurately. This is not the desired answer and so he is prompted: 'And you said it was some time in September?' Now comes the statement the prosecution want: 'Yes. As a matter of fact, I think it was the Friday night before the Watts were killed.'

The prosecution moves quickly to establish what type of gun Manuel showed him – one might say flashed – in the pub. Liddell explains that he noticed the lanyard ring was missing: 'He held it in his palm like that. I couldn't help but notice it.' Manuel had told him he was going to sell the gun in Glasgow, saying, 'Some bastard will blow their brains out with it.' He also had about six rounds of ammunition.

Manuel could not have been too careful when showing Liddell the gun, for a man came over and asked him if it was a .45. When the stranger left, Manuel worried that he might have gone for the police, so he followed him out but returned a little later to say he had gone for a bus. All this circumstantial detail strengthens the credibility of Liddell's evidence.

Now the court hears about the strange affair of the dead cow. John Lafferty states that he spent the day before the Watt murders drinking with Manuel in the Woodend Hotel. Manuel had told him 'he had shot a cow through the head', the shot going up the cow's nostril. What was the effect on the cow, Lafferty is asked. 'It just died, that was all.'

The cow story is odd and Leslie cross-examines, asking Lafferty if he believed it. No, he didn't, he replies: 'I couldn't imagine a cow standing and letting anyone walk up and shoot it like that.'

Leslie follows up: 'You know Manuel?'

'Yes.'

'Was he given to be a bit fanciful?'

'Yes.'

It is a neat piece of questioning. But if this makes the story seem unlikely, the Crown offers more evidence to support it. W.C. Jackson, a farmer, testifies that on16 September he found one of his cows dead. A little blood had come from its nose. He had notified the police in case it had died of anthrax. Examination by a vet ruled this out, so the carcass was sent to the knacker's yard.

We know from Muncie's memoirs that a considerable number of police were later given the disgusting task of searching through the rendered flesh and fat for the bullet – without success.

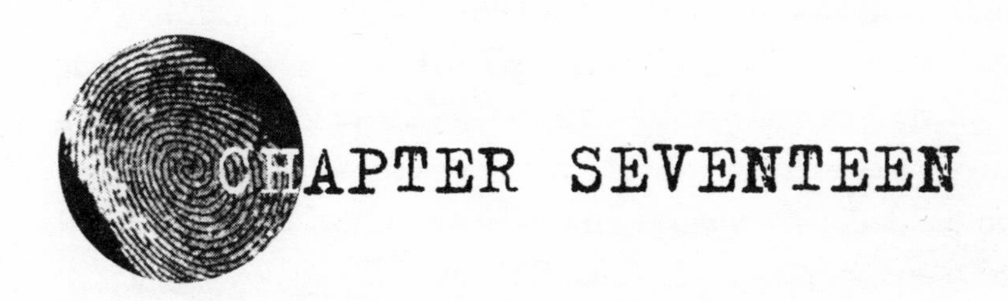

CHAPTER SEVENTEEN

The next day, the third of the trial, opens with the appearance of yet another criminal, Charles Tallis, who has been brought from Peterhead prison, where he is serving a three-year sentence for possessing explosives. His conviction on this particular charge will have some relevance to the trial: Samuel Manuel will claim Tallis tried to leave gelignite at Fourth Street on the afternoon before the Watt murders.

Tallis and Manuel have known each other for several years and have thieved together but now they are enemies, each determined to harm the other. Manuel believes Tallis refused to give him an alibi when he was arrested in the colliery case. In his special defence, Manuel has accused Tallis, Bowes, and another man, Martin Hart, of the break-in at the Martins' and, as the trial proceeds, he and his father will try to implicate Tallis in the Watt murders. The air between them crackles with hatred.

There has already been violence when the brother of Tallis's mistress assaulted Manuel in Barlinnie, apparently because he believed Manuel was trying to blame Tallis for some of his own crimes. 'I informed Chisholm that such information as he gathered from Tallis was completely false. He immediately punched me in the eye.' Well, such things happen in criminal circles.

Tallis starts to give evidence that the Crown hopes will greatly harm Manuel. In June 1956, when the men were still friends, Tallis says, the conversation, initiated by Manuel, turned to guns. Manuel said he had a .45 but the bullets he had were too small; they fell through the magazine. Tallis had suggested 'bushing' the gun, fitting an internal sleeve to decrease its bore. This discussion – if it occurred – took place well before Manuel was supposed to have acquired the gun that killed the Watts. Its sole relevance is that it shows Manuel had at one stage possessed a gun and wanted to be able to fire it.

Led by Ranald Sutherland, Tallis moves to the crucial days around the time of the Martin burglary and the Watt killings. In his special defence, Manuel has named Tallis as responsible for the Martin break-in. It is therefore important for the prosecution to establish that he could have played no part in it, nor in the Watt murders on the same night.

Tallis tells the court that his partner's son, Allan Bowes, was married in the early afternoon of Saturday, 15 September 1956. The wedding reception went on till eleven in the evening, when he and Mrs Bowes returned to her house. The newly-wed couple were with them and left between one and two in the morning. Tallis stayed with Mrs Bowes. The next day, he visited his sister in hospital, then went to the Woodend Hotel before returning to the Bowes' house. He, Mrs Bowes and the newly-weds drove to another pub about 20 miles away (thus qualifying to drink as bona fide travellers). They were there from about six in the evening until eleven and then went home. At about one in the morning, the newly-weds left them. Tallis did not go out again that night. What is more, he tells the court he has never been in Burnside, let alone in the Martins' house, in the whole of his life.

If Tallis is believed, it would have been impossible for him to have engaged in any criminal activity (except, perhaps, drink-driving) during the crucial time when the Martins' house was broken into and the Watts killed.

Now Tallis moves to implicate Manuel in the killings. He says that on Monday, 17 September – the Watts had been murdered during the preceding night – he went to the Manuels' house at about 1.45 p.m. He and Manuel went to the Crook Inn, where people were discussing the Suez Crisis and wondering if there was going to be a war. 'I happened to say, "There must be something special out, as I was coming through Bellshill in the bus and I noticed there's a special newspaper out, a special edition, and there seems to be a bit of excitement going on."' Two or three seconds later, he recounts, Manuel pulled at his sleeve and told him to drink up and come outside. When they got outside Manuel said, 'I have got to get back to the house immediately.' Tallis suggested it could wait but Manuel said, 'Oh, no, I have to go back now.' When they got there Manuel said, 'I've left something on the bed, Ma. I'll be down in a few seconds.' Tallis waited in the garden, talking to Manuel's mother.

When Manuel reappeared, they decided to go into Glasgow. As they walked along, Manuel showed him two rings and claimed they were 'the two hottest rings you will ever see in your life'. Tallis tells the court that he responded, 'I've seen hundreds of hot rings. I don't see why these are any hotter than any other rings.' Manuel made no answer and put them in his pocket. Tallis describes the rings for the court; his description more or less fits those stolen from the Martins'.

Sutherland asks if there was any further mention of the rings. At this point, Tallis shows how carefully he has prepared what he is to say. He tells Sutherland he is jumping ahead: 'Yes, but you have missed out a point here. When I got into Glasgow with him, we went to –' Sutherland cuts him off quickly: 'Well, if you just answer my questions, I think that will be all right.'

So Tallis states that as they were walking along the street in Glasgow he asked Manuel about the rings. He wanted to know more because by this time he had seen a newspaper report that the Watts had been killed and that nearby 18 Fennsbank Avenue had been broken into. Thinking about things, he had concluded, 'No wonder they are the two hottest rings I have ever seen,' and he said this to Manuel. He asked Manuel if he still had them and was told he'd put them down a drain while he, Tallis, had been looking in a shop window.

If the jury believes him, his evidence is extremely damaging. Harald Leslie immediately tries to cast doubt on it.

'You are pretty knowledgeable about guns?' he asks, following up on Tallis's statement that he'd recommended Manuel bush his gun.

It gets him nowhere; Tallis, like O'Neil, is practised at answering difficult questions: 'No, no. I am knowledgeable about fitting and I am an engineer to trade.'

'I beg your pardon?' Leslie asks incredulously.

'I am an engineer to trade,' Tallis repeats.

This seems so unlikely that he is asked if he was employed in September 1956. He replies that he was being paid between £18 and £20 a week as a toolmaker and setter, naming the firm where he was employed.

Leslie has no way of disproving this, so he asks Tallis more about his bushing advice. 'It is an understood fact of engineering that a thing should be a proper fit before it can be effective at any time,' is the devastating response. Tallis insists he has nothing to do with guns, that the only time he has handled a firearm was when he was in the RAF, and that was a rifle.

Then Leslie makes one of the simple mistakes that are to mar the defence case throughout. He says that Tallis's address is in Glasgow. No, Tallis corrects him, it is in Hamilton. It is a minor matter but it, and several similar errors, weakens the defence's position.

This is just skirmishing. Leslie now moves to a direct attack: he suggests it was Tallis who broke into the Martins' house. Tallis replies,

'A load of nonsense,' and he laughs when Leslie suggests that it was he, not Manuel, who had the rings after the break-in. And no, he says, he never arranged to get a gun for Watt. 'I never met the man in my life.' And no, he did not want a gun in early September 1956. 'I never wanted a gun in my life.' No, he never told Manuel he was to be paid for breaking into and wrecking a house in Burnside. Everything Leslie puts to him is flatly denied; it is an impressively consistent performance. Crucially, Tallis emphasises that he has never seen Watt, 'never been with him in my life, and I have never seen Peter Manuel with him either'.

He is handed Exhibit 106, the gun used in the killings. Rather petulantly, Leslie tells him to stop reading the label. Once again, Tallis wins the exchange: 'I am not reading the label. I am reading the maker's name on it.' His careful observation establishes for the first time in court that the gun is a Webley.

Question after question by the defence is rejected by a complete, almost contemptuous denial. Leslie tries to get Tallis to admit that he broke into the Martins' house: 'Did you not say that you were disturbed by a car coming out of number 19?'

'It is the first I've heard of it.'

'Did you know whose car was used in connection with the Watt murders?'

'No, I know nothing about the Watt murders, nothing at all.'

'Immediately after the Watt murders, did you have a gun to dispose of?'

'I never had a gun in the first place to dispose of.'

No, he did not try to get rid of a gun in the Manuel house. 'I distinctly told you that I have never had a gun at any moment in my life,' he admonishes Leslie.

What Tallis has said is supported by Mary Bowes. She denies that she was involved in the break-in at the Martins' and testifies that Tallis could not have left the house at night during the weekend of her son's wedding. Her younger son, James, also gives evidence to the effect that neither Tallis nor his mother could have left the house. The elder son, Allan, in supporting these claims makes one startling admission: he too had a gun – a P38 Luger, which he had acquired for two pounds when he was in the army. He'd kept it for about eight months, hidden from his mother, and then sold it for two pounds to an Italian café owner in Hamilton, with the assurance that, if he ever needed it, he could get it back for the same amount. By now, the jury understands that guns are neither scarce nor expensive in some sections of Glasgow society.

Now the flow of the trial heads towards William Watt. Manuel has named him as the killer of his family and the defence must persuade the jury that it is *possible* Watt killed them – no more. If they do that, the jury will not be able to convict Manuel of the murders. The prosecution, on the other hand, faces a double task: they must convince the jury that Watt is completely innocent and that Manuel is the killer. Watt's testimony will be of immense importance.

All along, there have been two popular views about Watt. One is that he killed his family and was only released from jail because the Lanarkshire police could not get enough evidence against him. The other is that he is completely innocent, the police made a mess of the investigation and it was outrageous that he was arrested and then freed without any proper explanation. To some people, the incompetent police were simply grabbing a second chance to get a conviction by accusing Manuel.

The prosecution begins by establishing Watt's whereabouts around the time of the murders. The week before, he had gone to stay at the Cairnbaan Hotel, run by a former Glasgow policeman, William Leitch, and his wife, friends of the family. On Sunday the 16th, he'd gone fishing, then visited acquaintances in the neighbourhood. After his return to the hotel, he had stayed up till after midnight.

Mrs Leitch testifies that at about 11.30 next morning she received a phone call from Watt's brother in Glasgow telling of the murders. Watt was out fishing so she sent a taxi driver to fetch him and went to pack his bag. When he arrived at the hotel, she gave him the terrible news. At first, he didn't seem to understand, thinking that something had happened to her daughter Marion. When he telephoned Glasgow, the news was confirmed. He became distraught but set out to drive home. Mr Bruce, the friend he had visited the previous night, went with him to keep an eye on him.

She tells the court that the road between the hotel and Glasgow, a journey of about 90 miles, was poor and winding where it ran along Loch Lomond, and she stated that there was a fault with Watt's car. The previous week, she had been in it with him and the lights had flickered off and on. Driving fast in the dark with faulty lights along a narrow, twisting road to commit three murders and then return would seem an exceptionally risky enterprise.

Grieve rises to question Mrs Leitch, aiming to cast doubt on Watt's character and suggest he had a reason for wanting his wife dead. It soon becomes clear that someone has been investigating Watt's private life; perhaps a police officer who believes Watt is guilty has passed evidence to the defence.

Grieve asks if Watt was 'sometimes . . . accompanied by ladies or a lady who was not Mrs Watt' when he stayed at the hotel.

'Never,' Mrs Leitch replies.

But, asks Grieve, had not a Mrs Milligan and Mrs Mulholland stayed at the hotel at the same time as Watt in the past? Mrs Leitch admits that Mrs Milligan had stayed there and that she was a close friend of Watt. The defence has made some progress. Watt is suspected of adultery and an adulterer may have a reason for wanting his wife dead.

Next, Grieve tries to get Mrs Leitch to say that Watt was far from upset at the news of the murders and again he makes some headway.

'Was Mr Watt not rather extraordinarily composed for a man who had suffered the tragedy he had suffered?'

'I am afraid I couldn't give an impression about that because I was upset myself.'

'You, being upset, assumed he would be extremely upset.'

'Yes, I put myself in his place.'

The prosecution acts to undo the damage caused by the hint that Watt had used the hotel to be with a mistress. Yes, Mrs Leitch says in response to questioning, it was true that Mrs Milligan had stayed there in 1954 and 1955 but she was accompanied by her sister. The two women shared a room and they had stayed on for a week after Watt had left. Watt had a male friend with him and they too shared a room. For now, the jury may be assured that these visits seem above board but the question of Watt's adultery will return. At least he and the prosecution team, who in effect are also acting as his defence, are alerted to the issue.

When Watt retired to his bed on the Sunday night, Mrs Leitch says, she loaned him an alarm clock so that he could get up at 5.30 a.m. to go fishing. At about 8.30 on the Monday morning, she heard a car coming to the front of the hotel. By the time she had gone downstairs, she found that Watt had had his breakfast and left. Her husband testifies that he had seen Watt's car outside the hotel at 7.45 a.m. and there was frost on the top of it. He adds the helpful observation that whenever they stayed at the hotel relations between all three Watts were good.

A young woman, Katherine MacLean, is the next witness. She was a waitress at the hotel and on the Monday morning was riding her bicycle to work. At about 8.05, she encountered a car coming the other way. It was driven by Watt, who was wiping the inside of the windscreen with his hand while the windscreen wipers left marks on the outside. The screen was clouded by mist or frost. A little after 8.30, Watt returned to the hotel to take his breakfast. This testimony supports Mrs Leitch's account of hearing a car come to the hotel at about this time.

Evidence about the erratic behaviour of the car headlights is given by Donald MacDonald, who runs the local garage. On the 16th, Watt had asked him to check them. When he could find nothing wrong, it was agreed that the car should be brought in the following day for a more thorough examination. He says the lights would go on and off for no apparent reason. Again, it is implied it would have been foolhardy to drive through the night to Glasgow and back with lights that might fail at any moment. MacDonald also testifies to Watt's state of mind when he received the news of the killings: 'It didn't seem to penetrate at the time and then he just sort of collapsed in a chair and cried.'

The next witness is Laurence Dowdall. His is a formidable presence, not only because of his high reputation as a solicitor but also because of his role in persuading some of the police that Manuel had killed the Watts. He has a complex professional role: he is acting for Watt but also for Manuel's parents and, of course, he had previously acted for Peter Manuel. Peter now regards him as an enemy and has instructed his counsel to attack his integrity, a task they must surely find deeply uncomfortable.

Earlier in the book, we gave Dowdall's account of how Manuel had written to him from prison, of their initial meeting, his visit to the Watt house, his growing belief that Manuel was the killer and how he had eventually arranged for Watt and Manuel to meet. Now, in court, Dowdall repeats what he had told the police about these events.

Grieve immediately suggests that Dowdall acted improperly. As Manuel was initially his client, he should not have revealed anything that Manuel had told him to Watt. Dowdall will have none of it. Manuel had been his client in connection with 'another criminal matter' but not in regard to the Watt murders. Therefore, 'the information he gave me that someone else had done it [the murders] I did not regard as confidential and I advised him to see the police about it.'

So, he is asked, did he himself go to the police? This is a dangerous question and one can only conclude Grieve asks it on Manuel's instruction. When he answers, Dowdall seizes the opportunity to depict Manuel in a bad light. Yes, he did go to the police, but before he did so he had asked Manuel, 'Well, what will you do if I go to the police?' Manuel's answer was: 'I shall deny that I said it.'

Grieve may regret his question but he continues trying to discredit Dowdall's account of his dealings with Manuel. Much of the initial case against Manuel depended on the fact that he was able to describe in detail the interior of Watt's house. Only someone who had been there could have done that. Grieve now claims it was Dowdall who gave this information to Manuel and not the other way round. He asks, 'Did you not in fact describe the Watt house first of all to Manuel?' Dowdall's counterpunch is telling: 'It is not my province to ask you questions but how could I, if I had never been there?'

Was money involved in the Manuel–Watt encounters? Dowdall says Manuel told him he was not after money from Watt for telling him about the murders. Similarly, he says, Watt had denied that he had given Manuel any money. All this is being brought out now to discredit in advance another of Manuel's claims: that Watt had given him £150. That is the end of the evidence offered on the third day.

CHAPTER EIGHTEEN

Next morning, it is Watt's turn to give evidence. He is almost as important a witness as Manuel and his appearance is awaited with feverish impatience. By malign chance, the prosecution has an unlooked-for opportunity to depict him as deserving sympathy. He is brought into court on a medical couch and with a doctor in attendance. He has recently been involved in a car crash and his injuries apparently prevent him from standing for more than short periods. Throughout his time in court, he will show obvious signs of pain as well as great emotional distress.

They start with his family situation. He tells the court that his wife underwent her heart operation against his advice but he was delighted when it improved her health. Just before she was killed, she had told him over the telephone that her sister was coming to stay and that she was very happy because of this. (This is significant because it will counter Manuel's claim that when Watt set out to kill his wife he did not know Mrs Brown was staying at the house.) He had gone to the Cairnbaan to recover from overwork and sciatica. He is asked about the car lights. He describes the fault. He thought there was a short circuit in the switch but he 'gave it a shake and usually it came on after that'.

He gives his account of what happened on the morning of Monday, 17 September. He had planned to get up at 5.30 and go fishing but, although he heard the alarm, he decided to sleep on for a while. When he awoke, it was 7.40. He misread the time and believed it was only 6.40. When he started out for the river, his car had frost on the windscreen. As he drove away from the hotel, he saw Miss MacLean arriving and realised he'd got the time wrong. He went to look at the river then returned for his breakfast.

Next, Watt tells of his reaction on learning of the murders. When he was called back, his first thought was that something must have happened to Mr Leitch and he prepared himself to comfort the man's wife. When she told him of the terrible discovery at his house, he could not believe it. He 'told her it must be ridiculous' because he had spoken by phone to his wife only the night before. He phoned his brother to check but he had already gone to the bungalow; his secretary confirmed the truth of it. At this point in his testimony, Watt begins to sob. After a while, he is able to continue and says he then phoned his house and spoke to a police officer.

He started to drive to Glasgow with Mr Bruce. After a few miles, he realised he wasn't safe to drive and they went to a police station for help. He was driven to Alexandria, where Lanarkshire police officers met him and took him on to Glasgow. He soon fell under suspicion. Eventually, he had to take part in two identity parades; following them, he was arrested and charged with the three murders. He spent 67 days in Barlinnie.

Dowdall had told him about Manuel and he arranged to meet him. When they first met, he told Manuel that if he was after money he should forget it. He also told him, 'If I thought you had anything to do with the Burnside incident, I wouldn't only lay hands on you, I would tear you into little pieces here.' (His choice of words is perhaps unfortunate here; some of the jury may think that 'incident' is an oddly mild way to characterise the murder of three of his family.)

He is asked how Manuel reacted. 'He sat bolt upright and said, "People don't do that to Manuel."' It is a phrase that seizes the attention because it seems to encapsulate Manuel's boastful egotism.

'What happened then?'

'I said to him, "Well, I suppose you have asked me to come along. You have something to help me?" and Manuel agreed he had.'

These initial exchanges took place at the Whitehall Restaurant but they soon left because Manuel was nervous. He scribbled something on a newspaper and passed it over to Watt. It read: 'I don't trust these two men at the next table. I think they are newspapermen. Act as if you know me.' Watt says he did not think much of this: 'I took the paper and threw it down on the table.' He now says something strange: 'I regret I wasn't able to keep this newspaper, because when I eventually did retrieve it the part that was written was torn off.' Yet, according to his own evidence, he left the restaurant with Manuel and was with him until early next morning. Did he go back next day and retrieve the paper? Or was there someone else (perhaps arranged for by Dowdall or the police) watching their meeting? And if so, did that person take possession of the scribbled note? Like so much that occurred between Watt and Manuel, it remains puzzling.

After they left the restaurant they went to a pub and then to another, where their main conversation took place. Manuel told him he knew who had carried out the Burnside killings. He also spoke of Watt's daughter and produced a photograph of a young girl, saying, 'There is your daughter.'

'I looked at it. To my amazement – I said, "That is not my daughter," but I recognised the photograph.'

'Yes?' Gillies prompts.

'It was a photograph of Anne Kneilands which I had seen in the newspaper.'

'A newspaper photograph?'

'No, a snap.'

He handed the picture back to Manuel, who tore it into small pieces.

His identification of the photo with Kneilands is devastating for Manuel's defence. If he had a photograph of her almost two years after her murder, it would strongly suggest that he was involved, perhaps that he had taken it from her body.

But is the story true? In his statement to the Govan police, Watt simply mentioned being shown a photograph. Only now does he identify it as depicting Kneilands. Whatever the truth of the matter, if his statement is accepted by the jury, it strongly links Manuel and the Kneilands murder.

Next, Watt tells the court, Manuel explained to him why his family was killed. It was all a mistake, he claimed: the wrong house had been raided and the wrong people murdered. Manuel told him that Tallis, Hart and Bowes had planned to steal the contents of a safe in the Valentes' house. Hart, a relative of the Valentes, had heard a rumour that it contained between five and ten thousand pounds. The plan was to kill everyone in the house except one person, who would be forced to show where the safe key was hidden and then killed. By any standards, this would have been an almost incredible piece of criminal planning.

The trio, Manuel told Watt, had broken into the Martins' house and then gone to the Watts', where they had seen Deanna Valente and assumed she was in her own home. They returned to the Martins' and then, in the early hours of the next day, broke into the Watt house, where Tallis shot the three women. It is worth bearing in mind that, according to Watt, Manuel claimed Tallis had told him all this.

Watt claims that Manuel revealed an astonishing knowledge of the inside of the house: 'He told me about every item of furniture in my wife's bedroom, my daughter's bedroom and in my sitting room. He told me all this in detail . . . He told me about the three-piece suite, he told me about the standard lamp and the coffee table, and he told me about the piano, where it was sitting, and he told me about a photograph that was on top of the piano.' He is asked if Manuel said how Tallis came to give him all this information and when he got it. But he replies that he has not finished telling how much Manuel knew about the house. Manuel had told him there was no safe in his house. But this was not true. There was one in the kitchenette under the kitchen table. 'I said to him, "Haven't you been in the kitchenette?" He says, "No, there was no safe in your house."' At the time, this testimony must seem strange to the jury. Why does Watt go out of his way to say something that suggests Manuel had *not* been in his house? Later, however, it emerges that the door to the kitchenette was the only one not open when the police entered the house.

'So it was then I said to him,' Watt continues, '"Now, look, you know far too much about the house not to have been there."

'"Oh, no," he says, "Tallis told me." He says, "Tallis came back after he finished and he was going like this [here Watt demonstrates a violent shaking of the hands]. You never saw a man like yon in your life, going like this, and he told me then about your house."' Then, Watt says, Manuel went on to claim Tallis had given him the gun and the two rings.

At this point, Watt began to question Manuel about guns. He told him he knew he'd got the gun used in the killings from Scout O'Neil. Manuel denied it.

'I says, "Yes, you did. I know you did, because I took O'Neil to the police, where the statement was made."

'"Oh," he says, "that gun. Oh, I have several guns."'

Two things are striking. First, according to Watt, Manuel admitted he had several guns. Second, Watt told Manuel he knew he had possessed the gun used to murder his family; yet after this they went on to spend another nine or ten hours talking and drinking together.

Watt then recounted how Manuel had told him, 'He could prove my innocence conclusively.' He had told him the story of the break-in in Bothwell and the bullet in the mattress, supposedly fired by Tallis. The same gun had been used at Watt's house. If the bullet could be found, Watt could be proved innocent, as he was away from Glasgow when the break-in took place.

He is asked, 'Did you ask Manuel whether the gun could be got?'

'Yes, I asked him where the gun was, what he did with the gun. He said Tallis gave him the gun. I said, "Where is it?" He said, "I threw it in the Clyde."'

And, of course, it was from the Clyde that the police, guided by Manuel, eventually recovered the gun.

And then there occurs yet another oddity in Watt's evidence. He says, 'But there was another very, very terrible side of the conversation too. He said, after he told me the gun was in the Clyde, he said during the time he was awaiting trial –'

'Don't pursue that,' he is quickly ordered by prosecuting counsel.

What on earth had Manuel said? What was Watt about to say and why did counsel prevent him?

The broad outlines of Watt's and Manuel's night together are described to the jury. After the restaurant and the two pubs, they went to Watt's brother's house and stayed there, talking and drinking, until the next morning. Watt then drove Manuel to Fourth Street at about five or seven, the exact time is unclear. Later, when Manuel gives his rival version of events, he does not disagree substantially about the length of time they were together. Manuel and Watt were thus in each other's company for about 11 hours. But, from all the court hears, the whole of their conversation might have occupied less than an hour. What else occurred during all their time together? Why was Watt so willing to spend all this time with a man he believed had killed his family? The jury may wonder about all this.

Watt goes on to explain that they met again later that day, this time with Dowdall, who urged Manuel to tell his story of Tallis and the others to the police. Manuel refused, so Dowdall suggested he should tell the Glasgow procurator fiscal MacDonald. Manuel rejected this proposal too. And that is the total of Watt's evidence about the second meeting. According to Watt, this was the last time he spoke to Manuel. The prosecution emphasises that there has never been any link between Watt and Tallis. 'Never saw Tallis in my life,' says Watt.

It is now the defence's turn and their aim is to cast doubt both on Watt's integrity and his story. They have hinted that he used the Cairnbaan Hotel to meet his mistress. Now he is asked by Grieve if he was always faithful to his wife.

'No, I was not,' he admits.

'Were you frequently unfaithful to her?'

'No, I was not.'

'Several times?'

'A few times, yes.'

He had gone to the garage asking for the car lights to be fixed and the tank filled on the Sunday before the murders. 'Were you not getting your car ready to go to Glasgow that night or the following morning?' Watt's response is robust: 'A load of nonsense.' He denies that he was on the Renfrew Ferry that night. 'That is a lot of nonsense, that is a lie,' he answers angrily. As the defence continues to draw a picture of him driving down through the night to murder his family, Watt responds furiously: 'My beautiful girls! Ghouls!'

Everything the defence suggests is 'a lot of nonsense'. 'I did nothing of the kind, a lot of nonsense. I was never near Burnside nor Renfrew Ferry. I was never on Loch Lomondside that night. A lot of nonsense.' And no, he had never got a gun from Tallis, that suggestion is also false.

Next, the defence tries to show that he was not truly distressed when told about the slaughter at his house. Surely, he is asked, he could not have been that upset if he'd been able to drive to Dumbarton, about 40 miles from the hotel, immediately on learning of the deaths? But Grieve has made a serious error. Evidence has just been given that

Watt drove only about three miles and found he could go no further. The bad mistake is pointed out to him.

DS Mitchell of the Lanarkshire force, who had been in the car for the second part of the journey to Glasgow, had raised doubts about Watt's demeanour. Watt is therefore asked if he had said to Mitchell, 'You don't think I did it?' because he had a guilty conscience. His reply is fierce: 'My conscience never has been guilty all my life. I never did a wrong thing all my life. Never once did I do a wrong thing in my life.' It is a sweeping claim, perhaps excusable by his highly emotional state.

Despite all Watt's robust denials, the defence continues to suggest he had a motive for killing his wife. Why did he ask the cleaning lady for the keys so he could get the insurance policies? Because the insurance agent had asked him for them, he replies. In any case, he adds, the sum involved was only a few pounds. He also wanted the keys so that the police could search the cabinet in which the policies were kept. They had, he explains, 'already searched the whole house except for this'. Again, this is slightly puzzling. The cleaning lady has said that the keys were kept in a jug in the kitchenette. If the police had made a thorough search of the whole house, why had they not found them? And why did Watt not know where the keys to his own cabinet were kept?

The defence takes him back to something he said shortly after the murders. Why had he told Mrs Collison that he thought he knew the killer's identity? His reply is surprising but reasonable. As there had been almost nothing stolen, he had reasoned that there must have been some other motive for the killings. He concluded that the killer 'must have been someone in the family' and considered whether his brother-in-law George Brown could have been the murderer. But 'the first name that came to my mind wasn't my brother-in-law. I had thousands of names in my mind; I had thousands of worries in my mind. I never slept. I was at it all the time, all that day, all that night.'

Grieve returns to Sergeant Mitchell's account of the drive back to Glasgow. Watt accepts that he could have told Mitchell 'if he thought he was coming to take back the man who committed the murder how wrong he was'. But he would have said this because Mitchell clearly thought that he had something to do with the murders. He recalled Mitchell saying something like, 'I thought I was going to bring back a broken-hearted and bereaved man, and I found a man with a smirk on his face and a man without a tear.' He is asked if he replied, 'I believe you are right.' His answer is vehement and embittered: 'A lot of nonsense . . . If he said that, it is an absolute invention – and quite like Mitchell, too.'

Grieve now turns to Watt's involvement with guns. Had Watt not gone to the police with a man called Charles Kerr in connection with a gun? He agrees that yes, he had, because he'd known Kerr had an unlicensed revolver. 'I was after revolvers, anything to do with revolvers, anything attached to this case.'

They turn to Watt's first encounter with Manuel. 'It was in December 1957 that you first heard about Mr Dowdall's meeting and communications with Manuel?' Grieve suggests. Watt contradicts him. He had heard about Manuel's first meeting with Dowdall while he was in prison. 'I had heard a lot about Manuel when I was in prison. I learned the type of man Manuel was when I was in prison.' It is a clear indication to the jury that Manuel was a criminal well known to other criminals.

Then why, he is asked, had he agreed to meet a man he believed had killed his family? Why had he spent so much time with him? These are very good questions. They may open a vast field of doubt about Watt's behaviour and possibly undermine his account of his dealings with Manuel.

However, Watt replies that he had seen Manuel at his request and because the police appeared to be doing nothing. 'I knew if I saw Manuel I was going to go after him, because I had come to the conclusion that Manuel was the man responsible for all my troubles, from the enquiries and investigations which I had made personally.' He adds, 'There was nothing done about it [i.e. about investigating the murders] unless what was done at the instigation of my solicitor.'

If that was the case, Grieve asks him, why had he not gone to the police? Watt erupts: 'I had spoken to the police about it. I had been into the matter with the police over that year. I was at the police incessantly about it. There was only one police officer who would listen to me and he listened very intently.' (Watt is most likely referring to Bob Kerr.)

Grieve persists: 'But instead of putting the matter into the hands of the police, you decided to meet Manuel and drink with him.' Watt repeats that he had spoken to the police; he had spoken to Hendry, who had dismissed the notion, saying: 'If there is anyone who knows Manuel, I do. If there is anyone who knows how Manuel thinks, I do.' He adds that, although he strongly suspected Manuel at this stage, he was not completely certain. He had met Manuel to question him, to get more evidence; that was why he'd gone to the Whitehall Restaurant.

This is challenged head-on by the defence: 'You knew perfectly well Manuel had nothing to do with it, didn't you?'

'I knew nothing of the kind. I was fully convinced he had.'

So, too, he adds, was the police officer working with him. He says the officer had assured him that he knew Watt was innocent and knew who did it.

The defence proposes something totally different: 'Did you eventually admit to Manuel in Jackson's Bar that in fact you had committed these crimes?'

'A lot of nonsense,' Watt almost shouts. 'It doesn't surprise me in the least if it came from him.'

Grieve suggests Watt had tried to get Manuel to help him frame someone: 'Were you not subsequently that evening with Manuel trying to manufacture some evidence against somebody else which would clear you?'

'Not at all. I have never manufactured anything in my life in so far as that is concerned.'

His denials continue. No, he says, he didn't give Manuel any money. He couldn't have given Manuel £15 from his bakery shop on the night they first met. (Manuel claims he was given this sum as a sweetener to persuade him to tell the Tallis story to Watt's sister-in-law.) He explains why this was not possible, why Manuel is lying: first, there would have been no cashier, as the shop would have been shut; second, no money was kept on the premises overnight in any case. Watt rejects again the suggestion that he was trying to come to some arrangement with Manuel, denies he was drunk when they parted, denies Manuel drove his car for him, denies he later gave Manuel £150 because he wanted someone else arrested for the murders. 'I had not £150 to give Manuel. All my money is on record, is recorded, everything that comes through. I touch no money in my business. Every penny that comes out of my business is on record.' Besides, he says, all the money he had was tied up in the business, which he was in the process of expanding. As for the insurance payout on his wife's life, that came to only £50 or £60.

John Watt's account of the night with Manuel supports his brother's and strengthens the prosecution's case. Manuel, he says, 'was very familiar with practically every stick of furniture in the house . . . even to a torch lying beside the bed . . . Vivienne's bed'.

When John has finished, the Watt murders are left for the moment and there follows another of those technical testimonies needed to lay the ground for later prosecution evidence. A local planning officer states that the distance between the Manuel and Smart houses was only about half a mile and it would take about fifteen minutes to walk between them using public roads. Isabelle Cooke lived only two and a half miles away. The jury is reminded of how close the sites of these crimes are, not only to each other but also to where Manuel lived.

The case moves now to the Christmas Day break-in at Reverend Houston's home. The minister and his wife unhesitatingly identify the gloves and camera found in the Manuel house as their property. The woman who gave the minister the gloves confirms the identification.

After this incursion into simple theft, the Crown turns once more to brutal murder. Isabelle Cooke's father has to describe how his daughter failed to return on the night of 28 December 1957 and the agony of waiting that followed. After her disappearance, the dread-racked days were broken by the police bringing him item after item of hers to identify, each adding to the horror as his family waited for her body to be discovered. Then, in the early hours of 16 January, Reverend Houston had come to tell them that their daughter's body had at last been found.

The prosecution turns to events around the time of her death. Evidence is given that at about 8.30 p.m. on the 28th witnesses heard a woman's cry coming from the general direction of the path Isabelle would have taken. Donald MacFarlane, a special constable, testifies that at about 11.30 that night he saw Peter Manuel. He had come along a railway line and then ducked under a fence to get to the road. He tried to hide his face but the witness recognised him. Leslie cross-examines him and shows that he is in error to say the moon was full that night and gets him to admit he needs to use glasses. The identification is under some doubt. Cameron asks him how far away he had been from the person he saw. About 15 ft, he replies. Police officers give evidence about finding items belonging to Cooke that had been spread over a considerable distance. It may be that the killer did this to confuse and mislead the police.

The final charge is that of murdering the Smarts. The Crown's contention is that the family was killed early on 1 January, although the bodies were not found until the 6th. The prosecution offers disturbing evidence that someone went in and out of their house in the period between the murders and the discovery of the bodies. Several witnesses testified to changes at the house between 1 and 6 January. A neighbour stated that the garage doors were open on New Year's Day and the car gone. Others attested to curtains being opened

Peter Manuel

Anne Kneilands

Isabelle Cooke

Sydney Dunn

William and Marion Watt

Frogmen searching the River Calder following
Isabelle Cooke's disappearance

The shallow grave in which police, having been led there by Manuel, found Isabelle Cooke's body

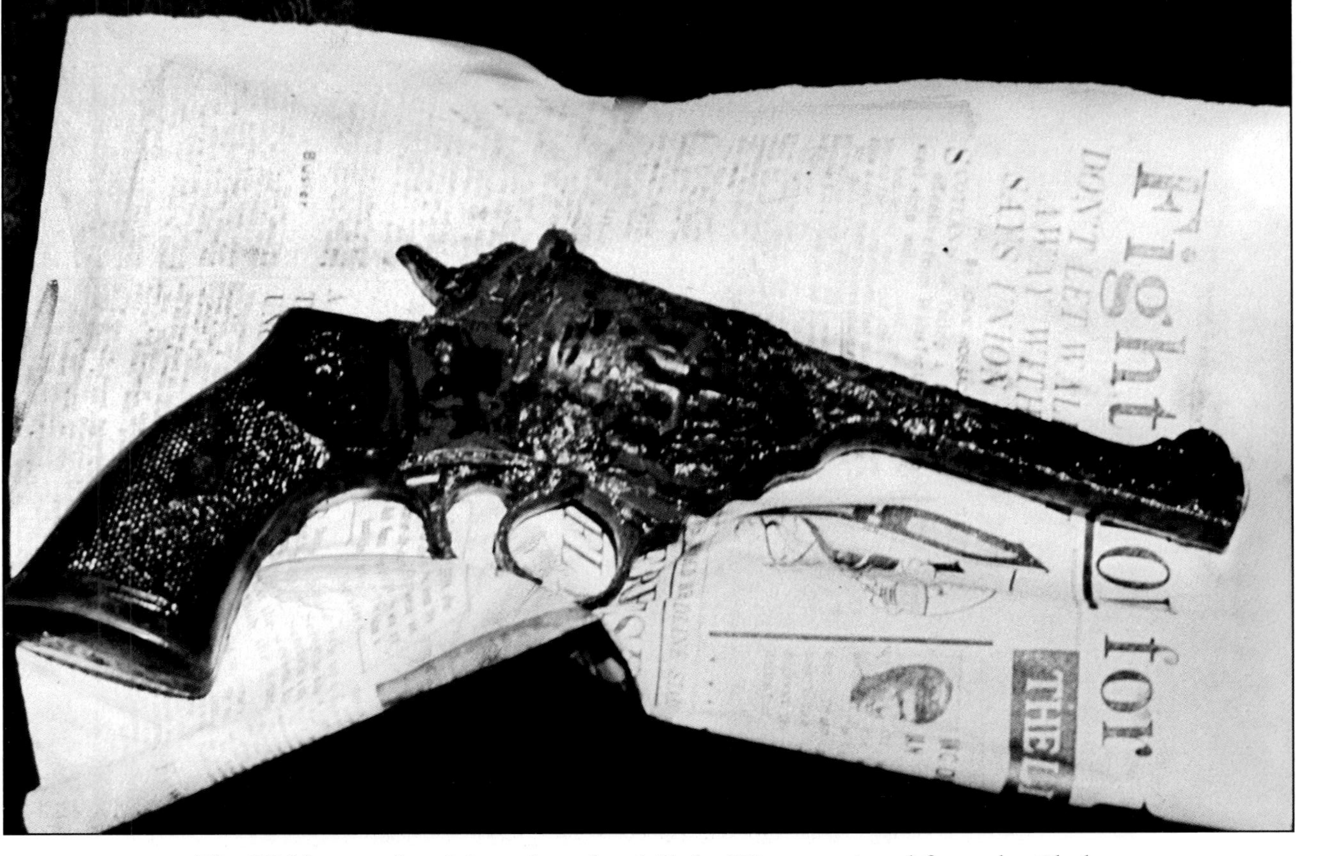

The Webley revolver Manuel used to kill the Watts, retrieved from the Clyde

The queue outside Glasgow High Court
on the first day of Manuel's trial

William Muncie, Tom Goodall and
Alex Brown, pictured during the trial

William Watt, injured in a car crash,
is carried out of court

A crowd gathers outside the court to hear the verdict

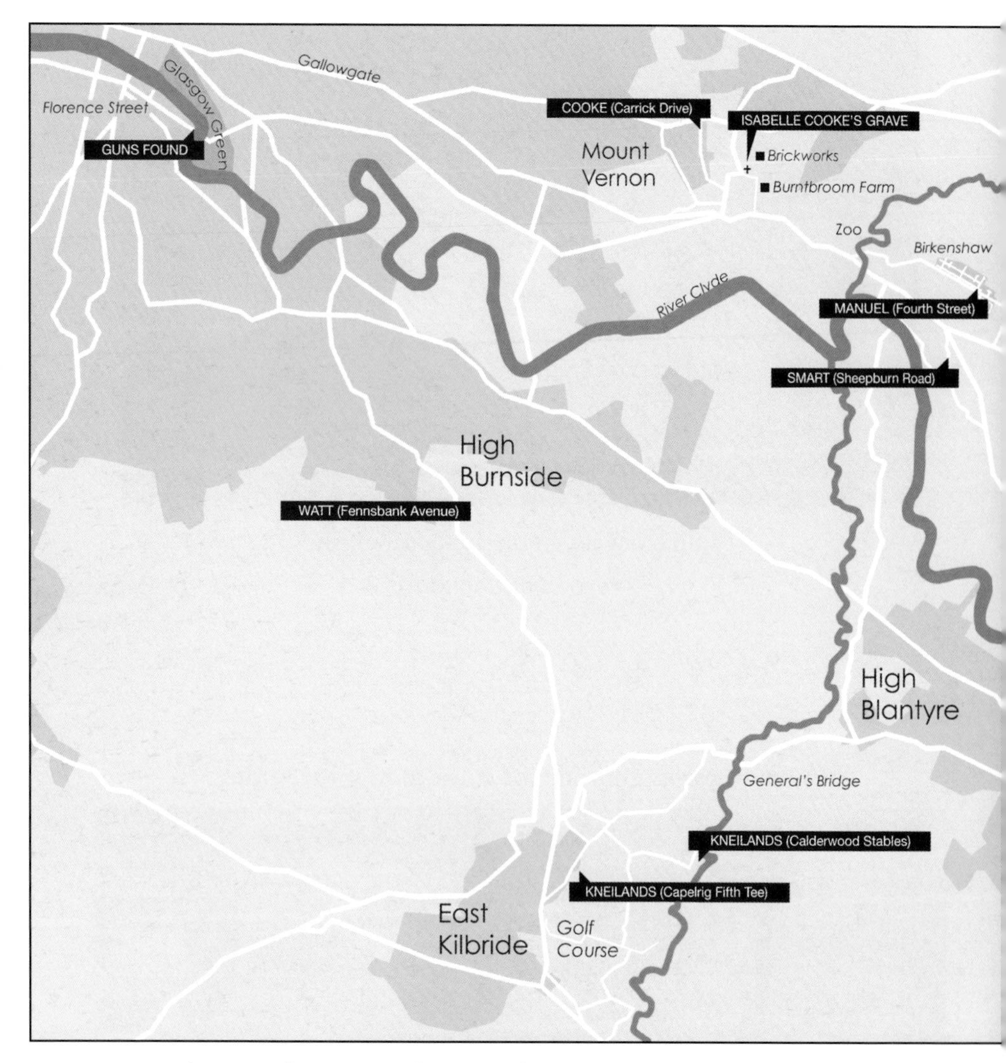

A map showing the area to the east of Glasgow in which Manuel operated (courtesy of Daniel Henrie)

and closed and lights switched on and off. The macabre implication is that whoever murdered the Smarts returned to the house from time to time and spent time there among the corpses of his victims.

Smart's car is also important: the prosecution case is that Manuel used it before dumping it in Florence Street. A taxi driver states that he saw a small Austin saloon resembling Smart's coming along Sheepburn Road with its lights off at about 5 a.m. on 1 January. The exhaust was emitting a heavy vapour, indicating that the engine had not been running for long. Testimony from other witnesses suggests that the car had been left at the Ranco car park by about eleven or twelve that morning. Another witness states that the driver of a small car had given him a lift towards Glasgow from near Law Hospital on the morning of 2 January, although he thinks the car was a Morris rather than an A30. PC Smith tells the court that he was given a lift on the morning of 2 January by a man he subsequently identified as Manuel. Other witnesses give evidence that the car had been dumped in Florence Street by the 2nd and that Manuel travelled by bus from Glasgow to Birkenshaw at about 9.15 that morning. The chain is growing stronger and stronger: if Manuel had Smart's car, he could not have come by it legitimately.

The money Smart received immediately before his murder is crucial evidence against Manuel. When Smart paid in his December wages cheque, he was issued with new Commercial Bank notes, blue in colour and numbered sequentially. He paid a five-pound note and ten singles to his firm to refund an advance. Seven of the pound notes remained in the firm's safe until the police took them. The numbers on the notes are vital to the prosecution case.

The police were able to establish the serial numbers of the notes Smart had received from the bank's records, the numbers on the notes in his firm's safe and those on the notes issued to the customer after him. If Manuel can be shown to have had notes from this sequence he can only have got them – somehow – from Smart. The Crown will maintain he took them by murder.

The next crucial task for the prosecution, therefore, is to link Manuel to the notes stolen from the Smart house. Witnesses testify that in December he was receiving small sums in National Assistance money. As he had no other legitimate source of funds, it was highly unlikely that he could have acquired a large sum by 1 January other than through crime. That crime, the prosecution argues, was the murder of the Smarts.

In his third confession, Manuel had written, 'I went through the house and took a quantity of Bank notes from a wallet I found in a jacket in the front bedroom. There was about £20 to £25 in the wallet.' At this point, the court has not yet heard about his confessions; the defence hopes – and the prosecution fears – that they will never be presented in court. To support the confessions, or to make them unnecessary, the prosecution has to find another way to link the Smarts, Manuel and the notes. The key to doing so is the Greenans' party.

On the evening of 1 January, the Manuel family went to an engagement party for the daughter of Patrick Greenan, Bridget's brother. There had been a twelve-year estrangement between the two families, perhaps caused by Peter's rape conviction, and the Manuels' presence at the party was indicative of a thaw in relations. A few days later, the Greenans found themselves sucked into a hideous murder case. How they must have regretted inviting the Manuels.

The first to testify is Mrs Greenan. She says Peter left the party at about eight and returned about an hour later with a parcel containing drink. Just how much drink he brought and how he'd paid for it will form another link in the chain. When he left at 11.20 p.m., he gave her a pound for herself. She believed he'd also given her husband a pound so that his mother could go home by taxi. Patrick, her husband, confirms that this was the case. His evidence is not quite what the prosecution needs because he states that it was a British Linen Bank note he received. He says that Peter had bought a dozen cans of lager for the party. One of his sons adds that Manuel had given his sister a pound to mark her engagement and had with him three packets of twenty Capstan cigarettes and a square bottle of whisky. He estimates Manuel had a bundle of five to seven pounds.

Manuel left the party with Mary McCamley and three other young people and they went to Mary's house nearby. She states that he had a square bottle of whisky with him and two or three tins of lager. He also had some pound notes, which he took out of his pocket.

'How many do you think they would be?' she is asked.

'Between five and ten pounds, I would think,' she replied, adding that they were new blue notes.

Next comes the key question: 'What was he doing with these notes when you saw him?'

'Well, he took them out of his pocket and read out the numbers that were on them.'

'How many of them?'

'Just three.'

'And how did they run, these three numbers?'

'Well, he read out the first number and then the second and third one. It was like six, seven and eight were the end letters [*sic*] in each pound note. One was six and one was seven and one was eight.'

'So the numbers appeared to follow one after the other?'

'Yes.'

Reading out the serial numbers from banknotes may seem an odd sort of party entertainment but the defence does not challenge it.

Manuel's generosity was not confined to his time at the Greenans'. The court is now told that when he and three others went on to a dance, he bought everyone's ticket.

Miss McCamley's mother is the next witness and provides a few moments of welcome light relief. Asked if she recognises Manuel in court, she answers, 'I don't know where to look for him.'

Cameron guides her: 'If you'll look between the two police officers –'

'I'm afraid I can't see him,' she replies.

Finally, she is allowed to go down to the floor of the court. 'Yes, I see him. I was looking all over the wrong place.'

She states that she refused a drink of whisky that Manuel offered her but accepted a 'clean' pound note from him. She thinks he had two or three more.

A young man called James McGorry also testifies that Manuel displayed blue, clean-looking pound notes at the McCamleys'. Part of his evidence repeats almost word for word what Miss McCamley has said: 'It was the last two or the last three numbers, they all came after, the likes of six, seven and eight,' he says. Manuel, he states, also gave away another pound at the dance. He had given McGorry about twenty cigarettes at the party and had about four more packs at the dance.

More witnesses from the party support all this. Manuel had a bottle of Johnnie Walker whisky (these bottles were square in section); he had new blue pound notes; he was giving away money. There can now be little doubt in the jury's mind that Manuel had a considerable number of new blue one-pound notes on 1 January, that he used them to buy quite a lot of drink and cigarettes, and that he was being extremely generous with the money.

The next witness is Joe Brannan, who describes himself as an unemployed miner. The court is not told two important facts. The first is that he had been arrested on a thieving expedition with Manuel. The second is that Brannan had been persuaded by the police to spy on Manuel.

By way of background, Brannan tells the court that he has known Manuel for about four years. They bumped into each other at the beginning of December 1957, just after Manuel had been released from prison, and met up again at the local labour exchange. On the Saturday before Christmas, Brannan says, Manuel told him he was going to Mount Vernon to do 'a snatch', which, he helpfully explains, 'is commonly known as snatching a lady's handbag'. He had been invited to join in but 'on those conditions, I refused to go'. This, of course, was well before the Isabelle Cooke murder and its only significance for the prosecution case is to suggest that Manuel was willing to snatch women's handbags and perhaps might kill while attempting to do so.

Brannan starts to say that on 27 December he and Manuel had taken a bus so they could see where the police were searching for Isabelle Cooke's body. He is quickly interrupted by the prosecution: 'Would it help you with your dates if I told you that Isabelle Cooke didn't disappear till 28 December?' Brannan's response is strange, perhaps hinting he has his story ready and does not want to be pushed from the prepared track: 'Well, I don't know if you are jumping –' Again he is stopped: 'I am asking what happened on the Friday after Christmas.' So Brannan tells the court that he met Manuel on the 27th and was told by him that 'he'd done a housebreaking in Mount Vernon at a minister's house' but had 'got only a small amount of money and a camera'. Damning – if the jury believes him.

On the 31st, Brannan encountered Manuel and his father in the Royal Oak pub. He and Samuel each bought a round of drinks: 'Two pints and a Nut Brown Ale,' he recalls fondly. Samuel had lent his son a pound so that he too could buy a round. This, of course, helps to establish that Manuel was broke at Hogmanay. But, Brannan states, the next day Manuel had money. He had arranged to meet him and, because he thought the man was 'skint', he was going to buy him a drink. In the event, however, it was Manuel who was generous. He had come to Brannan's house and given his two children two shillings each. They then went to the pub. Brannan was in the toilet when Manuel bought drinks but on his return Manuel told him he'd mistakenly given the barman a five-pound note instead of a single. The barman had pointed out the error.

Brannan wanted to know more about Manuel's financial circumstances, no doubt to pass the information to the police. 'I asked him how he was, how he was fixed. He said he had had a bit of pay.' Manuel added that he 'had to go in [to Glasgow] and see someone, as he was getting payment through the Mr Watt business. He got the money from the Gordon Club.' This confirms that Manuel claimed there was some sort of link between Watt, the club and money. Was it that Manuel thought he could get money from Dandy McKay by threatening that he had possessed the gun used to kill the Smarts?

Brannan is asked by the defence, 'You would be rather surprised, I take it, having seen Manuel borrowing, or apparently borrowing, money from his father on Hogmanay, that he had a five-pound note in the midday of the following day?'

'I was more surprised when he wanted to give the kiddies the two-shilling piece,' is his riposte.

At the pub, he says, Manuel bought a bottle of wine and a bottle of whisky and paid for these drinks with blue pound notes. The next time he saw Manuel was on 3 January.

'Did he say anything about the car?' he is prompted.

'Oh, yes, he said something about an Austin A30. He said he didn't think they went so fast.'

'Did he say what he had used the car for?'

'He said on New Year's night he went back up to the Woodend Hotel to get another quantity of liquor and take it back to the party again.'

The link between Manuel and the car is crucial, so the prosecution makes sure it is emphasised.

'Did you take it that he had used the car to get from the Greenans' house to the Woodend Hotel?'

'I didn't take it. Peter made it quite clear that he did use the car to get to the Woodend.'

'The car he described as an A30?'

'An A30.'

Manuel bought drinks with a pound note and later steak and sausages with another pound; he also bought half a bottle of brandy. If Brannan is accurate, Manuel was still in funds at that point.

Brannan continues, providing the jury with a detailed account of his contacts with Manuel. Talking of Wednesday, 8 January, he returns to the evidence he'd started to give when he'd been corrected about the date. He and Manuel boarded a bus, he says, in order 'to see the policemen wading and the firemen pumping the Calder River' as they searched for Cooke. Manuel had 'said it was a red herring they were looking for'.

On the Friday, Manuel told him he had to go into Glasgow to collect some money from the Gordon Club. He also suggested they should both go down to London. On the Sunday, the 12th, he went to the Manuel house, where he found Peter in a bad state. 'He was pretty down. He had got his nose busted and his face was all scarred at the side. That was an incident he had coming down the road when escorting a gentleman home.' Just what lay behind this mysterious reference is not explained. One presumes Manuel did not report the attack to the police.

Later that day, Manuel suggested they go to London on the Monday or Tuesday. 'He seemed quiet,' says Brannan. 'I think he'd had some sort of argument with his cousin Ron.' That was the last time Brannan saw Manuel before his arrest.

If his evidence is accepted by the jury, the cumulative effect must be enormously damaging to Manuel: he admitted stealing from Mount Vernon and planning to snatch a woman's handbag; he had been broke on New Year's Eve and immediately after the Smart murders he was in funds; he had indicated that he knew the police were searching in the wrong place for Isabelle Cooke's body; and soon after he wanted to get away from Glasgow.

Leslie tries to undo the damage by questioning Brannan's character. He gets some pretty sharp responses, but then Brannan is no stranger to being questioned by the police or lawyers. What was the exact date when Manuel proposed going to London? Brannan is evasive and unclear. Leslie asks, 'You have difficulty remembering dates, do you, if taken out of sequence?' Perhaps he is hinting that Brannan has learned his evidence by rote.

'I have difficulty remembering anything. As far as dates are concerned, it is difficult when you say dates, dates, dates.'

'It is difficult to remember?'

He gets the virtuous answer, 'I don't think so when it is the truth.'

'You weren't going to the coalmines in London, were you?' Leslie asks sarcastically.

'No.'

'What did you say your last job was?'

'A miner.'

'When did you last work in the mines?'

This gets the crushing response, 'December 1957.'

Leslie queries Brannan's attitude towards Manuel. 'I suppose the evidence you have been giving gives you some pain?'

'I don't think so,' Brannan replies.

Drinking and pubs obviously played a large part in their relationship, so he is asked, 'Are you still able to spend a considerable part of your time in public houses?'

'I wish I could but I am not in a financial position to do so.'

'Do you?' Leslie persists.

'No,' Brannan replies.

'When were you last in one?' he is asked.

'I was in one today.'

This may cast a little doubt on Brannan's character but it does nothing to deflect the thrust of his evidence.

He denies that his evidence has been influenced by what has been said in the papers because he doesn't 'read much in the papers'.

As for why he went on a bus to see the search for Isabelle Cooke, 'I just accompanied Peter for the sake of going with him.' (And almost certainly on the instructions of the police.)

'Did you just sit and look the other way?' he is asked sarcastically.

'Oh, no, no,' he answers.

'Why not?'

'If you hear a bang, you will automatically turn round and have a look at it and see where it's coming from.'

There is a cheekiness about Brannan, perhaps because he is confident that on this occasion he is on the safe side of the law.

When Brannan has left the witness box, further evidence is presented about the amount of money Manuel had on New Year's Day. One of the Egans, the family who run the Woodend Hotel, testifies that in the evening Manuel bought two bottles of whisky, two of sherry, twelve of lager and a hundred cigarettes. These cost him 'roughly about £8 17s 6d'. He paid with new Commercial Bank pound notes. Egan thinks Manuel also had some five-pound notes, although he is not sure. Manuel told the witness to give the change to his brother's girl. He adds that he doesn't think he had ever seen Manuel with so much money and had shown the notes to his brother, a statement soon confirmed by the brother, who says there were eight or nine notes. The honest barman who told Manuel he'd given him a five-pound note by mistake confirms that part of Brannan's evidence.

CHAPTER NINETEEN

One of the two guns recovered from the Clyde was the Beretta used to kill the Smarts. The story of how the weapon came into Manuel's hands is now told. It brings into court another fine selection of characters from Glasgow's underworld, all rounded up to give evidence against Manuel.

The first to appear is Billy Fullerton, who tells how he had obtained a Beretta and ammunition from a soldier in a pub in 1952. He'd immediately sold it for six pounds to John Totten, who wanted a weapon. He says the gun he is now shown appears identical to the one he'd sold, although he cannot be certain it is the same one. Fullerton is a notorious Glasgow gangster and the former leader of a ferocious 1930s Protestant razor gang, the Billy Boys. His religious fanaticism had not prevented him selling the gun to the dapper John Totten, whose appearance in court wearing a green tie, shirt and handkerchief proclaimed his allegiance to Celtic Football Club. At the time the gun changed hands, Totten was in need of protection and was grateful to Fullerton for finding it for him. Thereafter, he would occasionally open proceedings at his pitch-and-toss gambling site by firing a shot in the air to deter any potential troublemakers.

Leslie asks Fullerton why Totten had asked him to get a gun.

'Well, years ago I was a wee bit notorious,' is the modest reply.

'Notorious for your ability to get guns?' Leslie asks hopefully.

'No, my ability to fight – no guns.'

Totten appears next. He denies he asked Fullerton for a gun but says he bought it when it was offered because he'd heard a rival gang, who were trying to take over his gambling pitch, had armed themselves with guns. A little while later, he was arrested for fighting and sentenced to four years in prison. The gun was left in his house and he was worried about it being there. Another prisoner, Tony Lowe, had agreed to get it on his release. Totten seems unwilling to admit to any connection with a gun used by Manuel. He says that the gun he is shown is bigger than the gun he had, though he admits it is six years since he saw it.

His wife, the next witness, says that she gave Lowe a parcel that her husband had told her contained a gun. Lowe, fetched from Wandsworth Prison, relates that in 1952, in Barlinnie, Totten had told him that there were two guns in his house. 'So, being in a little bit of trouble, I asked him would it be all right if I could go to the house and collect the guns on liberation.' He had asked 'a chap called McKay' if he would come with him because he knew Totten's house. Mrs Totten had been anxious to get rid of both guns and their ammunition. The Beretta bullets were in a little cardboard box about three inches long; there were about twenty-five or thirty rounds. The guns were not wrapped when he received them.

Lowe and McKay took the guns to a house in Florence Street and left them with Andrew Thomson, who lived there. That was in December 1952 and it was the last Lowe saw of the Beretta until he was shown a gun by the police. He can only say that the Beretta produced in court is the same type as the one he got from Totten's house.

Thomson, the erstwhile custodian of the guns, appears next. According to him, Manuel came to the Gordon Club, where Thomson and McKay worked, and said Lowe had told him to collect a package from Thomson's lodgings. Both Lowe and McKay had previously stayed at his place and, he claims, Lowe had left a brown-paper package on a high shelf in the lobby. McKay drove Thomson and Manuel to Florence Street. While Manuel and McKay stayed in the car, he went upstairs, collected the package, handed it over and went off to be shaved.

He is a reluctant, even evasive, witness and claims he had forgotten that the guns were in his house. He answers slowly and speaks quietly.

The judge, Lord Cameron, is not impressed: 'Thomson, you are here to do two things, if you can: first, tell the truth.'

'I am telling the truth.'

'And the second is to tell it clearly. You are not doing the second. I have very grave doubts about you doing the first.'

However, he seems determined to distance himself from everything involving Manuel. The identification of Manuel as the person who collected the Beretta is crucial but Thomson refuses to confirm it. He states he is not sure he would recognise Manuel again. He only saw him very briefly and sat behind Manuel and McKay in the car: 'I don't think I would know him. I just spoke to him for a minute.' Cameron asks, 'Do you see anyone like him? What is your answer?' Thomson is obdurate: 'No.'

The next witness is Morris Dickov, another professional crook and possibly the owner or part-owner of the Gordon Club. He claims the place is a bridge club. What could be more respectable than that? Unfortunately, he is soon forced to admit it is a betting club. The police also know it as a sort of Crook's Rest, a social centre for criminals, where jobs are arranged and bent deals done.

Dickov recounts how a man came to the club and left an Uddingston phone number, asking him to tell McKay to ring Manuel at that number. He thinks this occurred a week or two before Christmas 1957. Later, he overheard McKay make the call. The phone was answered by a woman; Manuel was out. In questioning Dickov, the defence again makes a careless slip. Although Leslie has just heard him say that a man had come to the club in person and asked that McKay phone the Uddingston number, he asks, 'You don't know who was phoning the first time you got a phone call from Uddingston?' Dickov corrects him.

Samuel 'Dandy' McKay is another criminal, one famous in the Glasgow underworld. Now, like Dickov, he modestly describes himself as a clerk at the Gordon Club. He gives more information about Manuel and the gun. The request to call Manuel at home came 'exactly eight days' before Christmas 1957. After he'd called and spoken to Manuel's mother, Manuel came to the club the following day. They went with Thomson in McKay's car to pick up the gun. Thomson went inside, came back and handed Manuel a package. As they drove away, Manuel opened it and McKay saw it held a small automatic and a matchbox containing four or five bullets. He had seen in the *Daily Express* a picture of a Beretta that was 'exactly the same'.

He next saw Manuel sometime between 6 and 10 January, around midday. Manuel had said he wanted the money because he had to 'get out of the road and get down to England'.

'He asked for £150 off me [£150 seems to be a favourite sum of Manuel's]. He wanted to go to England. I told him he was not getting a halfpenny off me and I ordered him down the stairs.' It may be McKay did more than that: perhaps Manuel had tried to blackmail him into giving him money and he had beaten him up. This could explain the assault Manuel suffered just before his arrest.

In March, McKay says, the police had asked him to look at a number of handguns. The one he is now shown is like the one he picked out then.

Cross-examining, Leslie makes another mistake. A few moments earlier, Thomson said that once he had handed over the gun he had gone to be shaved. Yet Leslie asks McKay if Thomson was in the back of the car when Manuel opened the package. This sort of error cannot help the defence's case. The rest of Leslie's questioning does not shake McKay's story.

The prosecution now offers another witness to strengthen the links between Manuel and the gun. The licensee of the Mail Coach Inn identifies Manuel as a customer who joined a bar-room conversation about the Smart murders. 'This person dwelt at great length on automatic firearms and Berettas in particular . . . He spoke about the Beretta being a very treacherous weapon, in as much as there was some part of it recoiled.' This occurred on 8 January.

All this is very bad for Manuel: if the witnesses are believed, shortly before the Smart murders he had obtained a Beretta and at least four rounds of ammunition. After the murders, he had commented on the trickiness of the mechanism of that type of gun. Later in the trial, a police firearms expert will testify that the Beretta used in the Smart killings was defective. What the court does not hear are Manuel's pre-trial remarks to Ferguson Rodger, the psychiatrist. He had explained how the Beretta had to be loaded in order to fire shots in rapid succession.

It will not become clear why the next witness, Hugh McHugh, is called until much later, when Manuel and his father conspire to suggest that Smart killed his family and then himself. To make the connection with Smart that his story entails seem plausible, Manuel will claim he had helped Smart build his bungalow. McHugh testifies that he knows Manuel and that once when they'd arranged to meet at Sheepburn Road, he, McHugh, had used the Smarts' bungalow as a reference point in fixing the rendezvous.

'Did he seem to know where Smart's house was?' he is asked.

'No, he never knew where the Smarts' house was.'

The jury now has the sickening task of listening to the medical evidence. The reports have been prepared by Professor Allison and Dr Imrie. Allison appears first. His account of the injuries to Anne

Kneilands is particularly distressing. Her body was found some distance away from where she had died, the place marked by a pool of blood. She had suffered 'very extreme violence, because not only was the head smashed in and a large part of the skull reduced to fragments but blood and bone and brain matter were splashed to a distance from that pool near a tree stump . . . There was one point where a distance of eight feet from the pool a portion of brain or bone was found. Another tree at a distance of seven feet showed human debris.'

'Human debris': what was part of the living body of a young girl is here reduced to something comparable to inanimate rubble.

Gillies' questioning emphasises this extreme violence: 'That is, I take it, an unusual distance for portions of skull and brain to go?'

'It is an unusual distance,' Allison confirms. 'The violence necessary to fracture the skull would be very great violence.'

In a gruesome demonstration, he fits a piece of angle iron recovered by the police into one of the skull fractures, although he is careful to say he cannot be certain that it is the actual weapon that was used.

He testifies that a vaginal swab showed no spermatozoa and there was no evidence to show sexual interference.

Allison had examined all the murder victims. Marks to Vivienne Watt's head and face suggested she had been struck, perhaps knocked out, before being shot. The unnatural position of her right arm under her body supported this interpretation. There was bruising to her vulva, which could have been caused when her pyjama trousers were torn off; there were other indications that her nightclothes had been wrenched off. The bullet wound to her head was such that she might have survived for some time; her mother and Mrs Brown had probably died about 6 a.m. or earlier. Their deaths had been instantaneous or nearly so. Vivienne Watt's room might have been rearranged after her death 'to disguise there had been a struggle'.

Isabelle Cooke had a ligature (her bra) round her neck and a headscarf had been tied round her head with the knot forced into her mouth. She died from asphyxiation. Bruising to her face was consistent with having been struck. A vaginal swab detected no seminal fluid.

The evidence arising from Allison's careful, analytical examinations only heightens the horror. When he examined the Smarts' corpses, he noted that they showed 'greenish discolouration to the abdomen' and Mrs Smart's body, being stouter, showed 'many more evidences of decomposition'. There is a tiny amount of relief to be found in his suggestion that the Smarts had died immediately, asleep and unafraid. All the bodies were 'in perfectly natural positions' and there were 'no signs of struggle or disorder'. On the other hand, this only increases the sense of revulsion at the terror that Anne Kneilands, Vivienne Watt and Isabelle Cooke must have suffered.

Allison explains that he carried out tests on a jacket and a pair of trousers belonging to Manuel. In and around the left jacket pocket and the left trouser pocket were indications of blood, which had apparently been sponged off with water. The traces were too minute to allow further tests.

Leslie attempts to lessen the effect of this evidence and to prepare the way for Manuel's alternative explanation of the Smarts' deaths. He is following Manuel's instructions and his heart does not seem to be in it. He asks Allison if all the deaths were 'due to bullet wounds'. Allison gives the obvious answer: 'Not in all cases.' Leslie apologises for his elementary slip: 'I am obliged to you. Except in the case of the two girls.'

As far as the victims of shooting are concerned, 'You excluded suicide in all cases?' he asks.

'We excluded suicide.'

Leslie must know he is laying himself open to a crushing rebuttal but he asks, 'Upon what grounds, just in a word?'

'The wounds were actually in a position which is used by many suicides, but when a person shoots himself through the head he leaves the weapon behind, and had there been individual suicides in the six cases . . . then one would have expected to find six firearms lying around. There was not one.'

Listening to this, Manuel must realise that, if he is going to claim Smart killed himself, he will need to explain how the gun disappeared. By the time he comes to give evidence on his own behalf, he will have concocted an explanation.

Dr Imrie is next on the stand and his evidence simply reinforces what the jury has heard from Allison.

CHAPTER TWENTY

Detective Inspector Robert McNeil is the first of the police officers to give evidence about the Smart murders, Manuel's arrest and his behaviour in the following 48 hours. He describes the condition of the Smart house and the three bodies, the state of the windows, the garage doors and the salmon tin in the kitchen. He adds the significant detail that it was possible to open their back door merely by pushing against it. The only money found in the house was 2s 6d.

McNeil comes to the events surrounding the arrest. This is a crucial moment and he will have been warned that the whole direction of the trial will depend on what he now says and how he answers the defence's questions. He starts to give the police version of what happened. It is an account that will be repeated almost exactly by other officers.

They arrived at the Manuel house at 6.45 on the morning of 14 January with a warrant to search for money, banknotes and keys believed to have been stolen from the Smarts' house. They were a team of nine; seven entered the house. When they got to the house, Samuel Manuel was leaving for work and Peter was asleep. He was told to get dressed. Superintendent Brown formally cautioned Manuel, his father and his mother. Manuel had said to his mother, 'Phone Jimmy Bell, the reporter, and get Dowdalls [*sic*].' He told the police before they began their search, 'You can't take me. You haven't found anything yet.'

After Manuel had been removed to the police station, McNeil had found the gloves from the Houstons'. Samuel had claimed they were his, as was the camera found by Muncie. Samuel Manuel was arrested and charged with theft and reset. In the house, they also found a piece of paper with McKay's name and the phone number of the Gordon Club on it. They had taken all Manuel's clothes, among them the jacket and trousers that later showed traces of blood.

Key parts of McNeil's evidence concern what Manuel said at the house and that afternoon at Hamilton police station. Manuel, he says, had asked Brown what had happened to his father. He had been told he was detained at Bellshill police station. At this point, Manuel told Brown that he wanted to tell him about the money. He was immediately cautioned and told the police were investigating the housebreaking at Sheepburn Road and the murder of the Smarts. Manuel claimed Dandy McKay had given him the money and so McKay was brought from Glasgow and an identification parade organised. At about 7.30 p.m., there was another identification parade, then there was a third. Manuel was recognised as the man who had been spending new notes. At 11.10 p.m., he was charged with breaking into the Houstons' house and with housebreaking and murder at the Smarts'. The clothes he was wearing were taken for examination.

The next morning Manuel was remanded in custody for four days. Manuel requested to talk to McNeil and at about 2.50 p.m., he and Detective Inspector Goodall went to see the prisoner. Manuel said he had something to say: 'It is important and it concerns unsolved crimes in Lanarkshire.' McNeil warned Manuel that his position was serious and that he should have a solicitor. Manuel asked what had happened to his father. He was told that he had been charged with theft and reset. After a while, he said, 'Bring my father and mother here and I will see them in your presence, and after I have made a clean breast of it to them, you can take them away and then I will clear up everything for you and I will take you to where the girl Cooke is buried.'

This is the chance Leslie has been waiting for and he pounces. He rises and declares, 'My Lord, I do object to this line of evidence. Perhaps Your Lordship would hear me.' As he does so, the whole tenor of the trial suddenly shifts. Up to this point, the defence's cross-examination of witnesses has done little to weaken the prosecution case. Although it has been necessary for Manuel's counsel to attack Watt's evidence, as their client demanded, his robust replies and scathing contempt have not helped Manuel and have almost certainly alienated some of the jury. But now the defence's relatively desultory performance is replaced by ferocious attack. Their target is the legitimacy of the confessions and the propriety of their admission as evidence. If they can get the confessions excluded, a key part of the prosecution's case will vanish.

This is a matter of law and of law alone. It is up to the judge to decide it, nobody else. The basic question is how had the three confessions been obtained? Were they the result of police pressure? Had Manuel been offered an inducement to confess? When they detained him, did the police already suspect him of the Kneilands and Watt murders and the disappearance of Isabelle Cooke? If so, did this influence what happened to him while in custody? Besides all this, there is another legal point: did the search warrant allow the police to do what they had done or were some of their actions unauthorised by it?

Lord Cameron has almost certainly foreseen that these issues will arise. He and all the lawyers present understand fully the importance of the point Leslie has raised. In a recent case, Chalmers, a convicted murderer, had been freed on appeal because it was decided that his confession had been improperly obtained by the police.

Leslie begins his argument to have the confessions excluded by going over what happened when Manuel had been arrested. 'Never have such a battery of police officers of very high rank descended on a house to find if somebody was in it. And then it is the father who is taken after this.' He is trying to establish that by arresting Samuel and charging him, the police were starting to exert pressure on his son. 'Now, My Lord, that situation, in my submission, simply makes the [first] statement [made by Manuel] absolutely suspect, and any other activities which might follow upon it in the same category, and, upon that view of the matter, I would invite Your Lordship with all the urgency I can to investigate the circumstances under which these statements were made fully and outwith the presence of the jury . . . In my opinion, it cannot be said that those documents [the three confessions, listed for the trial as documents 140–142] or any statements by the accused were got as voluntary, spontaneous statements.'

Cameron agrees that the matter must be considered. He tells the jury to withdraw. If he decides that the confessions were improperly obtained, then they will never hear their contents. The whole nature of the case will turn on this decision.

The judge addresses the reporters: 'I can't forbid you to report [what will be said in the jury's absence] but I can only advise you as to what you should do in the interests of justice.' They do not write about the proceedings that follow.

McNeil returns, repeats the substance of what he has said and adds that when he told Manuel he could have a solicitor, he responded, 'I want to do this myself. I will write something out for you.'

Leslie begins questioning him but immediately makes two errors. McNeil was a detective sergeant at the time of the Smart murders, was he not? No, McNeil replies, he was a detective inspector. Was

Superintendent Hendry involved in the murder case in January 1958? McNeil points out that Hendry had retired on 28 December 1957. The mistakes are not serious but they suggest a lack of attention to detail.

A key question is how far the police regarded Manuel as a suspect in the Kneilands and Watt murders when they arrested him. If he was under suspicion, then it is possible that they pressured him to confess to those crimes. Leslie makes a small amount of headway when McNeil admits that Manuel had 'come under a degree of suspicion' for the Kneilands murder and was also suspected of the Watt killings. Leslie is also able to establish that Brown and Goodall were made aware that suspicion had centred on Manuel before they arrested him. (In fact, it is very unlikely that the two Glasgow detectives had not heard about the meetings at which Watt had told Kerr about Manuel.) McNeil also admits that the police had information suggesting that Manuel had acquired a .38 Webley from Scout O'Neil a short time before the Watt murders.

However, McNeil asserts that none of the police discussed the murders with Manuel before he wrote the first two confessions. He says that Manuel wrote the first confession without prompting or guidance. 'Then he said, "That won't do. I'll write another,"' and then wrote the second. There had been no promise that if he wrote the confessions the police would get his father released. On the contrary, he was told that that was a matter for the procurator fiscal.

Leslie's questioning is not helped by another slip. He asks, 'Who had statement 142 when his parents arrived?' McNeil points out that this, the longest of the three statements, was not written till the early hours of the next morning. Leslie apologises: 'I beg your pardon, 140.'

Leslie stresses that Manuel had no access to a lawyer or other source of advice. Why, he asks McNeil, was he not allowed to see his parents alone? Because, McNeil tells him, he was facing a capital charge, because there were no facilities at police headquarters to put them safely together and because Manuel had asked him, McNeil, to be present when he saw his parents. For good measure, he adds that Manuel had consistently refused to obtain legal assistance.

When his parents arrived, McNeil says, Brown also told him he could have a lawyer present. He reports what Manuel said, strengthening the case against him: 'He said to his parents that he found great difficulty in speaking to them and he said that he had never been able to speak to them freely, and his mother agreed with that. He said he had been fighting against this all his life and he had to fight it all alone.' Manuel had told his parents, 'There is no future for me, I have done some terrible things,' and confessed to them that he had killed Anne Kneilands and the Smarts.

During the night, Manuel had led the police to where he had buried Isabelle Cooke. Afterwards, in the car on the way back to the station, he had told them twice that 'he intended to write out a full confession and that would clear everything up'. At the station, Inspector Cleland had been called in and, in due course, Manuel had written the final, long confession.

After this, Manuel led them to the place where the guns were to be recovered from the Clyde and later to the General's Bridge, off which he said he had thrown Anne Kneilands' underwear and the piece of angle iron he had used to kill her. He also took the police to the site of the Gas Board hut where he had been working at the time of the Kneilands murder had been. After her murder, he'd hidden his clothes there before destroying them.

Detective Inspector Goodall, the next officer to be examined, throws more light on the question of whether or not Manuel had been denied access to legal advice. Brown, he said, had phoned Dowdall on the afternoon of 14 January only to be told that he would not be acting for Manuel but that another lawyer called Dunlop might. He had then phoned Dunlop. Later, it transpired that Dunlop would not act for Manuel. The police had actually tried to help Manuel get a solicitor.

Goodall rejects any suggestion that he and Brown initially suspected Manuel of the Kneilands and Watt killings. 'Manuel's name had been brought to my notice vaguely from time to time throughout the past year or so but we had no basis for suspecting that Manuel had anything to do with the Watt murders or others at that time.' But, Leslie asks, did he know that Manuel might have been implicated in the Kneilands murder? Goodall replies, 'I knew he had given some story to the newspapers concerning it, that was all. I knew nothing about the details of the murder.' He reinforces his denial: 'Both Mr Brown and I had a very open mind on the subject and we paid little – well, we paid attention but we kept a very open mind on the subject.'

He agrees that Manuel had asked to see his parents alone but only after they had been brought into the room where he and the police were and, he claims, 'he had no real objection to us remaining'. He adds something Manuel had said before he was charged: 'Mr Brown mentioned the missing girl, Cooke, and asked if the accused could be of any assistance in the matter. He said, "You seem to know a lot. I'll think it over. I may tell you in the morning."'

It is now Brown's turn. Leslie questions him about what happened when the police went to the Manuel house. Manuel, he said, had told his father not to allow the house to be searched. He was then removed 'because he was only going to be a hindrance and upset all that we were trying to do, which was to do the job quietly and efficiently'. He was told he was being detained for identification in connection with banknotes stolen from Smart.

Manuel had made two requests to see McNeil on 15 January, 'one in the late forenoon and one shortly after lunch'. The first two confessions had resulted. When Brown was told of them, he phoned Dowdall. 'I felt this was something which should be made known to the accused's solicitor, if he had one.' Dowdall had told him that he was representing Samuel Manuel and had referred him to Dunlop. He had phoned Dunlop at his home at about 7.30 that evening but was told he was not representing Manuel. He stresses that Manuel had been given every chance to get legal advice, although he admits Manuel had not been told that neither Dowdall nor Dunlop would act for him. He says Manuel had been told, in the presence of his parents, that 'he need not proceed further, or he could change if he wanted legal advice'. However, 'He said he wanted to do it that way and did not want a solicitor.' Furthermore, there was a notice posted on the inside of Manuel's cell door informing him that he had the right to a lawyer.

Chief Inspector Muncie fully supports Goodall's and Brown's evidence. He says that when the Glasgow detectives were called in by the new chief constable of Lanarkshire there had been no discussion of the Kneilands and Watt murders until after Manuel's arrest, although he does admit there may have been some mention of the Cooke case. Although he personally had suspicions about Manuel's involvement in the other murders, he claims, 'I didn't disclose that; there was quite an open mind kept on that.'

The police assertion that Manuel had not wanted a lawyer is reinforced by the next witness, Sergeant Robert Lyon, who says that Manuel 'told me that he didn't want a lawyer. He could ask questions a lawyer wasn't allowed to ask and he would defend himself.'

At this point, the judge intervenes to make quite sure what had been said: 'Did he say he could ask questions a lawyer couldn't ask?'

'Yes.'

In any case, Lyon related, when he had gone to the Manuel house the next day to fetch Mrs Manuel to see her son, he had found Mr Dowdall there and concluded he must be acting for Manuel.

Other police witnesses emphasise that the three confessions had been produced voluntarily. Inspector Cleland, who was fetched from his bed in the early hours of the 16th to take the final statement, denies he was given any instructions about what Manuel should write. He had told Manuel to put down the events in their natural sequence. The sole assistance he had given was to supply the name of one of two roads whose names Manuel did not know.

The police evidence is consistent: Manuel made it clear he did not want a lawyer, he was offered no inducements to write his confessions, and the Watt and Kneilands murders were not mentioned to him before he wrote them. If the judge accepts what the police have said, the jury will hear about the confessions and learn of their damning contents. Before he decides, however, Manuel must have his turn. Questioned by his counsel, he tells a very different story.

When the police arrived at his house, he was asleep. He was taken to Bellshill police station, where one of the detective sergeants tried to pump him for information. Then Superintendent Brown had taken over and accused him of spending money at the Woodend Hotel on New Year's Day. 'I said, "Yes, that is correct." He said, "I believe that was Peter Smart's money," and asked, "Are you going to tell me where you got the money?" I said, "No, I'm not going to tell you."'

Brown, he claims, told him he'd got the money from 'a man called Dandy McKay'. McKay was brought to the station to be part of an identification parade. There, for the moment, Manuel leaves the matter of McKay's involvement in his case. That evening, at about 11 p.m., he was charged with murdering the Smarts and stealing money from them.

Manuel's own account of what had happened next is quite definite. The police have lied, he says: he was put under pressure to confess. He also suggests the police were determined to prove he had committed no fewer than ten murders. 'Brown . . . told me I had committed ten murders and he said, "I intend to prove them one way or another."' Brown, he claims, 'also told me that he was contemplating charging my father with being involved in the murder at Sheepburn Road and also being involved in the murder of a girl called Isabelle Cooke and that if I did not write a statement to that effect to clear them, he was going to proceed with proceedings on those grounds against my father. And he further mentioned he would arrest my sister because he had found the money in my house and cigarettes – he mentioned the name of the cigarettes, they are an Edinburgh brand – that had come from the house at 38 Sheepburn Road in her possession.'

Leslie asks: 'Are you quite sure these matters were discussed that afternoon?'

'Yes, sir, they were hammered into me.'

If all this is believed, the confessions will have to be excluded. Leslie strives to emphasise what has just been said, pointing out that the police did not mention these matters. Manuel replies: 'They were definitely discussed; that was practically all that was discussed.'

Manuel goes on to provide more details of how the police supposedly tried to get him to confess. Goodall had been with him between 6 p.m. and 7.30 or 7.45 p.m. 'He told me about Mr Brown. He says, "He is a nice fellow and all that, he is doing a job, but you must confess to these eight murders because if you don't, he is going to ruin your family. I am giving you some friendly advice." And he started talking about the Anne Kneilands, the Watt case, the Smart cases and that girl that disappeared, Isabelle Cooke – he went through the whole lot.'

Leslie asks, 'Are you quite sure reference was made to those?'

'Yes, reference was made to these eight cases and two other cases in Glasgow.'

Next morning, the 15th, he learned that his father had been arrested and was being taken to Barlinnie prison. Although he had been told this the previous day, he had thought the police were bluffing. Now he realised they were serious. That was why he asked to see McNeil to discuss something important regarding his father. McNeil, he claims, told him, 'If you are prepared to write confessions to those crimes your father will be released from Barlinnie as quick as we can manage it and all charges against him will be dropped.'

Manuel continues, 'I said, "That is all very well but I would like something more definite than that. I would like to see them [his parents]."' He asserts that McNeil then told him, 'Well, you will need to give me something in writing,' and that 'he drafted out a sort of statement and I wrote it. That is number 140, I think.'

So, according to Manuel, not only did the police blackmail him by threatening to ruin his family but they had drafted the basis of his first statement.

He next gives his version of how he came to write statement 141. He says that McNeil went away with the first statement and then came back and said, 'This won't do. It's no use to us . . . I want you to write another one.' He claims that McNeil 'had this drafted out on a piece of paper'.

'It looked kind of strong to me,' says Manuel, claiming that he had inserted the proviso 'on condition that my father is released . . . and allowed to see me with my mother'. Although he copied out the police draft, he states, he did not sign it. Now, however, he points out, 'It is signed here.' He is claiming that the police forged his signature.

When his parents were brought to the police station, he adds, he asked to see them alone but was refused. McNeil had said this was because he was 'too tricky'.

'Now,' Leslie asks, 'it was said . . . that you wouldn't have anything to do with a solicitor. Is that so?'

'No, sir, I asked on several occasions for a solicitor and I was told by Brown that I wouldn't be allowed to see a solicitor until such time as he got what he wanted.'

When his parents arrived, Manuel says, Brown told him to read out his first statement. He only read it after this prompting and because he was concerned about his father's position. The key question is now put to him: 'Are these statements, numbers 140, 141 and 142, your own voluntary expression?' Manuel's answer is simple and emphatic: 'No.'

They return to the question of access to independent legal advice. 'No,' says Manuel, 'I had no access at any time. In fact, on the Wednesday morning, I deliberately asked for legal advice. I was taken to court, I was charged with three murders and even in court there was a couple of guys sitting, and I said, "What about a lawyer?" and they said "Keep quiet. You are not allowed to talk in here," and I was taken out.'

Had he asked for a lawyer when he was taken from his house on the morning of the 14th? Manuel says he cannot remember but he might have done.

'Did you get information as to whether a lawyer was coming to you or not?'

'Oh, I got told there were no lawyers coming. There was no question of a lawyer appearing.'

Gillies attempts to cast doubt on almost all of what Manuel has just said. Why had he not told his parents he was being denied a lawyer? 'I didn't think that at that time I should burden myself on my parents; I considered they were in enough trouble on my account and my sole purpose in writing that statement was to get them out of trouble.' Gillies repeats the question and gets the weak reply, 'It did not just occur to me at that time.' He says he asked for a lawyer no fewer than three times on the day he was arrested.

As Gillies' questioning proceeds, there are moments that reveal, as in a brief flash of light, Manuel's disdain for those who do not believe his version of events. He accepts that he had been told the day he was arrested that his father had been arrested in connection with stolen property. But, he states, 'As far as I was concerned there was no stolen property in my house.' Then, Gillies asks, if he did not think there was stolen property in the house, why had he asked his father about the gloves when he saw his parents at the police station? 'If you had listened to my testimony before, you would have realised that I told you on Wednesday at three o'clock I was informed . . . by Goodall and McNeil, that my father had been charged in connection with a pair of gloves and a camera and I gave McNeil the explanation for the gloves and camera.'

McNeil had told him that his father had claimed the gloves were his property. 'Which was not the case?' Gillies queries. Manuel's reply is a good example of his evasive way with facts: 'It was the case at the time I gave him the gloves. As far as he was concerned, they were his gloves, just the same as if I gave you gloves they would be your property.' That would depend, of course, on whether or not the gift rightfully belonged to the giver, a basic fact that Manuel seems to have overlooked for much of his life.

So why did he write the first confession? Because the police had said that if he did they'd do what they could to get his father released. He tries to show he had been clever: 'Goodall mentioned eight murders but I wrote the document without mentioning any murders.' Why had he written 'I promise you personally', that is, to Inspector McNeil? Because Goodall had told him to, he says.

This is far from convincing. He claims he wrote the statement based on what he had been instructed to say but also that he had done it to his own design. 'He told me what to write first and I sort of swung it round,' explains Manuel. 'I did not mention the crimes he specified, I just made it a sort of promise. But there was no definite statement in it regarding any crime at all.' He seems to wish to give the impression that he outwitted the despised police.

Manuel continues to assert that the police had made threats. Superintendent Brown, he says, told him that he was going to charge his father with the Smart murders 'and if he charged me with the Cooke murder, he would also charge my father with being involved in that'. Gillies points out that Manuel has claimed that Brown was with him from about 6 to 7.30 or 7.45 on the evening of 14 January. So, Gillies asks, 'If he says he was in Glasgow interviewing McKay, that cannot be true?' This gives Manuel a chance to show his vocabulary: 'I do not know what inference you put on suppositions.'

So why did the police bring McKay to Hamilton police station if it was all a put-up job by Brown? 'I cannot suggest why they brought McKay to Hamilton but I do know that in the afternoon Brown told me that he knew I had received money from McKay, and he claimed that in the preceding week there had been some sort of investigation round about Florence Street, in that area, in which McKay had come in for a reasonable amount of investigation from them.'

He denies he said anything about receiving money from McKay;

on the contrary, he claims, that was what the police had said to him. 'I made no statement involving McKay at any time.' He claims that Brown, however, said that McKay was one of two men seen in a car leaving the Smarts' house on the morning of 1 January and Manuel was the other. But if there was no mention of money when he, Manuel, and McKay were together at the police station, did not that strike him as odd? 'At that stage of the investigation, nothing struck me as odd regarding this fellow Brown's conduct.'

Manuel asserts that Brown said, 'I will crucify your family,' and, 'I will ruin your father and ruin your sister.' Later that night, he claimed, Brown 'told me I had killed Isabelle Cooke and buried her in a field . . . He said, "We are going to get you on that case too."' Manuel claims he was told 'they were going to "do" me for the Watt murders, Anne Kneilands' murder and a couple of other murders'.

His mother and his father now offer their version of events. Bridget Manuel is first. When she and Samuel arrived at the police station, she says, Superintendent Brown told them that Peter was going to read out a statement. When they saw him, Goodall urged him to read it. Peter asked his father if he had been released and why he had not told the police that he, Peter, had given him the gloves. No, she cannot remember if Peter had said anything about always finding it difficult to talk to them.

Samuel's testimony agrees with his wife's that Brown had told them Peter was going to read a statement. Peter asked him if he had been released and Goodall said this would have to be done through the procurator fiscal. Peter did ask to see his parents alone but this was refused. Goodall, he says, had to press his son to read out the statement. When first questioned about the gloves, says Samuel, he had only said they 'could be mine'. During all the time Samuel is talking, his son incessantly cleans his nails, never looking at him.

When Leslie summarises his argument for excluding the confessions he is subjected to some stern questioning by Lord Cameron. Then, to the great relief of the police and the prosecution, the judge states,

'Having seen and heard the witnesses I have no doubt in preferring the denials of the police officers to the assertions of the accused . . . I have come to the conclusion that no ground has been established for excluding the statements.' Cameron's preference for the evidence of the police and his expressed doubt about the defendant's veracity bodes ill for Manuel.

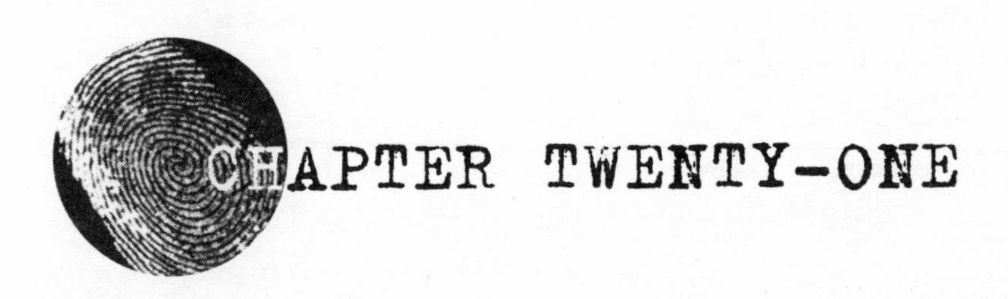

CHAPTER TWENTY-ONE

The jury is called back and McNeil re-enters the witness box. Led by Gillies, he explains to the jury how the confessions came to be written, adding to his earlier account new and startling details of Manuel's verbal admissions. This is the first time the jury hears about the confessions.

Manuel had promised 'to make a clean breast of it' once he had seen his parents. Having been cautioned and reminded that he could see a solicitor, he wrote out the first and second confession. Then he said he wanted to tell McNeil and Goodall about Sheepburn Road. He was warned this would be written down and this was done. Now McNeil reads from his notebook Manuel's full verbal confession to the Smart murders. It is unequivocal: 'I did it about six o'clock in the morning of New Year's Day. I got in the kitchen window. I went into a bedroom and got eighteen or twenty pounds in new notes and four or five ten-shilling notes in a wallet . . . I shot the man first and then the woman, and I then shot the boy, but at first I thought it was a man in the bed . . . I took the man's keys and then took the car. The car key was on a bunch on a ring, and I put it in the Ranco car park and took it to Florence Street the next night . . . I threw the gun in the Clyde and the keys in the Calder at the bridge. I think I threw the purse in there too.'

McNeil insists that the police reminded Manuel he could have the services of a solicitor and that Brown repeated this in the presence of his parents. Manuel told them, 'There is no future for me. I have done some terrible things.' He said that, once his parents had left, he would take McNeil and Goodall to Cooke's body. He told his mother and father that 'he had left the house on New Year's morning about five o'clock after they had all gone to bed', gone to Sheepburn Road and shot the three people. At this point, he says, Manuel's mood was subdued and he seemed repentant. He 'appeared very sorry not only for his position but for the trouble he was giving his family, and he appeared to be genuinely wanting to get everything cleared up'.

McNeil describes how Manuel led him and Goodall to where the girl was buried, warning them to avoid a hole as they approached. He said, 'I dug that hole. I had her body here but I was disturbed by a man and I had to take her away.' Next, he took them to where one of Cooke's dancing shoes was concealed underneath a heap of bricks; then he led them to the second hidden shoe. After taking careful sightings, Manuel commented, 'This field has been ploughed since I buried her.' They walked on and then he said, 'I think she is in there. I think I am standing on her.' It is a vivid and horrifying statement, showing the callous indifference of a psychopath.

While officers were excavating at the indicated place, Manuel showed them where one of Cooke's walking shoes was concealed along the nearby railway line. The detectives wanted to take Manuel back to the police station while the digging proceeded. He 'seemed at that point extremely anxious that the girl's body should be recovered'.

Before they left the field, Manuel said he would write a full confession and so Inspector Cleland was called to the police station and document 142 eventually produced. Now, the long confession is read out in full.

From this point, McNeil says, Manuel cooperated. First, he led the police to where the guns had been dumped in the Clyde. He also told them, 'You had better dig up another two witnesses, for I gave two men a lift on the Thursday morning from Law Hospital to Carluke. I intended to dump the car at Lanark.'

Manuel continued to provide evidence against himself even after he had received advice from Ferns, who had agreed to act as his solicitor. He indicated he did not want a lawyer with him when he took the police to the General's Bridge, where he had dumped items connected with the Kneilands killing, saying, 'I flung the bag down there,' and, 'I flung the piece of angle iron and her knickers away further down the burn. I used the knickers to wash the blood off my hands.'

Manuel described to them how he had chased, caught and killed Anne Kneilands. McNeil testifies: 'He had dragged the girl through the gate and she had run away from him in that field . . . he had chased after her and she had hidden. He ran past her but then he crept along the hedge, she came out from where she was hiding, thinking he had gone away, he caught her again and he took her. She ran away from him again across the fields to a road, she ran across a ditch into the wood or a wood, and he caught her in the wood when she fell into a waterhole.'

Manuel told McNeil that 'he had put his clothes in [the Gas Board hut]. I think he said he had changed in there, and he went on to say that he had put his dirty clothes in a piece of paper and had later burned them on the bing [a heap of mining spoil] at the rear of his house.' This statement is important. If it's to be proven that Manuel battered Kneilands to death, there needs to be an explanation of how he disposed of clothing that would have been muddied during his chase after her and spattered with her blood and brains. No such clothing was found when his house was searched.

McNeil tells the court that after receiving the confessions he walked at a brisk pace along two routes from Manuel's house to the Smarts'. One route took him ten minutes, the other half a minute more. The trip from the Ranco car park to Manuel's house took seven minutes. This shows how quickly Manuel could get to and from these places on foot. He testifies that when Manuel had been charged with the Kneilands and Watt murders he had replied, 'No, nothing,' to each charge. To the Cooke charge it was, 'Nothing to say.'

The testimony of McNeil is convincing, largely because it shows that there were things the police could not have known unless Manuel had told them. That, however, does not prove that Manuel was not pressurised to confess in writing. The jury must decide.

Leslie, although he does not know it, is nearing the end of his service to Manuel. As his time as defence counsel slips away, he tries vainly to weaken the mounting evidence against his client. McNeil rejects his suggestion that it would have been a fantastic change of front for Manuel to have refused to say anything to the charge of murdering Cooke just after he had led them round the site of her death. 'It was quite consistent with what I know of the accused's nature,' he counters.

Leslie asks McNeil if anyone else was involved in the break-in at the Martins', hoping to get some suggestion that the police suspected Tallis, Bowes and Hart. McNeil gives a careful answer, 'We have failed to trace any others but we have interviewed persons.' He does not say who these persons are.

The confessions are of course extraordinarily damaging to Manuel's case, so Leslie suggests that inducements were offered to make Manuel confess, that the police had prevented him seeing a lawyer and that they already suspected him of killing Kneilands and the Watts when they removed him from his house.

These efforts are in vain. McNeil gives him nothing: he agrees the other cases may have been mentioned to Brown and Goodall but states that the focus at 14 January was on the Smart murders and Cooke's disappearance. He says that Manuel did not ask for a solicitor and denies that the police prompted him about what to put in the first two confessions. Every suggestion Leslie makes is firmly rejected. When Leslie asks if it would have been reasonable for Manuel to be worried about his father's possible connection with the Smart case, he gets the cutting reply, 'He would if he had reason to believe that any of the articles from the Smarts' house were in his father's house.'

So far the case has involved a number of horrifying, sickening revelations and a conflict over a point of law. Now, at the start of the tenth day, there is an even more extraordinary development, one unsuspected by anyone involved – except for Manuel himself.

Goodall, the first witness of the day, is sworn in. Before he can begin his evidence, Manuel asks the judge if he can confer with his counsel. The jury retires; there is an adjournment. Then Leslie returns, looks at the judge and says, 'I am no longer in a position with my colleagues to continue the cause, the panel being desirous of conducting the remainder of the trial.' In other words, he and his two colleagues have been sacked and Manuel intends to conduct his own defence.

There is a shocked silence and then reporters rush out to phone in the sensational news. Leslie, Grieve and Morison gather up their papers and books and leave. A few minutes later, Leslie and Grieve are photographed almost dancing out of the building, their faces displaying relief, even joy. In years to come, Leslie will joke that he was the defence counsel sacked by Manuel – a distinction that invites congratulation rather than commiseration.

As soon as they have left, Lord Cameron arranges for Ferns and Docherty to sit closer to their client. The move is pointless; it soon becomes apparent he does not want their guidance.

The prosecution starts to question Goodall about the events of 14 January and Samuel Manuel's role in them. He says that Samuel claimed he had got the Houston's camera two years previously at the Barras, the famous street market in the East End of Glasgow. This claim justified the police charging him with reset.

Then comes the issue of the money. At the police station, Goodall tells the court, Manuel claimed all his money had come from Dandy McKay, who'd given him 'fifty pounds: six five-pound notes and twenty new blue one-pound notes'. He added that the notes had sequential numbers: 'the last three figures were something like 334 and 335'. Manuel said he'd got the money for 'showing him [McKay] the Sheepburn Road district, where he was going to break into a bookmaker's house'.

At that point, Manuel clearly wanted to harm McKay, probably because he knew McKay could tell the police he had sold Manuel the Beretta and possibly because a few days earlier he had refused to give him money to flee to London. Soon, Manuel will change his story: he will claim he got the money from Smart.

Goodall's account of how the first two confessions came to be written agrees in every way with McNeil's testimony. He too stresses that Manuel was cautioned and advised to consult a solicitor.

The prosecution turns to the night when Manuel took the police to where Isabelle Cooke was buried. Like McNeil, Goodall tells the court that Manuel wanted to remain until her body was unearthed. 'He appeared very upset [at the idea of returning to the police station] and said he couldn't go away until the body was found.' When one of the officers expressed doubt that they were digging in the right place, Manuel became agitated. On the way back, he told the officers he wanted to make a full statement and later wrote document 142. As he was being taken to Barlinnie, he indicated where he had thrown the two guns into the Clyde.

It is now Manuel's turn to ask the questions. He relishes the moment: now he is in command; now he no longer has to rely on intermediary lawyers; now he can question witnesses directly; now he is the focus of everyone's attention.

He starts mildly: did the police expect to find the gloves and camera at his house when they arrived on 14 January? Goodall replies that they had no particular knowledge of these items. The next question is startling and it reveals his strategy with regard to the Cooke murder: the police had framed him for it.

'Before you came to the house, did you know where Isabelle Cooke's body was?'

'Before we came to the house on the 14th? Definitely not.'

'You did not know where her body was?'

'That is nonsense to suggest it.'

Why did the police remove him from his house before they searched it? Surely a suspected person usually remains while a search is made? It is a foolish question. 'I think it was obvious when we went there that had you remained in the house you were going to be a perfect nuisance.'

Some of Manuel's questions deal with minor matters, pinpricks against the prosecution's case. Why had the police removed a bottle of champagne from his house? Because, Goodall replies, it was suspected it could have come from the Smart house. 'We had no evidence that there was liquor stolen from Sheepburn Road,' he adds reasonably enough, 'but a bottle of champagne is a bottle of champagne, and we took it just in case.'

The three written confessions have been admitted as evidence, so Manuel must attempt to discredit them. He points out differences in the signatures on the first two and accuses the police of forging his signature on the second. Next, he tries to suggest that different inks and pens were used on them and that they are therefore suspect. Goodall rejects all these assertions.

Manuel then claims the confessions had been forced from him.

'Did you not say to me that unless I was prepared to write statements and confessions Superintendent Brown would charge my father with being involved in the Sheepburn Road murder?'

'That is nonsense. That was never said.'

'Did you not make a statement that if I confessed to eight murders I would go down in history?'

'I certainly did not.'

Goodall is again forced to deny that the police knew where Cooke was buried and explains why the search had taken place at night: 'You said . . . that you could only go to the spot where you had buried her body in the dark, because you had buried her in the dark and the daylight would be no use to you.' He tells the court that Manuel indicated where they should dig two trenches to locate the exact place where he had buried the girl.

The police have claimed that Manuel showed them where Cooke's shoes were concealed: only her murderer could have known that. One was hidden beneath a brick in a huge dump of bricks. Manuel asks, 'There would be thousands of bricks scattered?'

'Yes.'

'And you contend that in the dark I just stopped and shoved aside a brick and pulled out a shoe?' He hopes the jury will not believe that he had such an outstanding memory for detail.

Goodall simply states, 'You did.'

'Just in the dark like that?'

'In the dark.'

Why had the police not taken spades when they went to the field?

'We had grave doubts as to whether or not you were telling the truth.'

Goodall is followed into the witness box by Brown. Gillies takes him through the long sequence of events from Manuel's removal from Fourth Street to the recovery of the guns. Manuel asks him a series of highly technical questions about the problem of loading and firing the Beretta with its missing spring. He seems more interested in showing off his knowledge of guns than in getting any useful answers. Brown simply deflects the questions, saying he lacks the expertise to answer.

Manuel again asserts that the search for Cooke was a sham. Brown rejects his claims and adds damaging detail: Manuel was handcuffed to McNeil and Goodall during the search because it was feared he would try to escape. It was not until the body was actually uncovered that the police believed Manuel had told the truth.

Once again, Manuel asks why he had been removed from his house on 14 January.

'Is it not a fact that when you came to that house you already had intentions of taking me from that house as quickly as possible?'

'No, you would have remained in the house if you had conducted yourself properly . . . You became aggressive, told your father not to allow us to search the house.'

The police had threatened him, he claims.

'Did you not tell me that you were going to hang me for ten murders?'

'I couldn't tell you that.'

'Did you threaten me in any way?'

'Never at any time.'

'Did you threaten to arrest my father and charge him with being involved in the Smart murders?'

'I did not.'

Nor, Brown says, did he threaten to arrest Manuel's mother and sister.

'Did you tell me that unless I was prepared to write statements and confessions to eight murders you would crucify my family? That is not a question that needs thinking about. You know whether you did or not?'

'I know I didn't. I never used the word "crucify" in my life.' (Brown's son has in fact confirmed to us that his father never used the word in that way.)

Exchanges like this offer the jury a simple choice: one of the men is lying through his teeth – which one is it?

Brown rejects each of Manuel's assertions. No, he did not threaten Manuel's family. No, Manuel did not ask to see a solicitor, although Brown did take it upon himself to get in touch with Dowdall. No, he cannot agree that there is anything significant in the slight difference between the signatures on documents 140 and 141. No, Manuel did not ask for the room to be cleared when he saw his parents. No, the police did not know where Cooke's body was before Manuel showed them.

Sergeant Lyon repeats what he said while the jury were absent: Manuel told him he didn't want a lawyer, he could ask questions for himself. Earlier in the case, this might have seemed difficult to believe. Now it is exactly what Manuel is doing.

Other police officers give evidence about how the confessions came to be written, how items belonging to Cooke were found, how they had followed McNeil and Goodall as Manuel led them to her burial place, how they attended her post-mortem examination. Manuel's examination of them is perfunctory but the sheer repetition of the same facts is damaging to him.

By taking on his own defence, he has got what he wants: he is Peter Manuel, Queen's Counsel, centre of all attention. As he returns to his cell, though, he may wonder just how effective his questions have been. However, he has an even more dramatic plan to turn the case his way.

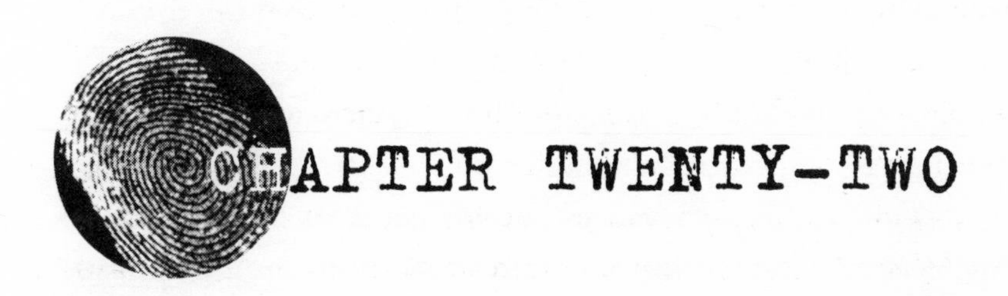

CHAPTER TWENTY-TWO

The next day, the 11th of the trial, Manuel causes another sensation: he asks for Watt and McNeil to be recalled. He explains that he feels Leslie failed him: 'My purpose is this, My Lord. At the time they were examined I strongly objected to counsel, the manner in which he cross-examined them, and I strongly objected to him at the time, and I stated he had left a great deal unsaid. He assured me he had done his best.' He wants to ask Watt about the two meetings they had: 'Although defence counsel had available a written report concerning these two meetings . . . he did not raise certain issues.' As regards McNeil, 'The particular points, My Lord, in relation to [him] were several instances in the past two or three years in which this man has been actively engaged in investigating me in connection with certain crimes.'

Cameron says he can ask about these two matters but no others. He is also allowed to call two prison officers and a civilian who witnessed a conversation he had with Brannan while on remand. The judge agrees Brannan too can be recalled.

The prosecution continues adding detail upon detail to its case. The farmer who owns the field where Cooke's body was found and his ploughman explain how and when the field was ploughed. The police and David Bell, the diver, testify to how the guns were recovered from the Clyde. Manuel does not ask them any questions. Detective Sergeant Sowter, the firearms expert, takes the jury through the evidence that proves the Webley and Beretta were used to kill the Watts and the Smarts respectively. He says it would be possible to fire two shots in quick succession from the Beretta, despite the absence of the spring in the magazine.

The key question – the hanging question – is how the Smarts died. Manuel asks Sowter if he has ruled out suicide. He has, influenced by the obvious fact that no gun was present at the scene. So, again, it's clear that the missing gun needs to be accounted for. Manuel gets Sowter to agree that, after death, someone must have pulled the blankets and sheets up over the victims, otherwise the fatal bullets would have passed through them. He continues, 'And on that basis it is quite possible that if such a person found himself in that house he could quite easily have removed a gun?' He is laying the ground for his claim that he discovered the Smart bodies and also the fatal weapon and removed it, fearing it might be linked to him. Cameron immediately points out: 'That would involve the person who adjusted the bedclothes giving no information to the authorities as to the finding of these dead bodies.' It is a highly damaging intervention. When he comes to address the jury directly, Manuel will attempt to neutralise it.

The next witness, Chief Superintendent Maclean, is a fingerprint expert. Manuel asks him if photographs of the inside of the Smarts' house and the number of glasses visible in them suggest someone else had been there. The officer will not agree that any such conclusion can be drawn.

Moving on to the Watt murders, he tells the court that the prints of a number of people, including Manuel, Bowes, Tallis and Hart were checked against those found in the Watt and Martin houses. There were no matches. This undermines to some extent Manuel's claim they were present in the house. However, in each house there was a single unidentifiable print. The one in the Martin house was on the lintel of the kitchen door; it was small and probably made by a woman.

Manuel wants to implicate Mary Bowes and, through her, Tallis in the Martin break-in. He has a clever idea. Was the unidentified print made by a toe, not a finger? He suggests that a woman had run across the garden, muddied her stockings and taken them off, leaving a toe print. 'Have you a wide experience of taking toe prints?' he asks Maclean. Unfortunately for Manuel, the policeman has. 'Quite considerable,' he replies, adding that the print was 'quite definitely not made by a toe'. Manuel's attempted explanation is ingenious, clever for the sake of cleverness, but Maclean's firm rejection discredits him.

Now William Watt is recalled, to undergo direct interrogation by the man he believes killed his family. Manuel begins by asking him if he recalls the time, during their first meeting, between about 7 p.m. and 9.15 p.m., when they were together in Jackson's Bar? Watt says he does. Does Watt remember their conversation? He does.

'Do you remember at one particular part of that conversation you professed that you were agreeably surprised?'

Watt looks to the judge for help: 'I beg your pardon, My Lord, agreeably surprised at what?'

'At meeting me,' Manuel supplies.

'No,' is Watt's response.

This is a typical Manuel tactic: to insinuate something that might put doubt in the jury's mind and also show himself in a favourable light – a person whom it would be surprisingly agreeable to meet.

He wants to convince the jury how much Watt had told him, how well they got on. He suggests Watt told him of a private ambition.

'Do you recall raising the matter wherein you alleged you had been selected or nominated as President of the Merchants' Guild of Glasgow?'

'No,' Watt responds.

The Merchants' Guild is an association of senior Glasgow figures. It is a mark of great civic distinction to be its head, whose status is second only to the Lord Provost's on formal occasions in the city. All this is a minor matter and it is easy to prove it is another Manuel lie. Watt has never even been a member of the Merchants' House or its sister body the Trades House.

Manuel's next question is much more to the point. 'Do you recall a subject under discussion between you and I wherein you outlined to me a plan whereby I would lead information to the procurator fiscal with a view to having a man named Charles Tallis and a man named Martin Hart arrested in connection with the murder of your wife?' Once again Watt addresses the judge: 'That is quite wrong, My Lord.' Manuel snaps back: 'The question has been asked by me, not His Lordship.' He gets the same reply: 'That is quite wrong.'

Now Manuel increases the pressure, using his questions to accuse Watt directly of being the murderer.

'Do you remember the part of the discussion wherein you described how you had carefully planned for months to kill your wife?'

'That is atrocious and a lie.'

'Do you remember a part of the discussion wherein you stated that so carefully had you laid your plans that it even involved changing your address?'

'That is a lie.'

'Do you remember offering to give me the biggest boost I had ever had if I pulled up my socks and played the game your way?'

'That is also a lie.'

'Do you remember describing to me that you could drive a car better than Stirling Moss?'

'That is also a lie.'

'Do you remember that you said to me that when you had shot

your little girl Vivienne it would have required very little effort to turn the gun on yourself?'

'No.'

'Do you remember describing to me the manner in which you killed your wife?'

'I never did.'

'Do you remember informing me it was your intention at that time not to kill your daughter?'

'I never did.'

'You made no attempt to kill your daughter?'

'I never did.'

'I asked you if you remembered at that time describing to me the killing of your wife and then I asked you did you remember telling me it had been your intention at that time not to kill your daughter?'

'No, that is a lot of nonsense.'

Clearly, Manuel is getting stark denial after denial. To some extent that does not matter: he wants to say things that sound plausible and plant in the jury's mind the possibility, no more, that Watt is guilty.

The role of Scout O'Neil is raised. Watt denies he ever paid O'Neil. All he did was give the man a pound for a drink and a suit because his clothes were in tatters. It is important to Watt and the prosecution that there is no suspicion that O'Neil has been bribed to give evidence harmful to Manuel.

Next, Manuel and Watt clash over the contents of the house, and the curious matter of the safe resurfaces. If, as Watt claims, Manuel was able to describe in great and accurate detail the inside of his house, why did he not see the safe?

'Do you consider it feasible that if I killed your wife, if I was in actual effect in your house, that I should take a note in great detail of the furniture and miss the obvious fact that there is a safe in that house?'

'You must have taken a note of everything because you knew everything about it.'

'If I had been there?'

'You knew all about every piece of furniture in three rooms in my house.'

The puzzle of the safe remains. For his final questions, therefore, Manuel resorts again to direct allegations of Watt's guilt.

'Did you mention to me the fact that you had deliberately removed your household from Muirhead to Burnside with the intention of having all close associates of your wife cut off for a short period before you killed her?'

'That is a lot of nonsense.'

'Is it?'

'It is and there is a reason why. We came next door to one of our friends there.'

'Did you mention that your only mistake had been using the Renfrew Ferry?'

'I never crossed the Renfrew Ferry.'

Brannan's evidence that Manuel was planning a 'snatch' at Mount Vernon has been useful to the prosecution. It would have been even more damning if the snatch was supposed to take place the day Cooke disappeared rather than about a week before. Manuel now tries to show that Brannan is a liar and denied in front of witnesses that he had told the police about the supposed snatch.

Brannan and another petty criminal, David Knox, had visited Manuel in jail and Manuel had asked Brannan what he had told the police. A prison officer who was present says Brannan had denied signing a statement about the snatch. When Manuel asked him what he would say in court he had replied, 'You will hear all about it.' A second prison officer gives Brannan's reply as, 'We'll see.' Cameron points out that Brannan had not denied he had made a statement, only saying that he had not signed one. Knox, the next witness, states that Brannan denied both making and signing a statement and said he would not make a statement in court.

This brings him to Brannan, once his companion on a thieving expedition but now a key prosecution witness. They face each other across the court and the questioning starts. Brannan agrees that he visited Manuel in Barlinnie every week in the months before the trial. We may conclude he did so under police instruction. Brannan had told him he had given various statements to the police, had he not? He had also assured him he would not stand by them in court. Brannan will have none of it: 'I told you that when I appeared in court I should tell the truth and the whole truth and nothing but the truth, as I stand here today and tell the truth again.' It is highly dramatic. But which of them is to be believed?

If Watt had killed his family, he would have had to drive through the night to his house from Lochgilphead and then return. The police had two witnesses who put him on the route south, a motorist on the road beside Loch Lomond and the operator of the ferry across the Clyde at Renfrew. Neither witness now proves convincing when questioned. The motorist says that he only caught a glimpse of the man he later identified as Watt, that the man he saw had the lower half of his face covered by his hand as he smoked, and that he had seen newspaper photos of Watt before the identity parade. The ferryman claims that Watt's car was a red Wolseley. He had identified it among a group of 30 cars at Hamilton police station by a scrape mark along the offside. He was convinced the car was a Wolseley as he had looked at it from the front. Although it is not brought out in court, all Wolseleys at this date had a distinctive illuminated name badge near the top of the radiator grille. Because of this, they were extremely easy to identify. However, it is shown that Watt's car was a Vauxhall and Manuel's attempt to prove that Watt raced to Glasgow to kill his family comes to nothing.

The next witness is Sergeant Mitchell, recently retired, who had helped drive Watt back to Glasgow on the day the murders were discovered. Previously, Watt made it clear he regarded Mitchell as a liar. Manuel hopes Mitchell can help him convince the jury that Watt killed his family.

When Mitchell first met Watt, Manuel asks, 'He did not appear to be to you at that time distraught or in a state of shock?' Mitchell replies that Watt had seemed so normal that he had initially mistaken the burly figure for one of the Dunbartonshire police.

He adds damning detail. He suggested to Watt that he should not say anything until he saw senior officers. 'He said, "Is it as bad as that? Do you think I did it?" or words to that effect.' Three days later, he claims, Watt said to him, 'Sergeant, the day you came to Alexandria, you thought you were coming up to bring back a man who had committed this murder.'

'I said, "No, Mr Watt, I went to Alexandria expecting to find a broken-hearted man but I found a man with a smirk on his face and without a tear.' Watt replied, "I believe you are right, sergeant." I said to him, "I know I am right."' Clearly, Mitchell still believes Watt was involved in the death of his family.

Mitchell and another officer had been involved in checking if a car could be pushed away from the front of the Cairnbaan Hotel without alerting anyone inside; they concluded it could. They had also driven from the hotel to Glasgow in just over two hours.

The prosecution acts immediately to remove any suspicion of Watt's involvement and to refocus the jury's attention on the evidence against Manuel. Gillies treats Mitchell as a hostile witness. He makes him admit the car had to be driven quite fast to make the journey in this time and that they had driven through the city and not used the Renfrew Ferry. As a test, it therefore had little validity.

He suggests Mitchell is prejudiced: 'May I take it you don't like Mr Watt?' Mitchell will not give a straight answer. He merely says he hadn't met Watt until Alexandria. Gillies repeats the question. He gets another evasive answer: 'I have no reason to dislike him.'

'Just answer the question,' he is commanded.

'I don't dislike Mr Watt,' he finally says.

All this evasiveness makes Mitchell seem shifty, his evidence unreliable.

The judge joins in, asking if the car they pushed away from the hotel was the same weight as Watt's.

'That I can't say.'

'Rather important to know, isn't it?' the judge asks.

Mitchell makes no reply. Gillies adds to his discomfiture by asking if it had tyres of the same dimension as those on the Watt car.

'I don't know,' Mitchell admits again.

'Not really a very scientific test,' is counsel's chilly comment.

And so, with a few brief questions, Sergeant Mitchell, formerly of the Lanarkshire police and Crown witness, is shifted quite brutally into the position of being an unreliable, even a hostile, witness and one whose suspicions of Watt can safely be disregarded.

Manuel tries desperately to salvage something. Mitchell was one of those who searched his house after the Watt murders. He gets him to agree that everything in his room as well as his shoes and clothing was examined but nothing was found that linked him to the murders.

George Brown, whose wife was shot at the Watt house, is questioned by Manuel about a remark Watt made to him that his wife, Margaret, had been shot first. Brown stresses that Watt was 'half asleep with exhaustion' when he said this. It does not damage Watt. Brown clearly does not believe he is a killer.

Now McNeil returns and is examined about the events following the Watt murders. Manuel hates McNeil but he wants to extract from him an admission that there was nothing to connect him with those killings and that the police were certain Watt had killed his family. Was he aware, Manuel asks, that after Watt was arrested the chief constable and Hendry held a press conference in which they said that all local suspects had been investigated and eliminated? McNeil denies knowing this. So why was Watt arrested? McNeil gives a careful reply: 'I was acting under the instructions of a superior officer who, having considered the information supplied by independent witnesses, had no other course than to apprehend the man whom that evidence pointed against.'

'Then why did you say at the time of the Burnside murder you thought I was connected with it?'

It is a dangerous question and McNeil treads warily. 'Do you really want me to answer that question? For it would not be in your best interests.'

But, Manuel persists, why is it that McNeil holds a certain view of him and not of Watt?

'The only reason I can actually give for it is my previous knowledge of you.'

But if they were wrong about Watt they might be wrong again. Has McNeil any doubt that he, Manuel, was the right person to arrest in connection with the disappearance of Isabelle Cooke?

'I have no doubt whatsoever.'

Manuel now calls retired Superintendent James Hendry, the man in charge of the investigations into the deaths of Kneilands and the Watt family, the man who, in some people's eyes, made a mess of things.

Manuel asks about police interest in him at the time of the Kneilands murder. He claims that the police had been watching his house before Christmas 1955 for two escaped prisoners who it was thought might come to him for help. If that were so, then it was highly unlikely he could have left home to kill Kneilands. Hendry denies knowing anything about a watch on the house but agrees that Manuel said he would tell them if the escapees turned up. After the trial, Hendry will say that Manuel had claimed a reward for telling the police where to find the same escapees on a previous occasion.

Manuel cannot control his vain desire to show how clever he is and how much he knows. As with earlier witnesses, some of his questions suggest he has special knowledge, knowledge that the jury may conclude could only be possessed by the murderer. He asks Hendry about the site of the Anne Kneilands murder and the ditch across which she ran, saying: 'It was actually a large gouge right along the whole length of the road, bulldozed out, about 15 ft deep.' He goes on to show more detailed knowledge of the area and then asks why the terrified Anne Kneilands had not run towards the lights of the nearby farm. Was this something that he had feared she might do when he was chasing her? Hendry gives the only possible reply: he could not say what was going on in her mind when she was running for her life.

Hendry admits that Manuel was suspected of the Kneilands and Watt murders but he totally rejects the suggestion that he had told the press that they had eliminated all other local suspects before they arrested Watt. 'No, certainly not,' he says firmly. Cameron helps strengthen his denial by getting him to agree that that would have been 'a very improper thing to say'.

But Hendry's weakness is that he did arrest and charge Watt. If the police were wrong, then they could be equally wrong now. And so Manuel asks: 'Did you feel confident that when you arrested William Watt you were arresting the man that shot his wife?' The judge saves Hendry from having to answer. He commands, 'Don't answer that question. That is not a question for this witness . . . What this witness may think or believe about any of the charges on which you now stand indicted is entirely irrelevant.' Still, Manuel has managed to ask the highly embarrassing question and to keep in the jury's mind the fact that the police may get things wrong.

But then Manuel gets it wrong himself: he asks Hendry if the police had fully investigated him for the Watt and Kneilands murders. He is told they had not. This suggests to the jury that if the police had looked harder, Manuel would have been charged much earlier.

Had Hendry believed or checked O'Neil's story of selling him a gun? He had checked it, Hendry replies, but, addressing the judge, he adds that the only way he could have obtained complete confirmation would have been to interrogate Manuel himself and, for a reason that is not stated, he was not able to do that.

Kinghorn, the chief officer at Barlinnie, testifies how Manuel arrived at the prison and shortly afterwards was taken away to show the police where Cooke was buried. The judge takes the opportunity to ask him about Manuel's physical and mental state when he was first brought into the prison. Kinghorn says he showed no sign of mental or physical illness or physical injury or any undue strain and that he showed no surprise at being taken out of Barlinnie so soon after he had arrived. Officer Kelly, who had also been there when Manuel was admitted, supports Kinghorn's evidence. It is two more bricks in the wall that is being built to prevent Manuel escaping the hangman on the ground that he is mentally ill.

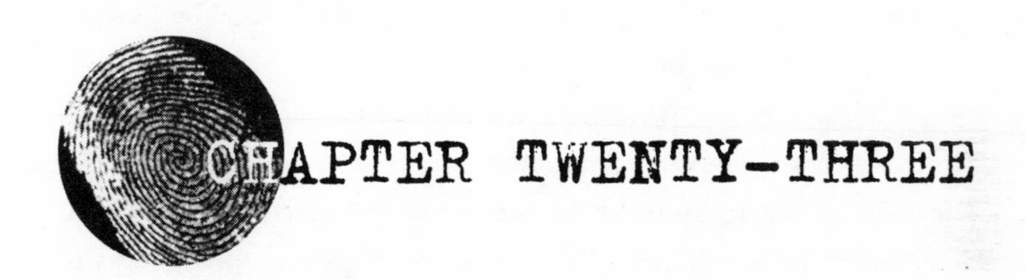

CHAPTER TWENTY-THREE

Outside prison, Manuel had craved notoriety but always failed to get all he desired. Now, at last, as a prisoner, he was front-page news around the world. Newspapers and writers were not allowed to buy his own story, so they sought other sources. Information – true or false – began to be provided, against the rules, by police officers and prison staff, and also by recently released prisoners or those still jailed, who could pass on gossip at visiting time.

One of these informants soon produced a gem for the *Daily Record*. He claimed that a quantity of cyanide had been smuggled into the block where Manuel was housed. How long, if at all, the newspaper sat on the story is not known but on 25 May, 13 days after Manuel's trial had begun, the paper alerted the Scottish Home Department, which quickly informed Barlinnie. Then the story somehow got out; later that evening the *Daily Sketch* began asking questions about poison in the prison.

At Barlinnie, strict measures were immediately taken to prevent any harm coming to their prize prisoner. He was removed from his cell on the pretext that he was to have a bath. While he was away, his cell was searched thoroughly. His clothes were taken away and he was given a fresh set. It was ordered that he was not to be given anything to drink that might have been handled by other prisoners. All his bedding and blankets were removed and replaced. Sixty Woodbines given to him by his mother on the previous Wednesday were confiscated and replaced from the prison store. In future, all cigarettes or tobacco sent to him were to be treated in the same precautionary way. The deputy governor, who was in charge during the governor's absence, also considered searching the other one hundred and eighty-four inmates in that part of the prison but, as he had only four officers available, decided against it. Twelve extra officers were drafted in to carry out the search the following evening. It was decreed that Manuel had to be thoroughly searched every evening when he returned from court. After each search, he was to be issued with fresh clothing from the prison store.

Meanwhile, the press was still driving things on. The following day, Monday, virtually every paper was telephoning questions about the supposed poison plot. More importantly, at about eleven at night, the *Daily Record* phoned the Home Department to say that its Glasgow office had received an envelope containing white powder. A letter that accompanied it claimed it was not cyanide but morphia sulphate, which would give 'a kinder death'. It added that the poison in the prison would never be found. At first, the *Record* said, it suspected a hoax but it then received a call from a person claiming to have sent the powder. The caller said the rest of the morphia had been smuggled into the prison inside a tooth-powder tin. To check the veracity of the story, they sent the powder to be analysed. The analysis confirmed it was poison.

On 27 June, Father Smith, Barlinnie's visiting Catholic clergyman, told the authorities of a plot to provide Manuel with poison if his appeal failed. A prisoner had told him he was to smuggle a small glass jar containing poison into the room where Manuel met his visitors. The prisoner eventually handed over the jar to the priest, who passed it to the chief warder.

Was there any truth in these sensational stories? It seems there was. After Manuel was safely hanged, the governor sent to the director of the Borstal and Prisons Service a report from the Glasgow city analyst. He stated that he had examined a bottle of powder sent him by the prison authorities. (To prevent its origin leaking out, they had transmitted it under the splendid code name of 'SNOB'.) The bottle contained, he reported, nearly 59 grains of a white powder that proved to be a mixture of a barbiturate drug and starch. He considered it had been made by grinding up sodium amytal tablets. Sodium amytal is an addictive drug usually prescribed as a sleeping tablet. Interestingly, it also had a reputation as a drug that in certain circumstances removed inhibitions about telling the truth. Because the sodium amytal formed 63 per cent of the total volume of the powder, the analyst believed it was 'sufficient to consist of a fatal dose'.

The governor explained that a prisoner serving a seven-year term had handed the bottle over to the chief officer (presumably it was given first to Father Smith), telling him that 'other prisoners had asked him to take the bottle of powder and endeavour to pass it to the prisoner Manuel'. He refused to name these other prisoners. The governor commented:

> I am of the opinion that this bottle had been in the prison for some considerable time, indeed before Manuel's trial, and it may have been the desire of the unknown prisoner to get this deadly material into Manuel's food so he would not appear in court. However, with the fuller security arrangements instituted before his trial the scheme may have been timeously frustrated.

Or perhaps, he added, whoever had the poison had simply seized the opportunity to get rid of it. Maybe prisoners feared that further searches might uncover other illicitly held items and felt it was best to give the authorities something to stop them from looking further.

Although we now know that there was poison within Barlinnie, it remains unclear whether there was in fact a plot to poison Manuel or help him commit suicide. Some of those imprisoned with him may have developed a hatred for him and wanted to harm him. The alternative possibility, self-harm with others providing him with the means, is highly unlikely. At the point in his trial when the alarm was first raised, Manuel was clearly relishing his time in court; a suicide attempt seems highly improbable. What he might have planned to do if the verdict went against him, if that possibility ever crossed his mind, is of course another matter. All we can say on the information before us is that there is a grain of truth, or more accurately 58¾ grains, in the story of poison inside the prison.

***

On the 13th day of the trial, Monday, 28 May, it is the turn of Manuel's mother. She stands in the witness box clutching her handbag, small, frightened, appearing almost numb with worry. Throughout her evidence, it is always 'Mr Brown', 'Mr Tallis', 'Mr Watt'. She is polite and deferential towards everyone involved, she even describes the seven policemen who invade her house as 'the gentlemen' – and she made tea for them all.

Led by her son, she describes the arrival of the police at their home on 14 January and immediately gives an insight into his mocking contempt for them. Mr Brown had asked, 'Where did you get all this money you have been spending?' Bridget says to Manuel, 'I think you told him you had tuppence on the sideboard.'

Her son takes her back to those moments in the police station when he read out his first statement.

'Can you remember what the statement contained?'

'Well, it was about crimes. You were going to clear up a few crimes and a few mysteries about things that had happened in Lanarkshire.'

She agrees with him that he said nothing about specific crimes.

Manuel asks whether he said anything else to her. A moment later, he must wish he hadn't. 'You asked me if I was all right and if everyone else was all right, and that you didn't know how these things happened, what made you do these things.' This is a devastating answer. Surely he was admitting to something far worse than break-ins and theft?

He tries to recover from the blow. 'Now, this is a particularly important point. Are you sure, absolutely sure, that you heard me saying that?' He gets the answer he needs: 'I am not sure.' He follows this up by implying that it was one of the policemen who uttered those dangerous words.

'Is it not a fact that you heard someone saying that?'

'Just a minute now. I am not sure.'

Wisely, Manuel leaves the matter there.

He moves on to the Watt murders. He wants his mother to support his story that Tallis was involved. Was she at home, working in the garden, on the afternoon of 17 September 1956 and did she see him come home with Charles Tallis that afternoon? He gets nowhere: despite putting the question several times, she keeps denying she was home or that she saw Tallis with him.

'And are you quite definite . . . I didn't return home with Charles Tallis?'

'No, you didn't.'

Although a chance to implicate Tallis has been lost, her evidence also casts doubt on Tallis's statement that he saw her that afternoon when Manuel showed him the rings.

He asks his mother about the police search of their house after the Watt murders at about 2 a.m. on 18 September 1956 (placing the time two and half hours before the search was in fact mounted). Immediately, she says something staggering: 'Well, they came – I was in one bedroom and you and your daddy were in the other, and they were looking for a gun – to see if you had a gun.' If Peter was sharing a bedroom with his father at the time of the Watt murders, how could Samuel *not* have been aware of his night-time comings and goings? It is inconceivable. Later, in court, Samuel will claim that both he and his wife are light sleepers; this makes it even harder to believe he did not know Peter was leaving the house in the middle of the night. The point about Peter and Samuel sharing a room is so important that Gillies gets Bridget to confirm what she has said.

'So Peter and his father were occupying one room?'

'Yes,' she replies.

Bridget agrees with her son that the 18 September search for the gun was confined to his room and the rest of the house was not searched. Perhaps the jury will take this as a suggestion that the police did not regard him as a serious suspect and it will be a small point in his favour. Alternatively, they may think the police were simply not thorough enough.

Manuel takes his mother through the events of Hogmanay and New Year's Day. She tells the court that he did not leave the house before 4.45 a.m. on 1 January, when she went to bed, and that he was asleep at 8 a.m., when she came downstairs. And, no, she agrees, she had not heard anything in the night indicating that someone had left the house or returned.

When Gillies rises, he first takes her back to the events at the police station when she and Samuel saw their son. She agrees Peter had said 'that he did not know how these things happened' but, she claims, he said nothing specific about unsolved crimes. 'He was talking about mysteries in Lanarkshire,' that was all. He didn't say, 'There is no future for me.' She does not remember him saying, 'I have done some terrible things.' He didn't say, 'I killed the girl Anne Kneilands at East Kilbride and I shot the three women in the house at Burnside.' He didn't mention Isabelle Cooke. No, he did not say he had left the house at about 5 a.m. on New Year's morning.

Lord Cameron now intervenes and effectively destroys any gains her son has achieved.

'I think you recollect him saying, "I don't know what made me do these things." Did he say that?'

'Yes, these are the words he said.'

Answering Gillies, she expresses strong doubt about the three confessions. The writing of the first only 'looks like his handwriting'. She doesn't think the second is in his writing. Then, on further questioning, she decides the first document does *not* look like Peter's writing, as one line of script is 'off the line' and he is always so careful when he writes letters. Of course, most of his letters to her have been written during his many years in detention; perhaps he had more time to write neatly in jail. She also thinks some of the signatures are suspect; some of the 'P's and 'T's are different and document 141 is signed 'Pete' and not 'Peter'.

When Gillies sits down, Manuel seizes the opportunity to question his mother again, going back to the damning remark 'I don't know what makes me do these things.'

'Did you hear me say that?' he asks.

'Yes.'

'Are you sure?'

'Yes.'

'Did you hear me say anything else?'

'No.'

'You just heard me say that?'

'Yes.'

He tries to get her to agree that Goodall might have said it. But she persists: 'I thought I heard you saying that.'

'You thought you heard me saying that?'

'Yes.'

This is bad for Manuel, rapidly getting worse. By his repetition, he is lodging the phrase more and more firmly in the jury's mind. Yet he tries again: 'The question is this. Did you hear me saying it plainly and clearly, or is it just an instance where you think you heard me saying it? You must know if you heard it or if you think you heard it.'

'I heard it.'

He is still unable to leave the matter. Was it not one of the police who said it?

'I think you said it,' she answers, slightly weakening her testimony.

'Well, that is what I am trying to get at. Is it a fact that you think I said it, or did I say it?'

Finally, he gets an answer that helps him: 'I don't know.'

'Then can I put it like this: did you definitely and plainly hear me saying, "I don't know what makes me do these things?"'

'Yes.'

'Then you can't possibly say you think you heard me saying it?'

'Yes, I heard you saying it.'

He has helped to condemn himself.

He finally leaves that issue and asks about the electric razor. She helps him: Tallis was living in their house when they returned from holiday and he was using the razor. This was well before the Watt murders.

Questioned by Cameron, she changes her evidence on one point: she had known Peter had been charged with murder when she saw him at the police station. He then asks a crucial question.

'When he was living at home . . . did he always appear to be in full possession of his faculties?'

'Yes.'

And by her answer, she helps close off one key escape route for her son: he cannot escape the gallows on the ground of mental illness.

The next witness is Samuel Manuel. He walks stiffly into the witness box and takes the oath. Then, almost immediately, he begins to lie for his son.

To any attentive listener, his probity is already in doubt. Bridget has just let slip that he and Peter shared a bedroom at the time of the

Watt murders. He must surely have known full well that his son's nocturnal comings and goings had coincided with three murders. Much later, after Peter was hanged, he would finally admit that he had indeed known that his son was out all night when the Kneilands and Watt murders took place and that he suspected his son was the killer. Despite this, in January 1956 he told the police that Peter was at home when Kneilands was killed. Now he is ready to lie for him again.

It is clear that Samuel is extremely hostile to the police and anyone who tries to harm his family. As we have seen, he can be vindictive, as when he encountered Mary McLauchlan at the bus stop and spat at her. As he tries desperately to exculpate his son, it becomes evident that, in a way, he too is on trial.

Peter begins with the Kneilands murder. Samuel tries to help his son and also depict the police in a poor light. Peter was a suspect partly because his face was scratched. But, Samuel states, he had the marks on 31 December, days before the young woman was killed. The police had come to their house five or six times and questioned Peter 'severely'. He says that 'it nearly came to blows one night', implying the police threatened violence. Yet despite their repeated visits, he says, they found no evidence against Peter.

Manuel then asks his father about what he offhandedly calls 'the Watt thing': that is, the cold-blooded murder of three people. Samuel sets out to blacken the character of Tallis. He testifies that on the afternoon before the Watt murders, Tallis had come to their house looking for Peter. He claims Tallis wanted to leave something in the house. Had he any idea, Peter asks, what it was?

'Four sticks of gelignite,' his father replies.

This is definitely not the answer Peter is looking for and he quickly tries to cover it up, saying, 'We don't need to go into that.'

Lord Cameron will have none of this. 'Four sticks of what? Gelignite?' One can hear his Lady Bracknell-like surprise.

'Yes,' Samuel answers him.

Cameron asks Samuel how he responded to this request.

'I refused to let him leave it in the house. I told him to get it out of there.'

The gelignite is an unhelpful distraction as far as Manuel is concerned and he tries again to get the piece of evidence he wants. He asks if Tallis had anything else.

'He mentioned he had a gun,' his father helpfully replies. Tallis with a gun just before the Watt murders: what better support could there be for his son's case?

He adds that Tallis was driving a light-coloured hire car. This could be important because witnesses reported seeing a similar car in the vicinity of the Watt killings. (After the trial is over, a newspaper will publish a receipt showing Peter had hired a car at this time.) Tallis, of course, has already said he was celebrating the wedding of Allan Bowes when Samuel claims he arrived with his high-explosive parcel.

Samuel is determined to depict the police in a poor light. When, at 2 a.m. on the day after the Watt murders were discovered, no fewer than seven officers came looking for a gun, 'I don't think they made a very severe search . . . It was mostly your bedroom they searched.' (Once again, the question of who slept where is raised but not pursued.)

Inspector McNeil had returned to the house some weeks later and asked for a pair of Peter's shoes (to check against a rather unclear footprint in the Martins' garden). 'He said it was only a routine call. Superintendent Hendry had sent him out but he did not know what it was about and he said any pair of shoes would do. He told me he knew you were innocent and he told me the date Watt would be tried, on 6 January, and he said any pair would do.' McNeil, he claims, came on the two succeeding Fridays and each time took away a pair of Peter's shoes. 'I gave him a new pair that you had never worn and I told him if he came back again he would need a warrant.' Then the police came back and took away 'every particle of clothing belonging to you' and some of his own, which they thought were his son's.

All this, if the jury believes Samuel, is a damaging description of police inefficiency. It also suggests that McNeil, an important prosecution witness, had doubts about Peter's involvement in the murders.

The search warrant, he recalls, was in connection with the Burnside murders. All through the trial, Peter tries to suggest that the police suspected him of the Kneilands murder and, in recent months, had tried to frame him for it. He asks if the warrant also mentioned Kneilands. Samuel says he cannot remember.

Lord Cameron queries this: 'How is that? I should have thought it would rather stick in your mind if you had policemen coming with a warrant about murders.'

'I beg your pardon?'

'How is it you can't recollect? I should have thought it was a thing that would stick in your mind. Have you got a bad memory?'

'I just can't remember whether that was on the warrant at that time or not.' When his son resumes his questioning, he offers an explanation of his defective memory: 'Because I didn't have my glasses on, I just read it kind of hastily.' It is hardly convincing.

The questioning moves to the electric razor. Peter needs to weaken the prosecution case by showing it had been in their house well before the break-in at the Platts'. His father responds as required: it was Tallis. Tallis offered to sell him the razor for two pounds in August 1956. Tallis offered a bonus if he bought it: he would include a gold watch that had belonged to his father. (By this point in the trial, nobody in court can think that this watch, if it ever existed, had been acquired legitimately.) So how long had the razor been in their house, his son asks him? At first Samuel says two to three years, then eighteen months, then goes back to the first figure. He says he had refused the splendid deal offered by Tallis but adds that the razor was later given to Peter, who changed its plug. All this, of course, keeps Tallis in the jury's mind as a crooked and a baleful presence in the Manuels' life.

The next step by Peter is to attack Brannan's testimony. He gave the dangerous evidence that Manuel was broke on 31 December yet flush with money the following day. Samuel rises to the occasion: it was just not true that Peter had no money in the pub, that was a pretence. Peter simply did not want Brannan sitting with them so they pretended he was broke. His father's loan of a pound to buy a round was an act; it didn't mean Peter had no money.

Whatever the jury may think of that, the next piece of evidence from Samuel is of a different quality altogether. It lays the foundations for Peter to claim someone else had committed the Smart killings – Peter Smart himself. After Brannan had left them, Samuel says, they were joined by 'two other gentlemen'. One of these went into the lavatory with Peter and then left. Samuel says he had never seen this man before or since, nor a photograph of him, but he wore a hat, was red-faced and grey at the temples.

They now come to the crucial matter of what Peter did – or did not do – early on the morning of 1 January. According to the prosecution, Peter had slipped away from his home, broken into the Smarts' house, killed and robbed them, and then returned home to the bed-chair where he slept. Samuel denies this was possible. He himself had gone to bed at about 3.30 a.m. and not heard anyone leave after that. He had been wakened at 5.45 a.m. by James coming to the bed they shared and had stayed awake till he rose at 6.30. Peter was asleep when he came downstairs shortly afterwards. If Samuel is believed – and it is an increasingly large if – then Peter could not have murdered the Smarts.

They move to 14 January, when the police came to search the house and eventually took Samuel and Peter away. Samuel says he was eager to get to work but was prevented from going. There is the matter of the gloves. According to the police, Samuel claimed they were his. He tells a different story: Brown had asked him, 'Do these belong to you?' and he'd simply replied, 'They could be [mine].' Later, Brown had said he was to be charged with reset. He was therefore surprised when next morning in court he discovered he was being charged with breaking and entering. His son asks him if he had ever been arrested before and he says he has not. He is lying. What cannot be revealed in court is that Samuel, like his two sons, has a criminal record, having been fined one pound for being a Peeping Tom in 1952.

The next step they take together is to throw doubt on the police account of the confessions. Samuel describes the scene when he and Bridget saw their son: 'You refused to read any statement and Mr Goodall kept hitting you on the shoulder like that and said, "Come on, now, Peter, read the statement, come on," and you said you were not reading any statement but finally they got you to read the statement.' The police, he claims, had also offered Peter reassurance. McNeil had said he would see his father would not lose his job and Goodall added, 'If you lose your job, I will guarantee another in Glasgow.' They had both told Samuel he would be released from custody next morning once he'd appeared before the Airdrie procurator fiscal.

Peter next turns to the words, 'I don't know what makes me do these things.' Had Samuel heard him utter them? 'No,' his father replies, 'you never made any such statement.' He repeats this denial and then he gives another hint of police inducement to make Peter confess: 'I heard Inspector Goodall saying, "Now, Peter, it will be all right. We will see you all right. You won't even get a trial," or words to that effect.' He adds that the police also told Peter, 'You will get treatment.' What did he conclude from this, his son asks? 'I took it to mean you were insane or there was something wrong with you.' He is suggesting that Peter was somehow tricked into reading out the confession because he was told it would not lead to him being tried for murder; he would instead be detained in a mental institution.

In any case, his son was not his normal self, says Samuel. 'It might be silly to say it – I felt you had a drink or a drug on you.' So, Peter asks, was he acting spontaneously and of his own free will? 'Oh, no, you were not acting of your own free will, everything had to be dragged out of you . . . you were different from what you usually are, your hair was all over your face, you looked very poor and dirty, you looked as if you had been getting a lot of bashing around.'

Samuel continues to contradict the police's evidence: his son had not mentioned Anne Kneilands, the Watts, the Smarts or Isabelle Cooke. Nor had he read out more than one document.

'Did you see another document?' Peter asks.

'Never saw another document.'

Not only did he not see another document but, he says, after Peter had read out from the single confession, 'Mr McNeil took me over for five and a half hours' questioning and on Sunday night he put me in an ice-cold room.'

He is quickly told he need not go into that, yet he insists on attacking McNeil, saying the man had assured him his son was innocent in the Watt case: 'He told me that, because I put it to him, I said, "Did you not tell me –" and the wife was there when I asked him this, I said, "Did you not tell me at the time you were investigating the Burnside murders that our Peter was innocent and when you took the shoes you would have to prove his innocence?" And he said, "Yes, I said that. When I arrested Mr Watt I was quite justified in arresting him. The man on the ferry –"'

Although this is an attempt to cast more doubt on the police investigations, his son tries to return him to the main line of his defence: 'You never heard me mention anything about any specific crime?' His father confirms that he did not.

This rejection of the confessions is reinforced by Samuel claiming that when he was questioned by the procurator fiscal, 'He read out a sheet to me and asked me if that was the document you read and I said definitely it was not.' The police had, he claims, inserted a bogus confession into the system. The procurator fiscal had also asked about the gloves and he'd replied they had been a gift from Peter, 'either Christmas night or the night after, I just can't remember. [Peter] threw them down and he said, "There's a Christmas present for you."'

Samuel's credibility as a witness depends on whether he lied about the gloves. So, Gillies asks, why had he not answered honestly and said how he came by them? If he had done, he would not have been arrested. His only response is to claim he was arrested because he would not leave the house. (This directly contradicts his earlier claim that he'd been eager to get to work to unlock the hut for the others in his gang.) Gillies will not accept this.

'You were asked if you could explain how the gloves came to be in your house?'

'I was.'

'And you gave a somewhat indeterminate answer?'

'Yes.'

The judge takes over; he too wants a straight answer. Why had he not said where he got the gloves?

'I made a mistake. I should have.'

'I know you did but I am asking why you made it.'

'Well, I had got a Christmas parcel too from America and I didn't know what was inside it.'

'You have already said that on Christmas Day, after your son came in at night, he put down this pair of gloves and said, "There is a present for you"?'

'Yes.'

'You must have been aware of that fact. When your attention was pointedly drawn to them by the police, you gave an evasive answer. Why did you not tell the truth?'

'I can't just say the reason I gave the wrong answer.'

'Why not? Why can't you give the reason?'

Finally Samuel gives a slightly better justification for his failure to tell the truth: 'I was excited at the time and I just said that they could be mine. I didn't know what the reason was at the time.'

But Cameron is relentless: 'You are not excited now. What was the reason?'

'Well, I had received a parcel from America and I thought the gloves could have come that way too.'

This gets the withering comment: 'Is that the best answer you can give?'

With these few questions, Samuel's credibility has been seriously undermined.

The questioning by Gillies returns to the night at the Hamilton police station and his son's supposed confessions. Samuel makes it clear that he felt the police were overreacting, trying to intimidate by their numbers. He claims there were initially about 20 officers in the room where he and his wife saw their son. On their way to it, they had to mount a staircase lined with uniformed and plain-clothes policemen. 'They must have come from the whole of Lanarkshire,' he adds bitterly.

He gives his version of what happened. Peter 'mentioned in it [his statement] he wanted to clear up about crimes and two or three mysteries'. So what, Gillies asks, did he understand by that? Samuel is totally unwilling to admit that he thought it had anything to do with murder, though by then he knew that Peter had been charged with killing the Smarts. He says he thought the police were dealing with 'jobs' – that is, burglaries – carried out by Tallis and Peter.

'The police had told me they understood Peter and Tallis were doing a lot of jobs in Uddingston. They knew they were doing them but couldn't prove it.'

'Did you think that might have been something to do with the murders Peter has been charged with?'

'No, because I knew he had never been out of the house on New Year's morning.'

'Are you seriously telling the court that when a statement was read by your son relating to unsolved crimes and mysteries in Lanarkshire, you took them to refer to housebreakings in Uddingston?'

'I did.'

'Is that your evidence?'

'Yes.'

Gillies' scepticism is completely justified. It is impossible to accept that Samuel would not have instantly associated 'unsolved crimes and mysteries' with the Smart murders and the disappearance of Isabelle Cooke, and perhaps also the Kneilands and Watt killings. Since Isabelle Cooke had disappeared, the whole area where he lived had been in turmoil. Vigilante groups were searching for the girl and patrolling the streets at night; every newspaper carried the story of the continuing investigation. Moreover, Samuel knew Peter had been suspected of the Watt and Kneilands murders. His story is simply incredible. Virtually everyone in the Glasgow area was horribly aware that these were the most important unsolved crimes; he could not have been immune.

As his examination by the prosecution continues, his credibility is eroded even further. He next claims that the first two confessions offered in evidence are not the documents read out by his son at the police station, implying they are fabrications.

The prosecution seizes upon this: 'Now, you're quite sure, are you, that neither of these two documents was read out by your son at that meeting?'

'Neither of them as far as I can recollect.'

'I am asking you whether you are quite sure. I am not asking you as far as you can recollect . . . neither of them was read?'

'Yes.'

'Are you quite certain of that?'

'Yes.'

He agrees Peter did read out a document but says that it took only a few seconds. He denies it contained the sentence, 'The crimes I refer to above are crimes of Homicide.' Nor could he recall his son saying words to the effect of 'I don't know how these things happened or what made me do these things.'

The prosecuting counsel changes the line of attack. If, as he has claimed, Goodall had said Peter would not stand trial, what would the trial have been for?

'Oh, it was whatever charges they would have against him, I suppose.'

'Of housebreaking in Uddingston?' Gillies asks sceptically.

'Yes.'

'Is that your position?'

Samuel must realise it is preposterous to claim that his son would be locked up in a mental institution just because he'd been breaking into houses. 'No, I am not saying that.' The question is put to him again. 'I didn't know what he was to be tried for. I knew he had been charged with murder at that day.' Finally, he offers a more plausible explanation of his poor memory of the events at the police station: 'I had never had a sleep for two days.'

The judge now turns to the crucial matter of how much money Peter had on 31 December, saying that he believed Manuel was drawing National Assistance at that time. 'I couldn't say,' replies Samuel. Cameron is sceptical: 'Did you not know perfectly well that he had been drawing National Assistance for some little time?' Again he denies he knew but adds that his son 'seemed to have quite a few shillings on him' on Hogmanay. He denies to Gillies that Peter said, 'That's a pound I owe you,' when he gave him money to buy a round. He also claims he did not see Peter with any money at the Greenans' party. The more Samuel says, the less trustworthy he is shown to be.

What happened in the early hours of 1 January is crucial and he is asked about it again. He claims he woke at 5.45 a.m., when James came up to share his bed, and that he rose at 6.30. His wife would have woken him anyway, as she usually did. He claims Bridget knew he was up and about: 'She heard me.' Both Gillies and Cameron seize on this remark and ask how he knew: 'I took it for granted.'

Cameron rebuffs him: 'I do not want you to take anything for granted here. How did you know she heard you?'

'How do you expect me to know what the wife –' he begins to protest.

'Answer the question. How do you know she heard you?'

Finally he admits, 'I do not know whether she heard me or not.'

He says one significant thing: 'We are both light sleepers.' But if they were light sleepers, Peter's nocturnal comings and goings over the years could not have escaped their notice.

He is questioned about the marks on Peter's face about the time of the Kneilands murder. His son had them, he says, on 31 December. Peter had told him he'd been in a fight. 'I wouldn't say they were there longer than four days. He heals very quickly.' But this is dangerous: does he not understand that this makes it even less likely that marks received on the last day of December would still be there to be noticed by the police on 4 January? In any case, he is lying. Later, after his son was dead, Samuel admitted to Superintendent Brown that Peter had been out all night when Kneilands was killed and had returned home with scratches on his face. He also confesses that a jacket and trousers belonging to his son had vanished: he suspected they might have been bloodstained.

The prosecution's questioning again turns to the role of Tallis and to Samuel's startling claim that Tallis wanted to leave a parcel of gelignite at the Manuel house.

'How did you know what was in it?' he is asked.

'He said that.'

Now he claims Tallis also told him other things about a gun. 'He told me about being out in the car a week before with a lady . . . I think he said Peter was with him . . . He said this lady stuck a gun into his side, kidding, and he said, "Yon woman would have used it."' This woman, Samuel says, worked in a dairy near Rutherglen; this identifies her as Mary Bowes. He says he thinks she kept the gun to protect the money in the dairy till.

'Did that [the incident in the car] strike you as being rather extraordinary?'

'It didn't strike me as being rather extraordinary. I was trying to get him out of the house.'

'With his gelignite?' he is asked sarcastically.

'Yes.'

He repeats that the incident occurred just before the Watts were killed. Moreover, he now recalls, Tallis told him he had a gun on him that day.

'How,' prosecuting counsel asks, 'did the conversation about the gun crop up?'

Samuel answers, 'He was a man who used to do a lot of boasting when he came to our house.'

He is questioned further about his relationship with Tallis and quickly gets entangled in contradictions. Neither he nor Bridget wanted him around, he says, especially when they returned from holiday in 1956 and found the man living in their house. Moreover, 'Peter told us if he came to the house we were to tell him he wasn't in.' If that was the case, he is asked (and, the jury may think, if he is not lying), why did he let Tallis in, as he has claimed he did, when he came looking for Peter on the afternoon before the Watt murders? 'For peace sake,' he replies. He also admits he was quite friendly with the man and didn't dislike him. 'I don't dislike anybody,' he adds. (He is forgetting his intense dislike of the police.)

Cameron wants clarification: 'If you didn't dislike Mr Tallis, could you tell us why you didn't want him around the house?'

'Well, we weren't very fond of him. We thought he wasn't company for Peter. The police told us that too, that he was a very rough man. Mr McNeil told me he wasn't a man for Peter to mix with at all.'

The idea that his son, with his string of convictions, might be corrupted by Tallis may raise a few smiles among listening police officers.

But if this was so, Gillies asks, then why did he tell Tallis that Peter was at the Woodend Hotel? Again the answer is evasive: 'I told him. It didn't mean he [Peter] had to meet him. If he wanted to meet him, that was his affair.' But, he is asked, if Peter had previously been so reluctant to meet Tallis, why had he told Tallis where to find Peter?

'The explanation is easy. He wanted to meet him [Peter].'

'That is your explanation?'

'He wanted to meet Peter, and I told him Peter was at the Woodend.'

Cameron will not accept this. 'You haven't explained at all. Will you kindly answer the advocate depute's question?'

'What is the question?'

He is told the question again and says he wanted Tallis out of the house. 'I wanted rid of him.'

Cameron: 'Couldn't you have said to him you didn't know where Peter was?'

Samuel gives a virtuous reply: 'I would be telling a lie then.' In the last few minutes, he has shown he has no reluctance to lie.

Among all this equivocation and evasion, the crucial thing is that he has claimed that Tallis had a gun just hours before the Watt murders. So, he is asked, if this were the case, why had he not told the police? After all, he knew they were looking for a gun when they searched his house only two days later. So why did he not tell them then?

'Oh, I don't know.'

'Didn't you think it was significant?'

He is evasive: 'I think they had searched Tallis's place.'

When he is pressed further, he still cannot explain his failure to tell about the gun. Instead, he talks about how the police searched his house: 'They drew up . . . the tick [mattress] of the bed.'

The judge will have none of this: 'Mr Manuel, nobody is asking you about the tick of the bed at the moment. I think you're probably aware of that fact.' He finally gets Samuel to admit that, when the police came, he did know that three women had been shot and that they were looking for people who had guns.

'Didn't you think it was important?' he asks.

'Yes, it was important but I understood they had Tallis under review at that time.'

'From whom did you understand that when the police came to your house on the 18th? Who told you?'

'We took it for granted.'

'Who told you?'

'I asked the police and they said they had been round all the people –'

'Who told you they had Tallis under review at that date?'

'Nobody.'

'Then can you answer the advocate depute's question? Why didn't you inform the police when they were looking for a gun which might have been concerned in that particular murder that a man had told you two days before that he had a gun in his possession?'

'I can't give any explanation.'

'Why can't you?'

'Because I just can't.'

The obvious reason why he did not tell the police is because his story is a pack of recently invented lies. Finally, he gives the court his best excuse: the police presence made him 'highly excited at the time . . . you get upset and you don't have your full faculties about you.'

There is also the key question of just when he had learned about the time of the Smart killings. If, at Hamilton police station, he was so confident that Peter was innocent because he had not left the house between five and seven in the morning, how did he know that was the crucial period? Sceptical listeners may conclude he knew that this was in fact when Peter had been out of the house.

At first, Samuel claims that Brown had told him this when the police arrived at their house on 14 January. But, pressed further, he agrees that this is untrue and that Brown had told him later. 'I can't remember that date. When you are in and out of prison you can't remember the date.' Next, he is forced to admit that he did not, at that stage, know that between five and seven was the crucial time. 'But he [Brown] told me. When I told him that Peter had been in the house all night, he said he was out between the hours of five and seven and that was when the murder was committed. But I can't give you the date.' He sticks obdurately to this story even when given the opportunity to deny his earlier statement about not being worried because he knew Peter was at home when the murders were committed.

The cross-examination by the prosecuting counsel and the interventions by the judge have left Samuel looking forgetful and confused at best, at worst an outright liar. Now his son tries to undo the damage. Very skilfully, Peter gets him to agree that, because he had been imprisoned in Barlinnie, he was upset and therefore could not be expected to remember all that had occurred at Hamilton police station. No, Samuel agrees, Peter had not mentioned anything about Kneilands, the Watts and the Smarts or Cooke that night.

As for not telling the police about the gun that he claimed Tallis was carrying, Peter asks, 'Is it not a fact that you thought on that occasion that it was not a very, shall we say, apt time to mention knowledge concerning guns?'

Samuel leaps at the heavy hint: 'I did think that.'

'That is why? You must be honest about it, you must not say, "I don't know."'

'Yes.'

'In other words, you were trying to cover up for me?'

'Yes.'

'You thought if Tallis had a gun there was maybe a possibility that I got it?'

'Yes.'

'And that is why you did not make any mention?'

'Correct,' Samuel replies.

Any small degree of plausibility in this excuse is quickly removed by the judge. He asks Samuel if he had told the police about the gun at a later date.

'No.'

'Never?'

'Never.'

'So you never came across the apt and appropriate time for telling the police?'

'I never told them,' Samuel is forced to admit.

If this looks bad, then so does Samuel's answer to Cameron's next question. Why did he not buy the electric razor? 'I was assuming it had been stolen.'

So was he surprised to find the same razor in the possession of his son?

'I noticed it in and around the house.'

'I did not ask that.'

'Yes, I was surprised.'

Well, if that was the case, did he take any steps to ask his son about the razor?

'No.'

They move from one stolen item to another: the minister's camera. Samuel admits he saw the police with the camera but denies he was asked to explain its presence in his house. While he cannot recall giving any statement about the camera to the police, he says he definitely did not say he bought it at the Barras.

'So if anybody said that you made such a statement that must have been a deliberate falsehood?'

'Yes, I never bought anything from the Barras.'

Cameron ripostes, 'I did not suggest you did, all I am suggesting is you made a statement you did.'

'No, I cannot recollect making any such statement.'

'May you have made that statement?'

'I don't think so.' This is hardly a satisfactory answer.

The question of his son's mental state is now raised by the judge. If Goodall had said that Peter would get treatment, did he think his son had his full mental capacity? Samuel says it seemed to him as if Peter was under the influence of drink or drugs. 'He did not seem to me to be the same person at all. Not the same person.'

There may have been a very good reason for that, Cameron suggests: 'Of course, he'd been charged with murder by then?'

Now, right at the end of his time in the witness box, the judge gives

Samuel Manuel a final chance to help his son. Cameron asks, 'If you could help me about his mental condition at the time?'

Samuel replies: 'Oh, well, I could not say about his mental condition. That is beyond me.'

Cameron becomes more specific: in the two years before January 1958, he asks, 'Did you notice anything unusual or abnormal about it?'

'No, I did not.'

'Are you sure?'

'Yes.'

Cameron wants to make this absolutely clear: 'Quite sure about that?'

'Yes.'

The judge offers him one last chance: 'Because if there is anything you can say or want to say, now is the time to tell me.'

'Yes.'

'Did you notice anything at all?'

'Never noticed anything out of place.'

'You are quite clear about that?'

'Yes.'

Perhaps pride prevents Samuel from admitting there was anything abnormal in his son, perhaps he now thinks he is normal. Whatever the reason, his answers have helped close off Peter's main chance of escaping the gallows.

Samuel is followed by Theresa, Peter's favourite in the family. Questioning her, he tries to establish that he could not have left home and killed the Smarts. During the family party, she had phoned a fellow nurse who was on duty and he had taken part in the call. It lasted from about two to four o'clock, he suggests, hoping to block out a good length of time. 'No,' Theresa replies, 'I think it was from 1.15 to 2.35.' When she went to bed, she tells the court, he was in the house, and during the night she had heard no comings and goings.

This is neither helpful nor harmful but now Cameron intervenes. As a trained nurse, has she observed anything unusual about her brother's behaviour during the past two years? 'Well, I wouldn't say any more unusual – to me it was his usual behaviour.' Cameron repeats the question and she answers, 'No, I don't think so. I mean, as I have known him, I have always known him the same.' That is, she has always known him as a boastful, fantasising thief who attacked women but showed a deep affection for her. Three years previously, she tried and failed to get him locked up because she believed he was mentally ill. Now he is on trial for eight murders. Poor Theresa.

Their brother James is next. He answers Peter's questions by saying they were together till 5.45 a.m., when he went up to bed. To Gillies, he confirms that his father woke up when he climbed in the bed he was sharing with him. His appearance is so brief that he is almost invisible; it is as if both sides have decided they do not want to bother with him.

The next witness is Robert McQuade, who is an acquaintance of the three Manuel men and a convicted criminal. In January 1956, he had gone to a local dance wearing a Teddy boy's long, velvet-collared coat and carrying three unusual accoutrements: two axes and a heavy cosh. For this, he got 60 days in prison. The testimony he gives supports Samuel's on one crucial point: Manuel had sold a gun to a man who might have been Peter Smart. The police are well aware that McQuade's testimony may be interesting; Muncie and McNeil went to Barlinnie and interviewed him on 11 May.

Led by Manuel, McQuade says they encountered each other in the Royal Oak on the evening of 31 December. Peter asked him to keep watch (there was a police station opposite the pub), as, he told him, 'I am going to sell this guy a shooter.' McQuade kept an eye out and Manuel went into the lavatory with another man. 'In about five minutes, he came out. I went back to my table and a drink came over [as a reward for his help].' The buyer of the gun was middle-aged and wore spectacles and a black hat. Yes, he answers helpfully, he did look like the newspaper pictures of Smart. 'Going on the newspaper photographs, specs and that, it definitely looked like him.'

This story of Smart buying a gun is, to say the least, highly unlikely but the prosecution needs to make sure McQuade and his story are totally discredited. Why, he is asked, if this man looked like Smart, had he not gone to the police and told them what had occurred? McQuade's reply depends for its credibility on his own criminal status: 'If I go to the busies, I am done for keeping the edge up [keeping watch] when the gun was getting sold. I was doing myself.' Besides, he claims, although there was a resemblance between the man in the pub and Smart, at that point he did not connect the two.

He admits that, when he'd seen Peter at the dance the following evening, he'd not said anything about the gun. However, he did ask, 'How did you get on and how did you knock it off at the New Year?' This is unwise; most of his listeners will know that 'knock off' can mean steal. He is asked to explain. He claims that for him 'knock it off' means to have a good drink. When asked if this is the usual meaning of the words, he remains mute. The judge forces him to answer and, cornered, he admits, 'You can steal. It means stealing.' But, he protests, that was not what he meant when talking to Manuel. Then he tries to retract what he has just said. If 'knock it off' means to steal, he claims, then it 'is a new one on me if it does'. If this is the case, Gillies asks him, why has he just told the judge it does mean to steal? 'It is a word that can mean various things,' he answers desperately.

Manuel tries to help him and gets McQuade to agree that the term does indeed have many meanings. Manuel adds cheekily that these various meanings 'might not be apparent to people less gifted in understanding this particular vernacular that you use'. Thus it is not a case of McQuade lying; rather it is the fault of the judge and prosecuting counsel for failing in their understanding.

Cameron takes up the questioning. 'May I take it it was a very unusual transaction selling a gun?' His two-edged question puts

McQuade in a difficult position: if he agrees it was unusual he will probably be asked why he had not mentioned it until now. If he says it was not unusual, he will be admitting to criminality. Eventually, he decides to go for a halfway position: 'Well, it was quite usual, not unusual.' That hardly convinces anybody that he is a reliable witness from the right side of the law.

He agrees with Cameron that he had heard about the Smart murders.

'Did you not think it was important to let the police know that a man unknown to you had acquired a gun on the night of Hogmanay?'

'Well –'

'Did you or did you not?'

'I wanted to keep out of trouble.'

'I didn't ask that. Answer my question.'

'It wasn't unusual,' is his only response.

Cameron repeats the question.

'Well, I didn't think it was very important and because I didn't think it had any connection with the Sheepburn Road incident.'

McQuade has trapped himself. He has just claimed to have been involved in the illegal sale of a gun which he thought had no connection with the Smart murders. He has also said that the supposed buyer of the gun looked like Peter Smart. So the judge asks the obvious question: 'When did you first realise it might be of critical importance?' He adds, 'If you understand my language,' just in case McQuade is 'less gifted' in this particular vernacular. McQuade gives the only answer he can: 'I didn't realise it had any critical importance until today.'

Cameron is relentless. Had he told the police about this transaction? No, he hadn't. Or anyone acting for Manuel? No, he hadn't.

'You knew it was an improper transaction and an illegal transaction, didn't you?'

'Yes.'

'But you thought it was of no importance.'

'No.'

McQuade's unbelievable story has probably done Manuel more harm than good.

CHAPTER TWENTY-FOUR

It is the turn of the final witness: Manuel himself. Day after day, he has been forced to listen as the evidence against him has grown inexorably. Now, finally, he can – he must – take centre stage. There is just one chance left: by testifying on his own behalf, he might convince the jury he is innocent. If he fails, he will hang. It is as simple and as final as that.

He is sure he will succeed. Over the years, in his imagination, he has created an image of himself as a master criminal, highly intelligent, able to out-think the police, able to out-argue the lawyers. Now he can speak for himself, tell his tale without interruption, talk directly to the jurors and triumphantly prove his innocence. After all the drear, bleak, mean years in and out of prison, branded as a petty thief and rapist, scraping a living by theft, sometimes dependent on dole money, now, at long last, he can show his true abilities. He imagines how people all over the world will follow his every word and appreciate his forensic brilliance.

He scurries eagerly across the court, almost leaps into the witness box and takes the oath. He begins to speak so quickly that he is asked to slow down for the sake of the shorthand writers.

He begins with the Anne Kneilands case and immediately shows both fluency and an amazing memory for detail – or, rather, an amazing ability to combine a sprinkling of indisputable facts with his own elaborate fabrications. Again and again as he argues his case, he will quote conversations and give precise details of where things happened and the exact times they occurred. It is deeply impressive – until one probes beneath the surface. Then all sorts of unlikelihood and contradictions come swarming out.

His defence in the case of Kneilands is simple: he didn't kill the girl and this is proven by the failure of the police to find any evidence against him.

He begins to tell his story. After Kneilands' body was discovered, he says, he was questioned by Hendry, who came to where he was working on 12 January. His house was also searched and some of his clothes taken away for examination. (He conveniently forgets to mention he had been detained for questioning shortly after her body was discovered.) But none of this police activity produced anything that could be used against him. There were difficulties, he admits. On 13 January, he learned that Corrins, the Gas Board foreman, had told the police he'd had scratches on his face the week before. He dealt with it: 'I had a few words with this fellow Corrins and he left East Kilbride. He went away to get a job in Uddingston.'

This is astonishing. Right at the start of his evidence, he is bragging that he threatened a man so badly that he left his job. His boast shows his complete failure to sense how his listeners will react. A characteristic of psychopaths is a profound inability to feel empathy with others. Time after time, as he addresses the court, Manuel will say things that demonstrate this mindset.

From a local reporter, he tells the court, he learned that Hendry thought he was the killer and that a witness claimed to have seen him in East Kilbride at the crucial time. It was for this reason that he agreed to have his photograph published in the local paper. If nobody came forward to say they'd seen him in the area, it would be in his favour. Nobody did come forward. He was questioned again about two weeks later, then again in the middle of February and then 'I never saw the man [Hendry] again. He just sort of disappeared.' His contempt for the police is undisguised. They had several attempts to get evidence against him; all had failed. He expects the jury to accept, therefore, that he is innocent.

The Watt case is next. He must convince the jury that he did not kill the three women and show that the evidence offered against him is a mass of lies. The prosecution has claimed that he fired a gun into the Platts' mattress, that the same gun was used to kill the Watts, that he drew it, with its missing lanyard ring, for Dowdall and, finally, he led the police to where he had thrown it in the Clyde. Each link must be broken and another explanation offered.

Speaking carefully, modulating his voice so he can be heard clearly, occasionally looking round the court to see the effect of his words, he says that in those days he was 'running around with a fellow called Tallis'. Tallis, he says, had two guns, both .38 calibre. One was a Webley. Tallis asked him to get ammunition for the guns but eventually obtained some himself. He goes on to describe how Tallis broke the lanyard ring from the Webley.

From this point, his story of Tallis, the gun and the Watt killings becomes increasingly complicated and increasingly bizarre. He claims that in early September 1956 (that is, roughly a fortnight before the Watt murders), Tallis told him he'd been offered a large sum to break into a house in Burnside: 'All I have to do is mess the house about, make it look as if somebody has been there a considerable time.' The man paying for the break-in had agreed to Manuel's participation and so Tallis asked him to take part.

He tells the court he refused the offer because it did not make sense. Despite this, he was interested in meeting the man behind this strange proposal. A rendezvous was arranged at the Woodend Hotel for the day after the Bowes' wedding. Unfortunately, he and Tallis missed each other at the pub so he never did meet the mysterious paymaster. He next explains that he could not have been involved in the Watt murders because, after closing time, he had escorted a woman to her home and then reached his own house at about 1 a.m.

His next step is to attempt to implicate Tallis even further. The next morning, he continues, his father told him that Tallis had been at the house the previous afternoon and had tried to leave a package containing explosives 'in your raincoat pocket in the lobby'. Later that morning, Tallis came to the house and asked him to dispose of two rings, which he claimed belonged to Mrs Bowes. He wanted to get rid of them as soon as possible. Manuel phoned a possible buyer, who was out. He was told where he could be found later that day in Glasgow.

He and Tallis went into town to wait, passing the time drinking and watching a film, appropriately entitled *The Long Arm of the Law*. (Detail, always detail – that is the essence of Manuel's narrative style.) He left Tallis in a pub and went to meet the potential buyer. However, on the way, he read in a newspaper that three people had been killed in Burnside. The paper said it was believed they had been battered to death. Back at the pub, he told Tallis, who then denied *shooting* the women. Manuel told him he was suspicious about the rings; Tallis should keep his mouth shut and in turn he would forget everything about the matter.

At about 2 a.m. the next day, the police had come to his house. Manuel cannot hide his arrogance and boasts about how he took control. He was in bed and his father said the police wanted him to go downstairs. 'I said, "Tell them to come up here,"' he says, and so eight or nine officers trooped upstairs to see him. They claimed they had received an anonymous tip-off that he had a gun. They searched his room and made a perfunctory search of the rest of the house. Nothing incriminating was found. He tells the jury that Inspector

McNeil had asked him, 'Have you got a gun?' He says, 'I had a gun at the time but I told him no.' He fails to understand how his listeners will react to his admission that he lied to the police about owning a gun.

On Thursday, 20 September, he was searching for sticky tape to seal a parcel (some books to send to a girl in hospital – a touching act of kindness) and looked in the space revealed by swivelling the top of the dining-room table. There he saw something wrapped in an oily rag: it was a .38 Webley Mk IV that had recently been fired, with five used cartridges and one unused. He went into Glasgow and threw it into the Clyde. He tracked down Tallis three days later and the man admitted he had left the gun there.

Manuel tells the court that Tallis now told him it was William Watt who had offered him the money to break into a house so it would appear someone had spent time there before going along to the Watt house. He and Mrs Bowes had broken into the Martins'. At about 3.30 or 3.45 a.m., Tallis had gone to meet Watt and handed over the Webley. Watt later returned it, saying, 'Charlie, there is your gun back. Get rid of it, for I can't get rid of it and I can't take the chance of taking it in my car.' The next day, Tallis discovered that Mrs Bowes had taken two rings from the Martins'. These were the ones he had asked Manuel to sell. She had been drunk and had panicked at one point, running across the garden: this explained the unclear footprint found by the police. Tallis said he had told Watt that Manuel would be with him that night. As Watt knew that Manuel had been questioned about the Kneilands murder, he told Tallis to put the gun in Manuel's house and tip off the police.

At this point, his story makes a sudden swerve. In October 1956, he tells the court, he received information that made him wonder if Tallis had lied to him and if Watt, then in Barlinnie, might after all be innocent. 'It occurred to me that perhaps this man Watt may not have had any connection with the thing at all, because all I had to go on was the word of Charlie Tallis which is not a reliable medium at any time [*sic*].' Well, Manuel would certainly know that a professional thief's word could not be trusted.

This new idea that Watt might be innocent prompted him to write his first letter to Dowdall. When they met, he told Dowdall that he knew a man who had been going to Burnside to break into a house on the night of the Watt murders. Dowdall, he says, told him that that man would be Tallis, as 'he'd heard all about it'. This is the start of an attempt by Manuel to enmesh Dowdall in the crimes and be revenged on the solicitor.

He claims that he told the lawyer that, according to Tallis, Watt had suggested the gun should be dumped in the Manuel house so that when the police found it 'they wouldn't need to look any further'. Dowdall had urged him to tell his story to the procurator fiscal, saying, 'Watt is in a very, very serious position,' as he had been charged with three murders and that 'There is only one man who can do anything about it and that is you.' Thus, Manuel gives himself a uniquely important role. However, he explains, he did not wish to repeat his story to the procurator fiscal because he had dumped the gun in the Clyde and, by showing the police where it was, he would implicate himself.

A week later, he continues, Dowdall had come back and told him he had to go to the police with his story or he would go himself, saying, 'Look, lad, this big fellow is going crazy in here [Barlinnie].' He threatened that if Watt cracked up he might tell the police that Manuel had sold him the gun. After more warnings from Dowdall, Manuel wrote to the procurator fiscal on 3 November. When he was interviewed by him, he complained of Dowdall's threats. 'Mr MacDonald said, "Well, Manuel, if he comes to me and tells me you sold Watt a gun, I'll be delighted to hear it."' Manuel suggests, in other words, that at that point the authorities were keen to get evidence to strengthen their case against Watt.

But there was more going on, testifies Manuel. Dowdall had invented a story implicating Tallis and Hart, and he wanted Manuel to repeat it to the procurator fiscal to help Watt. Manuel says that he told MacDonald that Dowdall had asked him to pass on this story.

He next tries to strengthen in the jury's mind the idea that Watt was up to his neck in the murder of his family. MacDonald, he claims, suggested to him that he and Watt were old acquaintances, that they had been seen drinking together in the Woodend Hotel for several months before the murders and that it was he who had sold Watt the gun.

Thus, if he is believed, the Crown was keen to accumulate evidence against Watt while Dowdall was trying to pin the blame on Tallis and Hart. Some of the jury are said to have looked puzzled at this point. One can see why.

Questioned by the procurator fiscal about Tallis, Manuel had told him, 'I don't know much about Tallis,' a statement listeners must find almost impossible to believe after all he has just told them.

Despite the fact that he had supposedly given all this information to the procurator fiscal, nothing much seemed to happen: 'Things more or less drifted along and apart from the fact that I got a right going over, the house was searched, the garden dug up, all my clothes were taken away again – apart from that, things drifted along anyway.'

Then, Manuel claims, he heard that Dowdall was telling the police that he believed Manuel had killed the three women and could describe accurately the interior of the Watt house. His informant, real or invented, was a policeman, who said Dowdall had 'tried everything he could to land this thing around your neck'. As a result, he met the solicitor and complained that this was no way for one's legal representative to behave but Dowdall persuaded him to meet Watt. Again, he quotes the exact words Dowdall is supposed to have used: 'It will be for your own good and I think I can assure you you will be making one of the shrewdest moves you have ever made.'

Everyone in court knows that his two meetings with Watt are of huge importance. Watt's evidence has strongly supported the prosecution case. Now Manuel must thrust the blame back onto

Watt. If, in doing so, he can also damage Tallis and Dowdall, it will be even more satisfying for him.

The account he gives of his first meeting with Watt is very different from the businessman's. According to Manuel, Watt claimed he knew Tallis was the killer and wanted Manuel to work on his behalf. He threatened that if he did not cooperate, 'There are two men who are prepared to go to the police and swear blind they sold you a gun just before my wife was shot.' When Manuel suggested Watt should tell the police that he knew Tallis and Hart were involved in the murders, Watt said he could not: the police were stupid; they had arrested him.

Watt, Manuel continues, was desperate to have someone arrested for the killings, banging on the table and urging him to tell the police about Tallis and Hart. 'He said, "I know all about it. I have known Tallis for years. I know what he is."' He also knew that Tallis had tried to frame Manuel for the murders. Manuel asked him how he knew that. 'Because I have got the cleverest lawyer in Britain and he is in cahoots with some of the highest-ranking policemen in Glasgow and Lanarkshire. He gives them information and they give him information, and I know Tallis tried to get you to sell two rings and he dumped the gun in your house.' Watt wanted him to get the gun back so it could be planted on Tallis.

So far, the story has wriggled and twisted. First, it seemed Tallis was being paid to break into a house to provide some sort of cover for Watt, who then shot his family with a gun belonging to Tallis. Then Manuel thought that Tallis might have lied and Watt could be innocent. Dowdall had wanted to rescue Watt so he had concocted a story implicating Tallis and Hart that he wanted Manuel to tell to the authorities. Then Dowdall had told the police that Manuel was the killer. Later, Watt wanted his help to frame Tallis and threatened that if he didn't, the evidence could be arranged to implicate Manuel. With all its sudden changes of direction and reversals, the account is very much like the highly contrived plot of one of the thriller films Manuel relished. The jury may find it equally fictional.

Now Manuel produces a further shift, adding yet more detail for the sake of verisimilitude. Watt had tried to get him drunk. He was 'slapping these whiskies into me all night long' and becoming 'a little drunk himself'. Watt, Manuel testifies, said they should go to his brother John's house. He supposedly added that John's wife 'hates my guts. She made a very damaging statement against me at the time I was arrested for murdering my wife. She made the most damnable statement that any woman could ever make.' Because of this, he wants Manuel to tell her about Tallis breaking into the Martins' house.

Manuel asked to be paid for this special service, so he was given fifteen pounds from the till in one of Watt's shops. They went off in Watt's car, 'a red Wolseley'. The court has already been told that Watt's car was a Vauxhall and that the Renfrew ferryman was in error when he described it as a red Wolseley. Perhaps Manuel is trying to confuse the jury and weaken the defence evidence about the car; perhaps, for once, he is misremembering.

At about midnight, he says, he and Watt went to the Glennifer Bar to await John. The woman behind the bar, says Manuel, was 'a spiritualist and she had been very helpful to Mr Watt over the last year. She had seen all sorts of marvellous things pertaining to what happened in his house on the night of the 17th.' Detail is added to vivid detail: 'A police sergeant came in. He had a few drinks and a talk with Watt.' When John arrived, they bought two bottles of whisky and, because Watt now seemed too drunk to drive, John drove his car while Manuel drove behind in John's van. Back at John's house, Watt was friendly, telling his brother Manuel was not what they had been led to believe and calling him 'chief'. Watt told his brother that Tallis and Hart had intended to raid the Valentes' house, believing the safe contained £5,000, but that they had been misled by seeing the Valente daughter in the Watt house. He kept turning to Manuel for confirmation so he said, 'That is correct.'

Watt, Manuel says, became very drunk, so eventually Manuel drove him to his house at Fourth Street, bringing him out cigarettes and cups of coffee until about 8 or 8.30 a.m., when he was sober enough to drive himself away. He didn't take him inside because: 'If I opened the door and told my mother I was bringing in Willie Watt, I think she would have a fit.' The idea that Bridget might have been afraid of Watt while daily seeing her murderous son is a curious one. He and Watt agreed to meet that evening.

In the early evening, Dowdall and Manuel met again at the Whitehall Restaurant. At this point there occurs yet another dramatic reversal of the story. Manuel claims he told Dowdall that Watt had confessed to murder: 'He told me everything.' That morning, when they were outside the Manuel house, Watt had told him that he had gone to the house to murder his wife, unaware that his sister-in-law was there. He had not intended to kill his daughter, only to tie her up so that she and the crime would not be discovered until the next morning. After the murders, he'd given the gun to Tallis because he did not want it in his car as he drove back to Lochgilphead. However, he had not instructed Tallis to plant it on anyone else.

Dowdall, says Manuel, said he had not heard this version from Watt. Nevertheless, the solicitor was still keen to protect his client, pointing out that Watt could 'sue the Crown for a tremendous amount of money' if someone else was arrested for the murders. The police could not arrest anyone else without admitting they had been wrong to arrest Watt, 'which is what we are after'.

At this point, Manuel says, he asked Dowdall about the story that Tallis and Hart had carried out the killing. Dowdall, he claims, did not directly deny that Watt could have killed the three women, only saying that Watt felt his position terribly, as lots of his friends had dropped him and business contacts had withered away. He mentioned the sum of £5,000 as an inducement to Manuel to support the Tallis and Bowes story. Thus, if Manuel is believed, Dowdall was trying to frame other people for the murders in order to get Watt a huge sum in compensation for wrongful arrest.

At this point, continues Manuel, they were joined by Watt and

Dowdall left. He and Watt went to a pub where Watt kept trying to get him to support the Tallis/Hart story. Both Watt and Dowdall had this version of events 'all word perfect about the names, the times, all the things these people were supposed to get . . . Watt said, "These two men are prepared to swear blind that they sold a gun to Charles Tallis a week before my wife was murdered. I have got these two tied up neatly."' But if Manuel did not do as he was told, the two (according to Manuel's story, it subsequently emerged that these men were Scout O'Neil and Dick Hamilton) would change their story and say they had sold the gun to Manuel, not Tallis. Two nights later, Watt gave Manuel one hundred and fifty pounds in five-pound notes to indicate how he could benefit by cooperating.

Despite all these baffling shifts and turns, Manuel's defence is simple: he did not kill the women, Watt did. Tallis and Hart were involved and Tallis tried to frame him for the crime by hiding the gun in his house. O'Neil and Hamilton's evidence against him can be disregarded because they have been suborned by Watt or Dowdall. Dowdall wanted him to help frame Tallis and Hart so that Watt would appear innocent and get compensation from the Crown. It is all highly ingenious. How convincing it is is another matter.

At this point, late on Monday afternoon, the day's proceedings end, leaving the jury with much to ponder. One wonders if they have managed to follow all the sudden shifts and reversals in the story they have heard.

Tuesday, 27 May, is the 14th day of the trial and everyone is aware that it is reaching its climax. Manuel has now to deal with the next charge, the break-in at the Platts'. He must break the damning link between the gun and the razor, the Platts and the Watts.

The truth of the matter, he says, is that the razor the police took from his house is not the one from the Platts'. It came from Tallis, who had been working for a firm that shared a canteen with Philips. He'd got the razor from someone there and passed it to Manuel between June and August 1956, well before the raid on the Platts'. He explains that if it had been linked to a murder gun, 'it would never have been in my house. I mean, it is just a thing you wouldn't have around if it had that sort of connection.'

Now for the bullet in the mattress. He first heard about this on 3 December 1957, when Dowdall told him a bullet had been fired into bedding in a house in Bothwell, adding that if they could find it, it would more or less establish that William Watt couldn't have fired it. Dowdall's earlier evidence is turned upside down: it was he who had told Manuel about the bullet, not the other way round.

Manuel tells the court that Dowdall explained he did not want to tell the police about the bullet as he would have to reveal his source. On the other hand, if Manuel decided to play ball with Watt, he could tell the police. Dowdall also urged him to question Mrs Bowes about the break-in and the bullet 'because this house is of vital importance . . . we can use it'.

Now Manuel picks up a puzzling weakness in the prosecution case: if a bullet had been fired into the bed, then surely the house's owners 'would see there was a bullet hole in the mattress'.

As for the two rings, well, he does accept that he had denied knowing about them when questioned by the police. This was because he suspected they had come from Fennsbank Avenue, as Tallis had mentioned planning a job there. Honour among thieves, it seems, had prevented him saying anything about them.

He has another point to make about the Watt murders. What the court has been told about how the killer gained entry is misleading. Whoever killed the women must have had a key 'because it looks rather odd that someone would walk up to a house, just walk up to it sort of openly, and smash in the front door and just walk in without waking anyone'. Anyhow, he asserts, whoever had the key, it wasn't him; he had been at home that night and was still asleep in bed when 'this man Tallis came to my house next morning'.

The gloves and camera found at the Manuel house have been securely identified as being stolen from Reverend Houston's house on Christmas Day and this presents him with another problem. He says he could not have stolen them because he was at home watching television at the time the manse was broken into. To support this, he lists all the programmes he watched – detail, more detail. Originally, he says, Dandy McKay had promised to get him a camera but had gone back on the deal. Fortunately, on 27 December, he met three tinkers in a pub and they offered to sell him the camera and threw in the gloves for nothing. He bolsters his account by describing the occasion in detail, even down to the fact that the rear lights of the tinkers' van were not working.

The next accusation concerns Isabelle Cooke. To set the scene, he reads out the full charge against himself, a horrid moment, perhaps a deliberate, relished piece of cruel bravado or perhaps the act of a man who simply has no understanding of how it will affect his listeners.

His defence against this charge is simple: he was not there; he did not do it. At the relevant time, he was watching a film in Glasgow. Earlier that day, his brother had reminded him, 'If you are going into the city this will be your last chance to see that movie,' so he went to see it. The film had a bleakly appropriate title: *These Dangerous Years.*

Finally, there is the Smart case. Smart and he were old acquaintances, he claims. They had known each other since November or December 1953. Smart began building his house in April 1954 and asked Manuel to help him apply to get it connected to the gas supply. In the end, he fitted the connection and then did further work on the inside of the house for Smart. All this is presented with the usual wealth of detail. After that, he says, he and Smart saw each other on numerous occasions and went together to the races. He recalls how they both did well at Brighton, betting at 20 to 1 on Lookout Second, ridden by Manny Mercer in the Hove Mile Handicap.

As so often with Manuel, the details seem impressive but the truth is another matter. After he was executed, the chief constable of Lanarkshire noted that Manuel's claim to have helped Smart 'caused extreme disgust among Smart's neighbours and friends who had assisted Smart in the building of the bungalow'.

A few days before Christmas 1957, he says, their friendship led Smart to ask him for a gun because he was worried about a prowler. After two arrangements to hand it over fell through, Smart finally received it at the Royal Oak on Hogmanay. He was pleased: first he handed over £15 in single notes, then he added more. All the money was in new notes. Smart went off with the Beretta; Manuel went home and stayed there all night. He had no opportunity to kill the Smarts; at all times, he had been with family members or asleep in the bed-chair.

That brings him to the party at the Greenans', where, he says, he played the piano and went to the Woodend Hotel to buy more drink. Again, his malice shows: the Egans have given evidence against him, so now he will claim they broke the licensing laws. When he got to their pub, Francis Egan, he asserts, said to him, 'Well, you will need to come into the kitchen because we are not supposed to sell you the stuff. It is a holiday, it is just like a Sunday.' He freely admits he paid with the money he had got from Smart: 'There was no reason why I should hide the money or anything. It was just straightforward money as far as I was concerned. I couldn't have got it from a better source.' Some of his listeners may think 'I couldn't have got it from a better source' is a singularly callous way to talk about a man he had shot through the head.

But there is more to his story. At the Royal Oak, he says, Smart had given him a house key. He was going away that night but remembered he'd made an appointment for a Mr Brown to call on him on Friday, 3 January. Would Manuel please go there and meet him? He'd leave out a bottle of whisky for Brown. Manuel agreed to do this good deed.

After going to the Greenans', then on to the McCamleys' and the local dance, he escorted a girl home and, at about four or half four in the morning, headed towards his own house. Then he decided that he would go to the Smarts' instead, drink some of the whisky left for Brown and bed down there for the rest of the night.

He let himself in and saw there were three bottles of whisky on the chiffonier and a bottle of sherry. Once again, he reinforces his story with detail: 'I remember the sherry was a sherry I had never seen before. It was called Romano Cabana.' He drank some whisky and then noticed the house was in some disarray; it struck him that perhaps the Smarts had not gone away after all. He offers an excuse for his odd behaviour: 'I had a good drink in me. I wouldn't say I was miraculous drunk but I had a good drink in me.'

He looked in the Smarts' bedroom then went into Michael's. He put on the light and saw someone was lying in bed, confirming his notion that the Smarts were at home after all. He went to leave but, as he was doing so, 'a wee sort of tiger cat bolted in'. He tried to put it out but failed. At this point, something made him go back into the boy's room. He put the light on and 'he just seemed to be sleeping'. Next, he went into the parents' room and put their light on. Then, 'there was no reason to look or listen any further because Mr and Mrs Smart were lying in bed and were dead. They were very dead.'

He now favours the jury with an account of his criminal skills. 'I suddenly realised . . . there would be fingerprints all over the place, so I went back into the bedroom and lying on a sort of dressing table was a pair of gloves . . . I took the gloves and put them on and went into the kitchen and got hold of an apron . . . and went right through the house and anything I touched I rubbed away, any trace of fingerprints on the front door, the vestibule door, the bottle of whisky. I rubbed everything I could have come into contact with. I even rubbed things I might not have come in contact with but I didn't take any chances.'

He went to look again at Michael: 'When you got to the bed and leaned over you could see blood on the wallpaper just on the far side of him and there was blood on the pillow.' There is little doubt that he had seen all this.

In the parents' room, he claims, the gun was lying on Mr Smart's 'chest round about his stomach' and his thumb was through the trigger guard. He saw what had happened: 'I mean it is straightforward. It was staring me in the face. I said, "He has done himself in."' So Manuel posits that Smart killed his family and then shot himself, using a gun Manuel had handed him the previous night.

He began to react. 'The first thing I did was I took the gun away. I grabbed hold of it and took it and there was a smattering of blood on one bit of the gun. I rubbed that off and it got on these gloves I had.' Again, this sounds as if he is recalling what actually happened. The Smarts' bedclothes had been pulled down. He tells the jury, 'They looked awful bare lying there, they looked, I don't know how to describe it because normally you would just leave them, but they looked cold, so I just took the bedclothes and just pulled them up over them.'

'Normally you would just leave them.' An extraordinary remark.

Now he had to get rid of the gun, telling himself, 'If this is found here you never know what will come out of it.' As he prepared to leave, the cat 'was still crying and snarling and messing about. [It] wouldn't leave me.' He went to find milk for it. When he found none (which reinforces the idea that the Smarts had intended to go away), he gave it a saucer of water. Then he decided to feed it. 'I don't know what made me feed the cat. I suppose it was walking in and seeing the people. I just did something.' There were two tins of cat food and one of salmon in the kitchen. He was going to open one of the Kit-E-Kat tins. Then 'I saw the salmon and I thought, "You might as well have that because nobody in here will be eating it."' Another strikingly callous comment.

He put the cat out and left. Manuel tells the court that the garage doors were open, implying that either the car was already gone or someone could have seen the open doors later and stolen it.

He next describes how he returned to Fourth Street and gives a startling insight into how he travelled about by night to commit his crimes: 'I didn't go up the road or up the street or anything, I crossed the road, down into a lane, over into a field, jumped a fence across the main road, over a back garden and up through some fields to my house. About seven or eight minutes it would take.' If the journey took only seven or eight minutes, then he is also, of course, indicating how little time he would have needed on the morning of 1 January to leave his house, kill the Smarts and return home. But by this stage in the trial, his urge to show the court how clever he is has overcome all caution.

He gives another clue as to how he operated. He says he hid the Beretta and the gloves in the park next to his house. It is highly probable that over the years he had hidden other items there, near enough to be reclaimed when wanted but safe from the eyes of his family or any police who searched his house. It only remained for him to dispose of the incriminating gun. Later that morning, he says, he took an old pair of Theresa's gloves, string and some brown paper, wiped off his prints, wrapped the gun inside the gloves and paper and then dropped the parcel into the Clyde.

Now, he says, he entered a period of deep anxiety as he waited for the bodies to be discovered. Perhaps he was in fact looking forward to seeing that he had made headline news. But day after day, nothing happened. 'On the Friday night again, I went and got every newspaper I could find, late editions, early editions and everything, and there was still no mention.'

This could not be allowed to continue. On Saturday evening, he says, he made an anonymous phone call to the Hamilton police. Speaking quickly, he said: 'There are three people dead in a house in Sheepburn Road.' His action was altruistic: 'I mean, you can't just let them lie there for ever, someone would need to get there quick.' But the police, if he did indeed call them, took no action. Finally, on Monday, his brother, who had been working near Sheepburn Road, came home and said three bodies had been discovered. A police report prepared before the trial describes James as a newspaper vendor. One wonders if he yelled the news of his brother's murders at his pitch.

He soon became aware that the police were after him. A few days after the bodies were found, Dandy McKay asked him if he had been questioned about Peter Smart's car, which had been dumped in Florence Street. He saw McKay again on 10 January and was told the police kept mentioning his name and trying to find people who had seen him in Florence Street. When he went to the Woodend Hotel, a waiter told him the police had instructed the Egans to keep any notes he spent; they had already taken away two pound notes he had used to buy drink.

But, Manuel says, he never tried to hide the fact that he had new notes. Contrary to what other witnesses have said, he claims that when Superintendent Brown was searching his house, he told him, 'I have had a lot of banknotes recently,' and did not conceal that he'd spent some of them at the Woodend on 1 January. Later, in the police station, he told Brown he'd had blue notes the numbers of which ran sequentially, although he refused to say who had given them to him. Brown, however, had told him that the money had come from Dandy McKay. He had denied this was so.

At base, his response to all the murder charges is simple: he has been enmeshed in a web of circumstances but he is completely innocent. He did not kill Anne Kneilands, Watt was the killer of his family, he was elsewhere when Isabelle Cooke was killed, Smart murdered his wife and son and then committed suicide.

The confessions remain to be explained away. To extract them, he says, the police bullied him, denied him his rights. Brown refused to let him have a lawyer, saying, 'I am the man in charge of this investigation. I am not a Lanarkshire policeman. You have got these people bamboozled. They can't make an impression on you. You have met your match this time and you are not getting a lawyer.' Manuel claims that he added, 'You twisted that fellow Hendry round your little finger.' Brown also accused him of being responsible for the disappearance of Moira Anderson, a young girl who had vanished from Coatbridge the previous year. To muddy the waters further, he claims Brown also said that Watt had paid him £5,000 to shoot his wife and more money to get him out of jail after he was charged with murdering his family.

The police had been relentless, Manuel tells the court. Initially, Brown and Muncie questioned him for about four hours. When Goodall took over, his approach was different: 'I know all about you, Peter. You are crazy . . . You have definitely killed these people but you don't know you are doing it. You are just going about the country killing people and you have some sort of quirk in your mind that you can, once you have killed somebody, you can shut it out of your mind . . . You are crackers. But we can't understand your motive. The only thing I can say at the moment is you just kill people as a sort of hobby, because some of these things, there is no motive.' With Manuel there is always the question of whether he is lying but some of this has a ring of authenticity. It also shows his curious compulsion, as the trial draws to its climax, to say things that damage his own case.

Goodall, says Manuel, told him Brown would get at him through his family. If he confessed, though, 'If you need treatment, you will get treatment.' Manuel adds, 'Actually, at the time, as far as I was concerned, I was getting the treatment.' Yet again, he fails to sense how such a facetious remark will be received by people who have just heard him accuse Peter Smart of killing his wife and son.

After many more threats against his family by Brown, continues Manuel, he was charged with the Smart murders. He adds resentfully that his clothes were taken away and he was made to wear a big baggy suit and a pair of police boots. Muncie then questioned him from midnight till four or five the next morning, demanding he write a statement. A few hours later, he was taken to court where the proceedings were improperly conducted: 'There were no charges read out, nothing . . . I said, "Excuse me, how about arranging for me to get a lawyer?" And this old character in the middle, he jumped up and he says, "You are not supposed to speak. That will be taken care of outside this court."'

Later that morning, he learned that his father was in Barlinnie, so he asked to see McNeil. When he failed to arrive, he repeated his request. At about 2.30 p.m., McNeil and Goodall came to his cell and, under pressure from them, Manuel tells the court, he agreed to write a statement on condition his father was released. He was warned that release was not a simple matter but assured it would be done. Manuel also asked to see his mother and father. The police agreed to this, so he wrote the first confession, document 140. 'I watched carefully how I worded it. It looked a good statement.' Goodall took this away and then returned, saying it was not enough. He gave Manuel a list of four cases, from Anne Kneilands to Isabelle Cooke, to incorporate into the next statement, document 141. He refused to sign this until he had seen his parents.

When his mother and father were brought to see him, he refused to read out the first statement until he was assured once more that his father would be released. Goodall had told his parents their son was 'crackers', saying, 'He doesn't know he is doing these things,' but he assured them Peter would get treatment. Later, Manuel was taken to Barlinnie, quickly released and driven into the countryside. Here, he claims, the police took him through a pretence of being led by him to Cooke's burial place. They already knew where this was. Goodall and McNeil took him to where her shoes were concealed and then to the place where she was buried.

Back at the police station, he continues, Goodall 'had a sheet of paper and he had all these murders on it, the lot of them, and he had them all written out in order'. He refused to write out a confession based on this text. Brown then threatened to 'fix your family' if he didn't do so. Finally, he agreed 'because at that time it seemed the stupidest sort of thing in the world to write . . . they were full of a lot of details that were absolutely idiotic, about giving policemen lifts in cars outside the Smarts' house and murdering people and burying them in parks.' And so Inspector Cleland was called in and Manuel wrote the third statement.

Now, as he comes to the end of this long account of what he claims had happened, he at last says something that seems heartfelt: 'I know I have given them a terrible life but at no time would I tolerate my family getting into any kind of trouble at all on my account.'

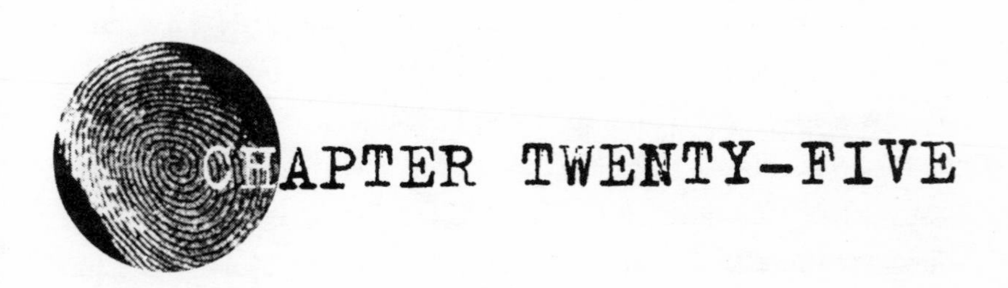

CHAPTER TWENTY-FIVE

The advocate depute rises and proceeds to cast profound doubt on everything Manuel has said. He asks a devastating question: did the police engage in a criminal conspiracy to manufacture evidence against him? Manuel avoids a direct reply: 'I have told the truth about what happened to me.' So were the three statements false statements if they implicated him in murder? 'Yes, they were.'

Manuel's statement that the police knew where Cooke's body was is almost impossible to believe. Gillies asks why, if they had known where the body was, they had kept it secret for 48 hours. Manuel says he cannot answer for the police but 'they would have left the body for a week or a fortnight under the circumstances that they were working if they would have thought they would have got a conviction to it'.

'In order to pin the murder on you, is that the position?'

'Yes.'

So the key question is asked again: does he claim the police engaged in a criminal conspiracy to manufacture evidence against him? 'Yes,

I do.' At this point, Cameron emphasises what this means: does this then amount to a conspiracy to have Manuel murdered? 'That is what it amounts to, My Lord.' This exchange presents the jury with a stark choice: if they believe Manuel, they must accept that the police have conspired to murder him. If they cannot accept that, they can find him guilty on the evidence.

The questioning moves to other matters. Asked about Corrins, Manuel says that the reason he had words with him was not because he'd told the police his face was scratched but because: 'He made a statement to the police that when he went into the hut that morning there was a pair of wellingtons covered in blood and he saw me taking them away.' This is a dreadful error, for it is the first the jury has heard of bloodstained wellingtons. Now he has mentioned them, they may think he was wearing them when chasing and killing Anne Kneilands.

Question after question is answered by a direct denial or by accusing others of lying. He claims the police lied when they claimed he guided them to the General's Bridge, from which he had thrown things belonging to Cooke and Smart. He makes the point that, as two officers recorded his supposed verbal confession in virtually the same words, since they agreed almost exactly with each other, they must have made it up. He denies he told Dowdall about the layout of the furniture in the Watt house or the bullet in the mattress and reiterates that Tallis left the Webley in his house. 'I don't keep guns in the house. I don't keep stolen property in the house.' Yes, he agrees, he did have a gun when the police had searched his home, but it was kept in another house. It was the Beretta used to kill the Smarts.

He cannot explain why Liddell said Manuel had shown him a revolver in the pub. Lafferty's story that he had shot a cow was a lie, motivated by enmity. The dead cow was Lafferty's doing: he and his brother had been stealing electrical cable and the cable had fallen on the cow and electrocuted it. Watt and Dowdall are lying when they claim he told them Tallis had shot the Watt women. Dowdall is lying when he says Manuel made him a sketch of the revolver. 'The guy that drew that can't draw,' he says contemptuously.

They move on to the discovery of Cooke's body and here the absurdities of Manuel's story become apparent. If the police knew where the body was, why did they not take spades and shovels with them? If they knew where it was, why did they have to dig in several places before they located it? He can give no good answer. He denies he made any remark to Brannan about a red herring when they saw the police searching along the River Calder. When the keys to the Smart house were found in the Calder, he claims, it was because they had been planted there by McNeil.

What about the evidence about how he came by the Beretta?

'I understand that the evidence given by Hamilton and Scout O'Neil, you say, was bought by Mr Watt. Is that the position?'

'Yes.'

Manuel says he had possessed the Beretta for two years; anyone saying he had recently got it from McKay is lying, bribed to lie by Watt.

He had not taken Smart's car, nor used it to collect drink for the Greenans' party, nor given PC Smith a lift in it, nor dumped it in Florence Street. He is asked why Smart had asked him to attend to the mysterious Mr Brown if he intended to commit suicide? Here he manages a feeble answer: perhaps he wanted someone to find the bodies. If, as he has claimed, he was given a door key by Smart, what happened to it? He can only answer that somehow he lost it.

If, as he says, the police spent hour after hour threatening him, trying to get him to confess, why did McNeil take so long to come and see him after Manuel asked for him? Possibly, he replies, to 'let me roast for a couple of hours. It is quite normal.'

Manuel's answer to all Gillies' questions is simple: he wrote the three confessions to stop his family being ruined, they were foisted on him by the police, the police and the prosecution witnesses are all lying. The police have conspired to murder him. He is innocent.

But by the end of Gillies' examination, he must feel shaken. This is the first time in his life he has been subject to a prolonged, careful trial and ruthless questioning in which all the inconsistencies and absurdities of his claims are held up and shown to be the fictions that they are. His view of himself is beginning to weaken, cracks are appearing and in the closing hours of the trial he will falter and stumble. His last and greatest chance to save himself from death has slipped through his fingers.

They are near the end. It only remains for the prosecuting counsel and Manuel to make their final speeches and for the judge to direct the jury.

The advocate depute starts. He is already in a strong position. As well as the vast amount of evidence that has been presented against Manuel, the jury has heard him claim that Smart killed his wife and son and then committed suicide.

Gillies begins with the three confessions: the jury can either believe Manuel's account of how he came to write them or they can believe the police's. If they believe the police, he reminds them, the confessions on their own are not enough to convict Manuel; they must be corroborated by other evidence.

In the Anne Kneilands case, Manuel's detailed confession to the killing is supported by the fact that he led the police to where they recovered the piece of angle iron that Professor Allison showed fitted one of the wounds to Kneilands' skull. If they decide he killed Kneilands, the jury will also have to decide if it was Manuel's intention to steal her handbag. If so, that was capital murder.

The law had been changed in 1957 so that the sentence of hanging was restricted to those convicted of murder in pursuit of theft, by shooting or explosion, while resisting arrest or escaping, or the murder of a police or prison officer. It could also be applied to those who had previously been imprisoned for murder in Britain. The killings of the Smarts and Watts were, therefore, automatically capital murders but the status of the crimes against Kneilands and Cooke was less clear-cut.

He reminds them how the Watt murders and the housebreaking at the Martins' and Platts' are tied together. The electric razor and the bullet in the mattress are key matters. Testimony has been given that Manuel obtained a gun shortly before these events, a gun that he showed off in a pub and which he told Lafferty he had used to shoot a cow. There was no evidence that Tallis had this gun but Manuel eventually showed the police where he had dropped it in the Clyde.

Manuel had named Watt as the killer of his family. But Watt had no motive. The evidence of the driver who claimed to have seen him at Loch Lomondside and the ferryman's testimony were weak. The state of Watt's car on the Monday morning showed he had not used it to drive to Glasgow.

Reverend Houston's camera and gloves were found in the Manuel house. Joseph Brannan said that Manuel had told him he had broken into a house in the same area and on the same day and got these sorts of things.

In regard to the Cooke murder, there is Brannan's evidence that Manuel had planned a snatch, the special constable who saw Manuel coming along the railway line and Manuel telling Brannan the police were searching in the wrong place for the girl. And finally, he had taken the police to where she was buried.

The money from the Smarts' house is important. It is hard to accept that Manuel was on close terms with Smart, as he has claimed. The jury has to choose: they can believe his story of how he got the cash or decide he got it by murder and theft. Evidence has indicated that he obtained the Beretta shortly before the deaths and had been driving Smart's car afterwards.

As Gillies ends, he and Sutherland must believe their case is very strong. The evidence against Manuel is overwhelming, and time after time he has produced explanations that are almost impossible to believe. The longer he has been examined, the more his claims have been demonstrated to be either highly unlikely or simply incredible.

And, of course, a verdict of guilty in only one capital murder will bring the death penalty.

When Manuel rises to make his final speech, he has already been defending himself for many hours. He has had only his excellent memory and his supreme inventiveness to rely upon and the strain is becoming apparent. As he concludes his defence, he begins to ramble and has to be reminded by the judge to cover particular matters.

He makes a few good points at the start, picking out weaknesses in the case against him. He denies that the scratches on his face were made by Anne Kneilands and asks why her fingernails were not examined for traces of skin. At the time, the police failed to get any evidence against him; this shows he is innocent.

The confessions were not made voluntarily; they were forced out of him.

He did not break into the Platts'. The fact that the son's scientific instruments were stolen yet valuables left surely suggests that the thief was interested in such things: Manuel is not.

Tallis is not to be trusted. He claimed he was shown the two rings only briefly but he was able to describe them in detail. He said he read about them in the newspapers on 17 September, yet Miss Martin said she did not tell reporters about them until some days later. Tallis must therefore be lying. (In fact, Miss Martin has misremembered.)

If he did not break into the Martins', says Manuel, then he did not break into the Watts' and, in any case, why should he kill the Watts? He had no motive. He did not tell Dowdall about the inside of the house; it was the solicitor who told him. The police had investigated him at the time and then they arrested Watt. The evidence that Watt had driven to Glasgow should be believed. The three people who claimed he had bought the Webley were not to be trusted. One of them, O'Neil, had been given a suit and money by Watt.

He did not break into the Houstons' house. He was at home watching television when the theft occurred. He had bought the camera and gloves from tinkers.

He was at the cinema when Cooke was killed. If he had killed her, he would have buried her clothes and possessions with her, not spread them across the landscape.

Witnesses who said he had taken Smart's car have given contradictory evidence. He would have been stupid to take it. The notes it is claimed he spent at the Woodend Hotel on 1 January have not been produced and he would in any case have been a fool to throw stolen money about there, where he was so well known. He had also had five-pound notes. These could not have come from the Smarts'. (In fact, there is no reason to think that Smart might not also have had some five-pound notes when he was killed.)

As for the confessions, well, he was not in the habit of confessing to the police. He had done so only because of threats to harm his family. Throughout Manuel's speech to the jury, Ronald Sutherland watched their reactions intensely. He would recall that he 'had never seen 15 more stony-faced individuals' in his life.

Now it is the judge's turn. The drama is drawing to its close. Manuel watches from the dock, his eyes occasionally cast down, as Cameron begins to address the jury. His fate is almost decided. Now the judge will attempt to sum up the case for and against him.

Cameron tells the jury that Manuel 'has presented his own case with a skill that is quite remarkable' and warns them they must be especially careful in considering the evidence because of this. He explains how they must reach their decisions: each case must be decided on the facts alone and the Crown must prove each charge beyond reasonable doubt. All the charges must be corroborated; a confession or the evidence of a single witness is not enough. The jury must consider each charge separately: a finding of guilt in one charge must not influence their verdicts on the other charges.

One matter must be dealt with immediately: Manuel's mental state. The jury may wonder if he is insane. But, he instructs them, the question of insanity is of no relevance at all here. No defence of insanity has been put forward and therefore the jury 'cannot and will not' consider the matter. But, he continues, there is still the possibility that Manuel suffered from diminished responsibility. Again, however, no evidence has been offered to support this view: no doctor has been produced to suggest it, nor have his parents or sister given any indication that they believed this was the case. And, he reminds the jury, they have seen Manuel for themselves. Thus, the question of Manuel's mental state is dismissed as something that need not concern the jury. Cameron ends by characterising his view of Manuel with the damning remark: 'A man may be very bad without being mad or near mad.'

He turns next to the confessions. The jury have to decide if they believe them. If they do, then they contain important evidence. He reads out key sections to make his point. The basic question is how the confessions came to be made. Manuel has claimed one thing, the police another. The judge puts the matter in the starkest of terms: if the jury believes Manuel's version, they are accepting that the police conspired to have him hanged. If that is the case, the three documents 'are the fruit of a careful, deliberate and indeed devilish conspiracy to provide a solution to unsolved crimes and to bring an innocent man on a charge of murder'.

As there is a direct conflict between the police's account of events and the Manuels', 'There is deliberate lying. There is no escape from that.' Can Samuel Manuel's evidence be believed? He has supported his son's story and testified that the electric razor came from Tallis and had been in the house well before the theft at the Platts'. In addition, he has said he would have known if his son had left the house at the time of the Smart murders and that he had not done so. 'So you see his credibility may be of vital importance.' Can he be believed? The implicit suggestion is that he cannot.

On the other hand, he tells them, there are strong reasons to accept the police account of how the confessions came to be made. Manuel may have decided to confess because he had become convinced the game was up. At his house, Manuel had said the police could not remove him because they hadn't found anything yet. The 'yet' implied that there were incriminating things to be found. On the afternoon of his arrest, the Egans told the police that Manuel had given them banknotes that were consecutively numbered, McKay said he'd sold him a Beretta and Special Constable MacFarlane had identified him at the scene of one of the crimes.

Cameron moves on to the individual charges. The first is the murder of Anne Kneilands. He instructs the jury to find Manuel not guilty. Although he has confessed to the crime, there is no corroboration. 'There is not one single iota of evidence that would positively link them [the pieces of iron gathered by the police] with the injuries inflicted upon Anne Kneilands.' Professor Allison's careful demonstration of how one of the pieces of angle iron fitted into the injuries in the victim's skull has been discounted. They must return a not guilty verdict.

The next charge, the theft from the Platts, he reminds them, is important because the weapon used to kill the Watts was fired into the Platts' mattress. Watt had been away at that time and nobody had suggested he had left Cairnbaan and returned at the time of the break-in. However, Manuel had told Watt about the bullet in early December 1957, yet Mrs Platt had not discovered it until near the end of that year. How did Manuel know about it?

Manuel claimed it was Tallis who told him about the bullet. He and his parents also said that the electric razor in their house came from Tallis and that it was there before the Platt break-in. Cameron reminds the jury that Samuel 'later got himself into trouble through not being frank about the gloves'. In other words, his evidence on this matter needs to be treated with considerable scepticism. Conversely, Geoffrey Platt had identified the razor as his and that identification was important.

In his special defence in the Martin case, Manuel had named Tallis and Mrs Bowes as the perpetrators. They denied their involvement. Was it likely they would have gone out to steal on the day after Allan

Bowes' wedding? Tallis had said Manuel had showed him the rings immediately after the break-in and claimed he had learned from a newspaper that they probably came from the Martins'. Manuel had pointed out that Miss Martin had said she did not discover they were missing until some days later.

The Watt murders were horrible. The jury must ask themselves if a husband and father would do such a thing. There were witnesses from Lochgilphead who described Watt's distress on learning of the deaths. Sergeant Mitchell, on the other hand, said he did not appear upset. What of the two people who had identified Watt on the road to Glasgow? Cameron indicates that he does not consider their evidence can be relied upon.

He summarises Manuel's version of how the Watt killings occurred and casts doubt on it. Why would Watt kill his family and then hand the gun to Tallis? 'What an extraordinary coincidence that he [Watt] should, of all people, have made an arrangement with Charles Tallis . . . as a means of getting rid of what? The thing that could hang him, the revolver.' Tallis, he reminds them, is a man who is so untrustworthy that Samuel Manuel wouldn't buy a watch from him. And if Manuel is believed, what does Tallis do with this gun once Watt has handed it to him? He hides it in a table in the Manuel house and tips off the police. 'You may have difficulty in accepting that sequence of events,' he tells the jury.

Manuel has claimed he had no motive for killing the Watts. But perhaps, the judge suggests, the apparently motiveless murders might be explained by his story that the intruder's aim was to get money that was believed to be in the Valentes' safe.

All in all, he considers, the Crown's case is formidable. Manuel has displayed a considerable amount of knowledge of the crime and of the interior of the Watt house. In prison, he revealed a great many details to Dowdall and even drew the revolver used in the murders. Later, he told Watt all about his house and other relevant matters.

The prosecution had produced testimony to show that Manuel had obtained the gun used in the murders before the break-in at the Platts'. There was O'Neil's and Hamilton's evidence about how Manuel had come by the gun. Could they be trusted? Manuel has claimed Watt suborned them to tell their tale and Watt has admitted giving O'Neil a suit and a pound. 'It may very well be that O'Neil is of such a type that his evidence can be purchased for sixpence, far less than a one-pound note and a suit,' is Cameron's crushing comment. Yet if these two witnesses are dubious characters, there is the evidence of Manuel showing off the gun in the Crook Inn, telling Lafferty that he had shot a cow, drawing the same sort of gun for Dowdall and showing the police where he had thrown it into the Clyde.

Manuel's story of the murders changed, Cameron reminds the jury. He first claimed Tallis, Bowes and Hart were the killers but has since altered his story to accuse Watt.

He turns to the theft from Reverend Houston's house. According to Brannan, Manuel told him he had stolen a camera and gloves from a manse. They have to decide if Brannan's evidence can be trusted. When he saw Brannan in Barlinnie, Manuel was certainly eager to learn what Brannan had told the police about it. That might suggest Brannan was telling the truth. As for Manuel's story that he'd bought the camera and gloves from tinkers in a pub, well . . . 'One thing I would say to you: it is quite obvious that old Manuel told lies about this; if the police are correct he told lies about the camera.'

Manuel had initially admitted in writing that he murdered Isabelle Cooke. The jury had to accept or reject that confession. If they accepted it, it was supported by strong corroborative evidence. According to the police, Manuel had shown them where he had concealed three of Cooke's shoes. He had also led them, in the dark, to the place where she was buried, saying, 'I think I am standing on her.' He had warned them of an uncompleted grave nearby. If they believed that evidence, it proved his involvement in the girl's murder. Brannan had stated that Manuel intended to carry out a snatch. That might lead the jury to conclude that Cooke could have been killed during an attempt to steal her handbag; the crime then became capital murder. He suggests this might be going too far, that a simple murder verdict might be safer.

He reverts to the question of Manuel's mental state at the time. Was he in full possession of his faculties? 'Where is there a shred of evidence to suggest that on 28 December 1957 he was suffering from any form of mental disease whatever?'

The final charges concern the murders of the Smarts and thefts from them that made the crimes capital murders. Manuel admitted that he had been in the Smart house and that he had the Beretta and had thrown it into the Clyde. There was no doubt he had money that came from the Smarts. He had given his own explanation for having it.

Cameron brings out the absurdities and weak points in Manuel's defence. Samuel and James Manuel have provided him with an alibi but both, of course, are close relatives. James's evidence has lacked a key element: he did not testify that his father was awake from 5.45 to 6.30 a.m., as Samuel had claimed. And how can they remember with such accuracy events that took place several months ago? It would only take Manuel a matter of five to ten minutes to reach the Smart house from his own. A slight difference in the timing of the murders would therefore destroy the alibi.

He expresses doubt that Smart and Manuel were friends and went to horse races together, as Manuel has claimed. Manuel has said that he handed over the Beretta to Smart and was given the new pound notes in return. But Smart was dead and could not give his account of the supposed transaction. Samuel and McQuade had supported Manuel's story. Cameron comments acidly on his view of the reliability of McQuade: his 'appearance, demeanour and testimony may be a very ample certificate of his character'.

Then there is the claim that Smart, as well as buying the gun from

Manuel using new notes, also asked him to look after 'Mr Brown' and gave him the keys to his house. But if Manuel had a key to the front door, why were papers and post piled up behind it? He suggests the jury may find this aspect of the story hard to accept. It was also implied that someone otherwise unconnected with the murders stole Smart's car and later dumped it in Florence Street: does that sound convincing? The details in Manuel's confession of what was in the house – the biscuits, wallet, jacket, etc. – fitted with what was found there by the police. Brannan has said that Manuel mentioned he had not known an A30 could go so fast. The Egans had said he had spent £8 17s 6d on drink.

There is no dispute about whether the Smarts were shot with the Beretta Manuel has admitted he possessed on 31 December and later threw into the Clyde. Does the jury believe Manuel had arranged to meet the mysterious Mr Brown, who has never been found? He reminds them that the gun and the car were found where Manuel said he had dumped them.

The jury retires. After two hours and twenty minutes, they return. Outside, a crowd of over a thousand people awaits their verdict; inside, almost ninety reporters are poised to rush the story to their papers and news agencies.

The male foreman stands and reads out their verdict on each of the counts. They unanimously find Manuel guilty of capital murder in the cases of the Watts and the Smarts, guilty of the non-capital murder of Isabelle Cooke and, as the judge instructed them, not guilty of the murder of Anne Kneilands. By a majority verdict they find him not guilty of the break-in at the Houstons' and return a not proven verdict. They return guilty verdicts in the cases of the break-ins at the Platts' and the Martins' and find him guilty of stealing Smart's car.

The black tricorn hat is placed on Cameron's head and he begins to pronounce the sentence.

The crowd outside quickly hears the news and it is passed around the city from mouth to mouth. The Saltmarket, one of the main thoroughfares, is blocked by people discussing the verdict, and men and women jump off buses to find out what has been decided.

James telephones the verdict to Theresa. Their parents have been hidden away in an Argyll hotel by the *Empire News.* A reporter from the paper tells them of the verdicts. At least one newspaper has been so certain of what the jury will decide that it has already set everything up in type.

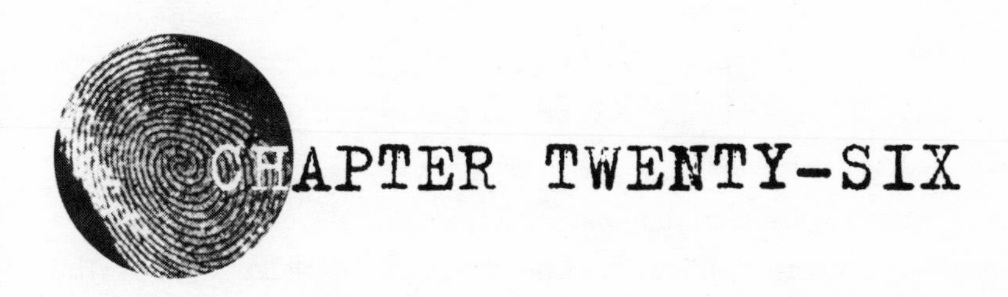

CHAPTER TWENTY-SIX

'The sentence of this court is that you be taken from this place to the prison of Barlinnie, Glasgow, therein to be detained until the 19th day of June next and upon that day, in the said prison of Barlinnie, Glasgow, and between the hours of eight and ten o'clock, you suffer death by hanging, which is pronounced for doom.'

One newspaper reported that as soon as Lord Cameron had finished speaking:

> The tiny group in the dock erupted into motion. A policeman swept back the dock gate . . . another lifted the folding seat. Manuel spun round on his heels – and, before more than a handful of people in the nearest seats had a chance to see his face – ran down the sixteen stairs to the basement cell.

The high public drama of the trial was ended, the spotlight turned off. Manuel would never again be free, never again have a public audience for his fantasies and lies. But even in the condemned cell, he could make his plans and manipulate those around him.

He was hurried straight from the court to the special cell, ready in Barlinnie. This, made by combining three ordinary cells, contained a bed, a table and chairs for him and the prison officers who would keep watch over him. It was provided with a radio and a cupboard and equipped with washing facilities and a toilet. Books, playing cards and dominoes were supplied, palliatives against the grimness of his situation. He was to spend most of the rest of his life in this cell, allowed to leave it only to see carefully checked visitors, go to hospital or religious services, attend his appeal and, finally, to be hanged.

The execution chamber was directly across the corridor, adapted from an ordinary cell and the one directly beneath. A beam for the rope and noose had been fixed into the upper cell and a hole cut in its floor for the trapdoor through which Manuel would hurtle. He was fully aware that the place where he was due to hang in four weeks' time was only a few paces away, a constant reminder to him, if one were needed, of his status as a condemned man.

The police and judicial authorities were determined that Manuel should not escape justice. From the moment he entered the cell until the moment of his death, he was under constant observation. Teams of three warders, each working an eight-hour shift, were with him night and day. They watched over him, chatted with him, listened to his tales, played cards and dominoes with him and, most importantly, they were supposed to write down anything of significance that transpired. The book in which they recorded their observations survives. In accordance with standard prison nomenclature, it bears the chilling title 'Death Watch Journal'.

Now that Manuel was condemned to death, one crucial task faced the prison authorities: they had to keep him alive until the hour fixed for his execution. If he was to be hanged – and at this point there was still a slight possibility that he could appeal successfully or, if that failed, a still more remote chance that he might be reprieved – it was essential for him to survive fit and well until the time appointed by Lord Cameron. Then and only then could he be killed according to the proper process of law.

All the prison staff – and his fellow prisoners – knew this. The officers' vigilance was made even greater by the fright caused by stories of a plot to poison Manuel. He was the most notorious killer the prison had ever held. Heads would roll if anything went wrong. Everyone involved had to make absolutely sure that he came to no harm, either by his own hand or someone else's. Dr Anderson, the medical officer, believed his main duty at this time was to see nothing bad happened to Manuel – that is, until the moment of his execution.

On the face of it, this should not have been a difficult task. In his cell, Manuel was constantly supervised by enough men to overpower him. If more were needed, they would rush to the cell in response to the alarm bell. His food was checked, he was made to undergo regular medical examinations, even his bowel movements and urination were watched and recorded. All visits were supervised and access to the prisoner was strictly controlled. And, of course, there was virtually no way he could escape from his cell in the high-security prison. Manuel, however, was making plans.

Things started smoothly. The first entry in the death watch journal is dated 29 May, in the evening immediately after his trial. It states: '9.5 p.m. [*sic*] Prisoner listened to the news. Heard verdict [that is, of his own trial]; then continued to read. Quite cheerful.'

The trial was inevitably at the forefront of Manuel's mind and he had strong views on how it had been conducted. That evening, it was also noted that:

> [He] talked occasionally about the summing up of case. He considered that Lord Cameron had given him a raw deal, in considering Anne Kneiland [*sic*] case independently. He

> read and talked alternately till 11.10 p.m. He then went to sleep and appeared to sleep soundly thro' the night.

No doubt to the relief of those watching over him, Manuel appeared to settle into a routine. To some extent, he was prepared; after all, he had been locked up for most of his life since the age of 12. In his first days in the condemned cell, he was described by his watchers sleeping soundly, listening to the radio and especially to pop music on Radio Luxembourg (the officers noted he had 'a good knowledge of the current lists and artists'), playing cards, doing crosswords, eating most of the food brought to his cell and being taken to see his parents in the deputy governor's room. When Manuel saw his parents for the first time, he complained that the judge had not allowed him to say anything after sentence was passed. 'Perhaps he thought you'd said enough,' was his mother's perceptive comment. He was also called on by Father Smith, the priest who visited the prison. His mother had begged Father Smith to try to persuade her son to confess his sins. The priest spent many hours with him but found him intractable. He was with him at the end.

In those early days, Manuel was regularly reported to be 'cheerful' or 'quite cheerful'. Strange, perhaps, for a man a few weeks away from death, but then before the trial he had also seemed totally insulated from the harsh reality of his situation. Did he manage to blank things out? Was his mind still filled with excitement about all the attention he had received? Or did he think he could escape hanging? We can only guess; the brief entries give no clue as to what was going on in his mind.

Whatever Manuel's feelings about his scheduled execution, there was a temporary respite. He had lodged an appeal, so his hanging was postponed until the Appeal Court made its decision. This may well have contributed to his cheerfulness. Meanwhile, to help pass the time, he smoked numerous cigarettes and read books from the prison library. Not that everything he was given to read was to his taste. He complained to the authorities, 'I don't know why I am being given so many books about the sea, they must think I was a sailor. I prefer books about women.' The first part might be taken as a joke; the second is chilling. Every few days, Governor Anderson and Father Smith paid visits. The trial still occupied Manuel's thoughts and he continued to speak about it.

Nor was he completely isolated from the outside world. Apart from the radio and visits from his family and friends, he was also allowed to receive mail, though he complained he was not given newspapers, which he described as his 'favourite reading matter'. They were full of stories about him; of course he wanted to see them. The ban was relaxed and the *Glasgow Herald* delivered daily.

The entries in the journal were written by the prison officers with a brevity and blandness that excludes almost any sense of how they regarded their charge. Yet sometimes, suddenly, one gets a clear sight of Manuel, the fantasist, the boastful liar, the self-vaunting crook, the strutting, cocky little man who always strove to impress people with his superiority: 'Prisoner cheerful and spoke of his many experiences during the war'; 'Manuel spoke a lot about his exploits and experiences with the US Army'. These were his old fantasies, of serving in the US forces, of being an American, of having led a heroic life. 'He talked freely about his trade and visits to America and Majorca.' All fantasy, all lies, all unbelievable – and all typical of Manuel.

How did the officers receive all this? Did he fool them? Were their entries written tongue in cheek, with a sense of irony? After all, they had a good idea of his criminal record and some of them had served at Peterhead when he was imprisoned there. They must have known he was a habitual, unstoppable liar. But, one assumes, they listened quietly to his tales and passed no comment. There is a common Glasgow expression, 'Aye, right,' that uses two positives to create a negative expressing disbelief. Perhaps, as they listened to his stories, they silently repeated, 'Aye, right,' to themselves.

Letting Manuel tell these tall stories may have helped keep him from brooding on other matters and perhaps it helps to account for the curious cheerfulness that was noted with such regularity. On 18 June, for example, the record states: 'Prisoner in very good humour.' Perhaps it came as no surprise to his watchers that, once again, he was telling them about 'his travels abroad'. Some fabulists appreciate an audience for their inventions. Manuel now had a captive one, men who were almost as much his prisoners as he was theirs. Cunning Manuel, clever Manuel.

For the whole of this period, the picture sketched – and regrettably only the bare outlines are drawn in the brief entries in the journal – is of Manuel calm and cheerful, passing his time quietly but without the slightest hint that he was able, or willing, to think about his crimes or his impending fate. His hours are spent talking, sketching, playing cards, reading and smoking heavily. Once he attends a church service. He sees some of his family again in the deputy governor's room; it is not recorded what they talked about.

There are, of course, a few minor things that don't go too well with him: on one occasion he refuses to be shaved and it is clear that he has developed a strong dislike of the prison soup. Well, one can't have everything in such circumstances. Usually, however, he is recorded to be sleeping well. He is often still asleep at six in the morning when the shifts change over.

Then, on Friday, 20 June, within a few hours, there are dramatic changes. One way or another, Manuel seems to be slipping away from the trap in which the authorities believe they have captured him.

It is the early afternoon and he is lying on his bed; suddenly, one of the prison officers notices that he is frothing at the mouth and appears to be only partly conscious. The medical officer is called and arrives seven minutes later. The vicinity of the cell is cleared of other prisoners and Manuel is immediately removed to the prison hospital. There the contents of his stomach are pumped out, although he tries to resist this. The medical officer's immediate suspicion is that the prisoner has swallowed soap and is faking some sort of attack. But there is also the frightening possibility that he has somehow managed to poison himself. His stomach contents are sent to be analysed. He is taken back to his cell. He was due to have seen his legal team later that afternoon to discuss his appeal, which is set to start on the following Tuesday. The prison records state that Ferns and Mr R.H. McDonald, the QC who had been provided for him, could not see him because he was 'in a dazed condition caused by his own actions'.

The sudden change in Manuel's behaviour sets off a frantic burst of activity among the authorities. The Scottish Prison Service and the Scottish Home Department are quickly alerted by the governor. Alarm bells begin to ring. Everyone is horribly aware of the enormous public interest in Manuel. A thing like this could cause them a massive amount of trouble. So, at 6 p.m., a press statement is produced. It outlines what has happened: the 'slight' frothing at the mouth, the treatment by the medical officer, after which 'he recovered'. It stresses that, despite this incident: 'While in prison he has been eating well and his general health has been good.'

Consciously or unconsciously, Manuel has put himself in a position where he is able to manipulate those responsible for his custody. He can make them rush around, worry about him, fear recriminations from the public and those higher up in government service simply by appearing to be in some sort of daze, even just by lying on his bed and doing absolutely nothing. Cunning Manuel, clever Manuel.

If the authorities hope this initial brief incident will be the end of the matter, they are quickly disappointed. By early that evening, it becomes clear that a profound change has started to come over the prisoner. Manuel, who had previously been reported to be so talkative, so cheerful, so calm, now begins to withdraw into himself. From this point on, he will show no response when addressed; he will be impassive, remote. Most striking of all, from this point on the usually loquacious Manuel cannot or will not speak. Manuel silent: a previously unknown phenomenon.

The first definite indication of this disturbing new pattern of behaviour comes just before seven o'clock. When he is informed that his mother and father have arrived to see him, a visit he requested a few days earlier, 'he would not speak'. The officers in the cell again tell him that his parents are waiting to see him but still he 'would not speak' although, it is noted, 'he was able to sit up without assistance'. He does not go to see them.

Is this all an act or is he genuinely disturbed? Has he suddenly understood the horrors of his deeds and the almost inevitable terror to come? Is he withdrawing into himself to escape a reality that is too appalling to face? Or is he faking, trying to find a way to escape the noose?

To investigate the matter, new medical examinations and checks are quickly initiated. At ten past eight, he is examined again by the medical officer and forty minutes later two officers take his pulse and his temperature. These sorts of tests will be repeated regularly over the coming weeks. Although it is clear that prison staff strongly suspect he is faking, they must nevertheless give him their most careful attention – and be able to prove they have done so in case there is an inquiry later.

There are a few slight indications that Manuel is not completely out of things. A little later that evening, he accepts a proffered cigarette. (Puzzlingly, it is noted that he then sat up in bed and 'put on his underpants'. What on earth was he wearing up to that moment? Pyjamas? Or was he naked?) Accepting cigarettes is to be his only regular response for the next 18 days. Yet even this has its abnormal aspect: he smokes with his fingers outstretched and the lighted end held towards his palm. Officers have to light his cigarettes and remove the burning stubs from between his fingers to prevent him harming himself.

That night it is observed, for the first time, that he seems very restless in his sleep. Something has definitely changed. From this point onwards, Manuel's behaviour, as recorded by the death cell officers, becomes more and more strange. We give a few examples. He ignores a telegram brought to the cell: 'Prisoner took no notice and refused to read same.' 'Prisoner was sitting up in bed. He slapped the bed in jerky movements at the same time emitting slight groans. His head dropped on chest, cigarette had to be removed from his hand by Officer Joiner.' 'Prisoner started jerking back and forth holding his stomach and wimpering [*sic*]. Actions became more violent and struck his head against the wall.' The officers on duty ring their alarm bell for assistance and two more arrive to provide support. 'Prisoner was sitting on edge of bed. He looked under bed occasionally and was shaking arms and head about.'

There is an immediate legal problem: the change in Manuel's behaviour begins on the Friday afternoon and his appeal is due to start on the following Tuesday. Is he fit to attend it? If he isn't, can it legally go ahead without him? Manuel is visited by Ferns on Saturday and by McDonald on Sunday, wishing to discuss his appeal. He mutely refuses to see them.

The authorities are deeply concerned. Urgent phone calls are made, press releases prepared and memos carefully written. It is considered imperative that Manuel is examined yet again by psychiatrists.

It is arranged for two psychiatrists and Dr Anderson to examine him on the Monday afternoon. Ferns is told he can organise an examination by an independent doctor if he wishes. After seeing Manuel, the three doctors advise that they believe he is fit to attend the appeal, although, they say, 'it would be unfortunate if he did attend the public hearing because of his appearance'. They give their interpretation of what has happened to him: his behaviour 'is indicative of a hysterical reaction to his present situation'.

On the Tuesday, Manuel goes under escort to Edinburgh for the first day of his appeal. He is advised by McDonald not to enter the court, so he sits silently in a back room. A press photograph shows him tie-less and dishevelled, looking far from the smart, almost dandyish figure he has always tried to present in the past.

The next morning, he is asked three times if he wishes to attend the second day of his appeal. He makes no response and so he is kept in his cell. His absence from this key hearing again causes some disquiet to the authorities. McDonald argues the case in his absence.

The appeal goes catastrophically; the three judges reject all his counsel's arguments without so much as retiring to consider them. The death sentence will stand. The warrant is signed. Manuel is to hang on Friday, 11 July.

Often there is a keenly sceptical tone to the prison officers' brief notes on his behaviour. After all, they were experienced (perhaps 'hardened' would be a better word) officers who knew a great deal about Manuel and his crimes. One of them notes, 'I am not sure if Prisoner heard the rejection of Appeal on the wireless as it was toned [*sic*] down at the time. A few minutes later Prisoner sat up and started pulling his usual funny faces.' A few hours later: 'Prisoner quiet during the evening not so much acting as usual.'

Careful checks on Manuel's health continue. From time to time, some of his urine is sent for analysis. His mental state remains the main concern. Not only is he still withdrawn but he walks in a curious, shambling, uncoordinated way. He sits on his bed cross-legged; his limbs and face twitch.

On 26 June, the day after he has been told of the failure of his appeal, having apparently slept well, Manuel still will not talk, although those watching him think he seems more settled and appears thoughtful. Perhaps this thoughtfulness is caused by the appeal decision – that is, if he has grasped it. He refuses to read his mail and 'did not talk at any time and is always acting in the same strange way'.

The same day, there is an examination arranged by the Medical Commissioners of the General Board of Control for Scotland. This is done thoroughly: their two experts, doctors Craigie and Mill, scrutinise the records of his previous offences and the times he has spent in detention, going back to his first years in approved schools, and study past medical and psychiatric reports. They interview the governor, Father Smith and six prison officers 'who have some special knowledge of Manuel's character and behaviour both in Barlinnie and Peterhead'. They also scrutinise the death watch journal.

Two prison officers who served at Peterhead describe to them Manuel's unstable and aggressive behaviour there. One says he had frequent temper tantrums and would smash everything within reach; the other recounts that he would threaten and assault prison officers and smash crockery and windows. Father Smith, on the other hand, points out a striking contrast between what Manuel has done and how he can appear to those who do not know about him. He says that if he had not been aware of Manuel's criminal record, he would have considered him 'a nice lad who could conduct himself well in any company'. Now, however, he has changed. The doctors report: 'Father Smith said that to him Manuel now looked the typical picture of a madman.'

The two psychiatrists try to interview Manuel, telling him why they are there. He shows no reaction and remains mute. After 30 minutes, they feel they are doing no good and leave.

The question is this: is Manuel genuinely mentally ill? If he is, then perhaps he should not be executed. The verdict of the two experts is that 'his symptoms and the nature of their origin and onset do not conform to any recognisable or accepted form of mental illness' and that the symptoms 'have been more consciously than subconsciously developed'. In other words, he is probably faking. They conclude, 'We do not believe he is insane at the present time.' And if he is not insane, he can be hanged.

They also offer an explanation of why Manuel's behaviour changed so suddenly. Manuel, they think, had formerly seen himself as 'an attractive and clever personality . . . [he] came to have an exaggerated idea of his abilities and an overweening vanity. He courted the limelight and his ruthless egotism reacted badly and often violently to frustration and authority.' However, 'His morbidly inflated "Ego" was built upon a personality which was fundamentally inadequate.' Therefore it was perhaps to be expected that he might crumble once he took in the fact that he had been sentenced to die. This is a convincing account of Manuel's personality and the likely reaction once his lies and invention could no longer save him.

One distressing aspect of this withdrawal by Manuel is the fact that when members of his family visit him, he takes absolutely no notice of them. Here they are, coming to see him, aware that he is soon to hang unless a reprieve is granted, and he seems not to know them, will not talk to them. For them, it must have heaped misery upon misery to an almost unbearable level.

At first when Manuel began to withdraw, his family were kept away from him. Initially, his mother was told he was not in a fit state to see people. For several days, she telephoned daily only to be told that he did not wish to have visitors. Finally, the governor suggested that she should write to her son appealing to him to see her. He promised her letter would be read to him. When this was done, Manuel showed no reaction. Eventually, the authorities decided that unless he expressed a definite refusal, by word or gesture, not to see his family, they should be permitted to visit.

The first visit under this regime took place on 29 June. It must have been a ghastly experience for his mother, because, according to a medical report written shortly afterwards, Manuel appeared not to know who she was 'and her efforts to secure recognition or any other verbal response failed'. Mrs Manuel became incensed. She slapped her son's face, pulled his hair and said that 'he couldn't fool her'. He made no response. Interestingly, the compilers of the report note that pulling his hair usually aroused his anger. It is impossible not to feel a terrible sadness for Bridget in such a situation.

She asks if she can come again with his sister, 'the person with which Manuel perhaps has the closest link', and this is agreed to. The result, when his sister eventually sees him, is the same. On the day his mother visits, Manuel wets his bed. Later, while he is being shaved, he speaks for the first time in nine days. He says, 'Fuck the bull.' That is it, nothing more. After that, he throws his clothes about, punches the bed, moans and only quietens down when extra officers arrive.

The authorities wish to be doubly certain about his mental state and so yet another examination is ordered. It takes place on 30 June. This time, Dr Angus MacNiven, who has already interviewed him five times, is one of those consulted. He, Craigie and Mill are with Manuel for 15 minutes. Once again, his lack of response prevents any communication.

In their report, doctors Craigie and Mill mention two incidents that have helped convince them that 'the symptoms that he is at present displaying are assumed and consciously motivated'. One is that when a prison officer was shaving him, he said to Manuel, 'You know who I am anyway,' and Manuel smiled and called him by his obscene prison nickname. Another was Mrs Manuel telling her son that he couldn't fool her, which was reported to them by Father Smith.

Dr MacNiven submits a separate report. Whereas he had previously considered that Manuel showed some psychopathic attributes, now he concludes that he is definitely a psychopath. However, he believes that this does not bring him into the area of diminished responsibility as the law defines it. He concludes that 'the probability is that his abnormal behaviour is deliberately assumed and that it is not a manifestation of insanity' and that 'in my opinion, the accused is not at the present time insane'. MacNiven's reports are careful and balanced and he is at pains to point out the great difficulties and areas of uncertainty in such diagnoses. Later, he will refuse a fee for his services; it is clear he is moved, perhaps even troubled, by the case.

If Manuel is not insane he can, as the law stands, be hanged. But the recent Royal Commission on Capital Punishment has drawn attention to the problem of psychopaths who kill. In some cases, it is suggested, a reprieve might be considered. No legislation on this matter has yet been proposed but the issue has been raised and it has to be considered. The Permanent Secretary at the Scottish Home Department, Sir William Murrie, does so in summarising the situation for the Secretary of State. He concludes: 'Though he is probably a psychopathic personality, this is not of a degree sufficient to justify a reprieve, even taking into account the views of the Royal Commission on Capital Punishment.'

Eventually, the prison authorities receive the analyst's report on the material pumped from Manuel's stomach at the very start of this episode. It 'did not contain soap, disinfectants, barbituric or acidic drugs'. Perhaps Manuel really is genuinely ill? The deputy governor clearly does not think so. He writes: 'Manuel continues to act the goat and is keeping up the appearance that he is oblivious to all that is being said and done around him.'

In the death cell, things get worse: 'Prisoner roused, refused to put his clothes on, was aggressive, moody and violent at times. He twitched his body and made absurd noises. Eventually allowed us to put on his trousers, vest and socks.' He was medically examined again. At least he did speak once more. When he got his dinner, he said, 'Chips.' In his sleep, he was 'puffing and blowing'.

He again sees his mother and father. They are together for 25 minutes but he does not speak or show any sign of recognising them. In the cell, his silence is maintained, though it is noted that 'his facial and bodily contortions were not quite so frequent as yesterday'. Is this an indication that his state is changing for the better? The next day, a further slight change is almost eagerly noted. Officers have become used to their additional duty of removing burning cigarette stubs from between the prisoner's fingers. This time, 'He looked up to see who it was. This is not what he usually does, he normally looks anywhere but at the officer.' Eye contact might indicate something – but what?

And then, the following day, what has been his recent utterance is repeated: 'Chips.' And on 3 July, he responds for the first time in 13 days, albeit silently, to a direct question. When asked if he wants to go to the toilet, he gets up and does so. And, once more, he speaks: 'Chips.'

The authorities remain concerned about what is going on inside the condemned cell. A senior official in the Prisons Division of the Scottish Home Department sends a memo to the governor stressing that, as a matter of urgency, *all* incidents involving Manuel must be recorded and if anything unusual occurs, the governor is to telephone one of four nominated officials, whatever the time, day or night.

Most of Manuel's time, according to the journal, is spent sleeping or sitting on his bed and smoking. At 5.30 a.m. on 4 July, just seven days before he is due to hang, 'Prisoner sat up and again said, "Chips."' Not the most varied or extensive conversation for the officers.

The watching officers are still looking for anything that might suggest that his apparent obliviousness is an act. Any possible indication of pretence is eagerly seized upon: when he burns his finger on 'hot grease on chips, his reaction was immediate' and 'after he appeared to go to sleep a smiling expression was noticeable on several occasions'. Does the fact that a man a few days away from hanging reacted normally to a burned finger or smiles in his sleep indicate he is sane or mad, fit to hang or not?

We know from other sources that not everything that happened to Manuel got into the journal. It is a brief and very selective record and it is therefore unclear how far it can be trusted. A separate report, for example, noted that Manuel, when he heard one officer tell another he wanted a decent book to read, went to the shelf, selected one and handed it over. 'It was a book of a high standard of literature.' (Sadly, neither title nor author was recorded; it would be interesting to know the literary taste of both Manuel and the official who recorded this.)

The early-morning exclamation of 'Chips', first heard on 4 July, looks like it might become habitual. It rings out in the cell again at 5.45 a.m. the next day. Later on the 5th, a further slight change in his behaviour is noted. He shows an interest in new books that have been brought to his cell, looking at them for an hour, and it is recorded that: 'The Prisoner has been exceptionally calm and more settled in all respects. Although he did not speak he showed more interest than usual.' More importantly, he has twice retuned the radio to a programme of his liking. Yet, lying on his bed that evening, 'every few seconds he jerked his head and arms'. He began to hiccup and later 'gave a groan and turned his face up, he had large bubbles at the left side of his mouth'.

The fact that he has retuned the radio is leapt upon to confirm that his withdrawal is a pretence. The next day, one of the officers who was present writes a memo to the governor, copied to the Director of Prison and Borstal Services for Scotland: that is, sent to the very top of the prison hierarchy. The officer states that he wishes to report 'the following notable incident' that occurred on his watch.

> On several occasions [I] remarked to Officer Bruce that I was unable to tune it to station Radio Luxembourg. The prisoner who had been showing keen interest went over to the set, commenced to adjust it and did in fact tune into the station Radio Luxembourg. He stood by the set for a short period until he appeared satisfied with his effort then returned to a sitting position on his bed. At 9.30 p.m. the prisoner again repeated the above procedure.

Such reports, although they may look rather like clutching at straws, must have strengthened the authorities' belief that Manuel was faking.

Meanwhile, they had to deal with another matter involving his mental state. At this time, the use of the death penalty was the subject of great public debate. Both within and outside Parliament, there was strong pressure for the end of all capital punishment, and each death sentence immediately led to demands for a reprieve. The Scottish Home Department received a number of letters and petitions for this in Manuel's case. From a hotel in Glasgow, the Manuel Appeal Committee wrote asking for his reprieve and claiming correctly that he was an American citizen. The American connection appeared again in the shape of a letter signed by a couple of dozen US service men petitioning against his hanging. It looks as though it had been passed round, perhaps in a canteen, at one of the US bases in Britain.

The senior civil servant who passed details of these letters to the Secretary of State noted that there were seven letters claiming Manuel was innocent, including two from 'an anonymous sufferer from delusions about Freemasonry, address unknown'. He advised the Secretary of State that 'none of this is worth troubling you to look at' except for one letter that records the deliberations of 60 schoolteachers who had met in Glasgow to consider the case. This letter raises in a most cogent way the basic question of Manuel's sanity and whether it was right to hang him. The writer argues:

> A criminal of Manuel's undoubted intelligence might have killed in order to avoid detection, but it would have been for some discernible motive such as profit, or revenge. We found, however, that the common feature of his crimes is their irrationality . . . The view of many was expressed by one of our number who declared that as Manuel had shown early in life the danger signals of hyper-sensitivity to minor set-backs and the consequence to brood on 'persecution', the counter-balancing bragging exhibitionism, and at the early age of fifteen the outbreaks of violence common in such

> forms of mental disorder, the fact that this wretched lad was not kept under restraint for his own sake, and for that of the community, is an indictment of our present system.

This is a remarkable analysis of Manuel's behaviour and it reads as if it came from direct knowledge of him. Hindsight is easy, of course, but how many people might have lived if, as the writer of this letter suggests and Inspector Muncie had hoped when he encountered him in the years before he took to murdering, Manuel had been institutionalised from an early age? The letter ends rather darkly in regard to his family: 'We all agreed that in a decent home the parents of a boy showing such tendencies would have seen to it that he got the benefit of such treatment as is possible.' None of the letters or petitions did him any good.

Early on the morning of the 6th, there were more 'chips'. At 5.15 a.m., Manuel lay awake and repeated the word over and over again. Later, he spent nearly 25 minutes with his mother, father and Father Smith but again he did not speak to them or appear to recognise them. A couple of hours later, he became 'very upset' and tried to bite the arm of the nurse officer who was taking his temperature. He also spoke once more, though only in his sleep: 'Take this road and behind the tall building.' If all this was disturbing, at least he continued to take nourishment: most of his meals seem to have consisted of fish and, of course, chips.

Much of the material above has been taken from the death watch journal. We have quoted it frequently not only because it is the most comprehensive record we have of Manuel's behaviour at any time in his life but also to indicate something of its limitations. What was going on here? Was his withdrawal genuine? Was it all pretence, as several eminent psychiatrists and many cynical prison officers believed? And how far is the record accurate? How far is it the result of conscious or unconscious selection and censorship by the officers involved?

The journal does record the next key event in Manuel's rapidly shortening life. On 8 July – that is, three days before the date set for his execution – he was visited by the governor and the chief prison officer. They were accompanied by the senior magistrate of Glasgow and the town clerk. This was a highly formal, very important visit and it sealed his fate. The magistrate read to him a letter stating that the Secretary of State was unable to discover sufficient grounds to advise the Queen to stop his execution. There would be no reprieve; he would hang.

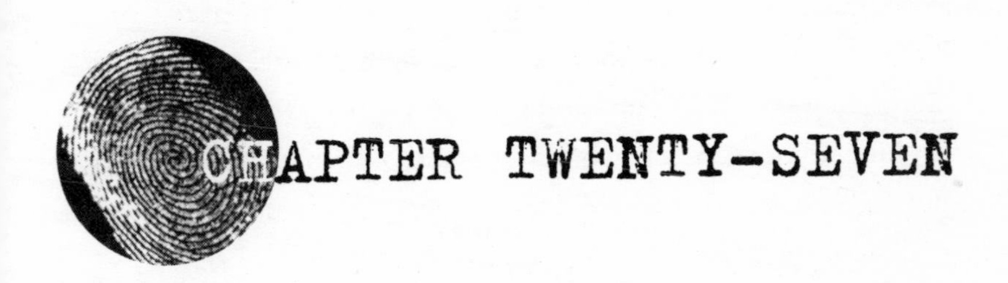

CHAPTER TWENTY-SEVEN

Thus, Manuel's last hope was gone. Despite this, he 'did not respond in any manner' to those who brought him the news and he still appeared to be cut off from what was going on around him. That evening, he was 'quiet, calm and restful' and he did not show 'any emotional change' although he knew – if he had taken it in – that there was no chance any more of escaping the noose and the drop.

It is not clear exactly how his family learned that the final chance of a reprieve was gone. It may be that they heard it over the radio or read it in the evening paper, because one of the city magistrates leaked the news to reporters either just before Manuel was told or shortly after. This gross breach of proper behaviour rightly caused great annoyance at the Scottish Home Department.

Then, on 9 July, just two days before Manuel was due to be hanged, things changed. The alteration began slowly. Around 10 a.m., it was noted that he seemed 'deep in thought'. Around midday, he was asked if he wanted to play cards. Without speaking, he signified that he did and he spent most of the afternoon doing so. He signalled the score on his fingers and it is reported that he smiled a lot. The officers on duty made every effort to get him to talk but he could not or would not, although one of them recorded that 'he conversed in a form of sign language'.

In the evening, Samuel, Bridget and Theresa visited him. He did not speak but wrote two messages, the first on the flyleaf of a prayer book, almost certainly one brought in by his mother. This says, 'I am feeling OK today. I was told it is July 9th. I can remember back to June. I got cracked by an officer called Sutherland. He is not here now.' Then came the second message:

> Get hold of Timmons [his MP] tonight. My appeal was carried through by a QC who was engaged in an advisory capacity only. Tell him I want a medical examination (neutral). My head is broke; I feel it. I only found out yesterday that nearly three weeks have elapsed since Sutherland and I fought. Doctor here is no use. He's cuckoo. An officer told me they pumped my stomach and found nothing.

In other words, he has suddenly recovered from an assault by a prison officer and wants to be allowed to mount another appeal.

More dramatic changes were about to occur. When Manuel was returned to his cell, he went into one corner, pulled back the lino and then, as one of the officers present related in a special report to the governor, he 'pointed to a stain on back of lino, then signalled that he wanted writing paper and a pencil'. With these he wrote, 'Said I would get burned.'

> I asked him who said that and he said, 'Sutherland.' I asked him what happened and he wrote on the table that he

> punched Officer Sutherland then Officer Sutherland drew his stick and hit him, he fell into the corner and then Officer Sutherland kicked him. He then wrote, 'The other screw banjoed [struck] Sutherland.' I asked what happened after that and he wrote, 'I got washed and Joiner asked me to forget it I laid on my bed that is all until this morning.' I asked, 'When did this happen?' He wrote, '1 o'clock on the wireless. It was Friday the QC was due.' Then he wrote, 'No soap.' I asked if he knew what day this was. He nodded his head. I asked how he knew. 'This morning wireless Broadmoor,' he wrote.

'That is all until this morning.' Having supposedly returned to full consciousness, Manuel repeats his claim that he was attacked by one of the warders. The last 19 days, the failure of his appeal, all the medical examinations, the visits when he had shown no recognition of his parents – all those things had happened without him being mentally present or even aware of them.

Interestingly, none of the above appears in the death watch journal, only in other reports. If one had to rely solely on the journal, none of this would be known. Just how much else was left out? How far can we accept that what did get into the journal is accurate?

Clearly, there was much that had to be investigated in all this. The duty cell officers, almost certainly believing it was all nonsense, continued to note in the journal things that might indicate Manuel was lying about his mental state. The next morning, 10 July, they reported that he was talking freely, asking them why there were three officers in the cell and then loosing a 'flood of questions appertaining to occurrences over the past 2 weeks'. 'Appertaining to occurrences' – the pompous words of minor officialdom. Despite his claim that he had been unaware of what had been going on around him, they noted, he nevertheless 'accurately recounted general conversations held between various officers in the past week'.

The next key stage in his alteration came after he had been examined yet again by the medical officer. He told his warders that 'he wished to make a complaint in the presence of the Governor and Medical Officer'. This was to be his last attempt to escape, his last attempt to cause trouble.

And so, at 9.45 that morning, less than twenty-four hours before Manuel was due to die, he was seen by the four most senior prison staff: the governor, the deputy governor, the medical officer and the chief officer. To them he repeated the story of how he came to lose so many days. This time, he provided much more detail. According to this version, he got into an argument with Sutherland about the cell radio and Sutherland said he should be burned. Manuel slapped the officer on the face and was pulled away by Officer Joiner. He went into the lavatory to cool down and then sat on his bed. At this point, claimed Manuel, Sutherland hit him with his baton. He grappled with the officer, his nose was bleeding, Joiner intervened again. Manuel told the authorities, 'Sutherland began crying and rampling about having already been in trouble for hitting someone with a stick.' This refers to an occasion at Saughton Prison when Sutherland had used a baton to subdue a prisoner. The incident was well known to many in the prison population.

Joiner asked Manuel if he wanted to see the governor. He said he did but his complaint was never made, for, he claimed, from that point onwards, he could recall nothing. 'I don't remember anything after that. I don't remember going to the appeal. I knew it [the incident] happened the day before the QC was due to see me.'

But now, Manuel wanted to make it clear, he was back, suddenly once more fully aware of things. 'Yesterday, I remember playing cards and remember the priest visiting me. I remember asking Mr Crammond [an officer] about different things. I don't remember the magistrates coming to see me [to tell him there was to be no reprieve] and I don't remember being seen by any doctors. I couldn't mind [recall] what happened yesterday morning. I remember seeing the doctor.'

Manuel also claimed he had a sore on the top of his head that was painful when pressed and that his left eye was also sore. There were other problems: he said he couldn't see or hear very well. Dr Anderson examined his head and found a small abrasion, which he said was not very old.

Two psychiatrists examined him yet again, this time to see if the claimed assault by Officer Sutherland could have caused his strange withdrawal. Dr Inch reports that it was in 'the highest degree unlikely that Manuel suffered any damage to the central nervous system' and Dr Craigie concludes that his symptoms 'did not in any way conform to those which might have resulted from a head injury inflicted in that way'.

Then there was the important matter of his appeal. In his view, this had not been conducted properly and therefore the appeal judges' decision should not be allowed to stand. He claimed that he had told his solicitors that he intended to handle the appeal himself. McDonald was to be there only to advise on points of law.

He spoke directly to the governor about this. He wrote down what Manuel said and then phoned his statement through to Sir William Murrie. 'This thing [his fugue, withdrawal, whatever it should be called],' Manuel claimed, 'has messed up my appeal.' At the date of the appeal, 'I was in need of expert medical advice rather than legal advice.' If he hoped any of this would invalidate the decision of the Appeal Court, he was wrong; it stood. The last bid had failed.

Manuel, when talking to the senior officials, perhaps deliberately gave the wrong date for when his withdrawal started, or, if we accept his version of events, when he was struck on the head by Officer Sutherland. He placed the events a day too early, although a few hours before, talking to the warders, he had dated it correctly. The exact date is critical: his withdrawal actually began at the very time he was due to confer with his counsel on how the appeal should be handled. The officer who went to rouse him, and who discovered him frothing at the mouth, had gone to prepare him to see McDonald.

The appeal and the subsequent failure to get a reprieve are the two keys to his withdrawal and to his return. The change in Manuel began on the Friday; the appeal was scheduled for the following Tuesday. Whether he was to die or live would almost certainly depend on the result of the appeal; a post-appeal reprieve was highly unlikely. Manuel must have come to understand – perhaps he had been told by his lawyers – that his appeal had little chance of succeeding. Even if, as he claimed, he had planned to represent himself, he must also have been forced to accept how unsuccessfully he had done that at his trial. The prosecution had torn great holes in his story and the jury had refused to believe his fabrications. His chances of doing any better at the Appeal Court, facing highly experienced senior judges, were small. Rather than going through with it and having to endure the humiliation of depending on his QC to steer him through the legal issues, he chose another route. He would avoid all that by pretending to be mentally incompetent and saying, if need be, that this had been caused by one of his guards assaulting him. (The little detail about Sutherland 'crying' because he had 'been in trouble' for assaulting another prisoner is a typical piece of Manuel malice.)

His sudden 'recovery', his apparent return to consciousness, was triggered by the fact that, the previous day, he had been told that he was not going to be reprieved. The game was up and he had lost. All that remained was to try to cause trouble by claiming he had been assaulted.

None of this, of course, did him any good. The prison authorities, supported by the Scottish Home Department and their political masters, had no doubt that he was fit to hang, and hang he would. It was made totally clear to him that his last attempt to escape had been futile. Now, at last, he began to act normally, or what passed as normally for him.

So, verdict given, sentence passed, appeal rejected and now his attempt to escape the noose under the pretence of madness failed, Manuel was moving rapidly towards his death.

But death had to be achieved in the proper way. This was a judicially sanctioned killing, and therefore the process – the noose carefully arranged under the right ear, the plummet through the trapdoor, the sudden snapping of the spine – had to be done quickly and efficiently. And also, of course, the paperwork had to be correct, exactly correct in every detail, before, during and after the event.

The intense bureaucratic care and caution with which Manuel was sent to his death can still be witnessed. On the cover of the Scottish Home Department file that holds many of the key records, someone has written in large red letters the command: 'Do Not Destroy Ever'. Manuel himself was to be destroyed, of course, but the relevant paperwork had to be preserved. Those involved in his death wanted to be quite sure that they could prove that everything had been done according to the strict requirements of the law. After all, their task was to kill a fellow human being. In a paradoxical way, the file shows how determined they were to take the very best care of Manuel – until that final moment when the trapdoor suddenly fell away beneath his pinioned feet and the rope snapped his neck.

Preparations for his death had begun well before the warrant had been signed. Of course, these arrangements could always be cancelled if the appeal succeeded or a reprieve was granted but meanwhile it was sensible to get things moving. So the governor had already telephoned the hangman Harry Allen and his assistant Harry Smith to ask if they would execute Manuel. Once the death warrant had been issued, he sent them telegrams asking them to carry out the hanging on the morning of 11 July and followed these with formal letters of appointment. All was ready.

By 1958, judicial hanging was a fast and almost mechanically efficient operation, the techniques honed and refined over many decades. Its speed was the result of practice and careful preparation.

The basic aim was to snap the prisoner's spinal cord so as to kill him or her instantly. The distance he or she fell at the end of the rope was crucially important. If the drop was too great, there was a risk that the head would be torn from the body. If it was too short, slow strangulation instead of a broken neck could result. To get the length of the drop exactly right, calculating it to a matter of inches, the hangman took into account the prisoner's weight, state of health and strength. A set of tables helped him with his calculations. He also made sure that the rope was already stretched so that it would not lengthen under the victim's weight as he plunged through the trapdoor.

Hangman and assistant, taking time off from their regular jobs (for hanging was a part-time vocation), usually arrived at the prison the day before the execution and there covertly observed their victim. They operated as a practised team. Information on the weight, health and any physical disabilities of the prisoner would already have been compiled by prison staff, and using this and their own observations, they worked out how best to carry out the hanging.

When the appointed time came, usually just before eight in the morning, the hangman and assistant entered the condemned cell. There they fastened the condemned man's hands at his sides. He was quickly taken the short distance to the gallows, the hangman usually in front, his assistant behind. The assistant pinioned his legs, placed him exactly over a chalk mark on the trapdoor as the hangman slipped hood and noose over the prisoner's head. They moved quickly off the trap and the hangman pulled the lever to open it. The helpless prisoner dropped through, the rope dislocated his spine between the second and third vertebrae and he died instantly. The aim was to have the prisoner dead within two minutes of the executioners entering his cell. The faster things went, the better.

What of Manuel, as his death came closer? The Barlinnie death watch journal records in its matter-of-fact, petty bureaucratic way some of the events of his final hours. We cannot know what was ignored by the writers, what they did not record. As it is, the journal gives only a superficial account of Manuel's final hours. Perhaps it is better so. Nevertheless one is fiercely aware of the huge gaps between the words, of what the writers were unable or unwilling to record in their painstaking handwriting.

Take the entries for the day before his execution, starting at a point when he had less than 24 hours of life left to him. At 11.45 a.m., Father Smith entered the cell and left five minutes later. At noon, Manuel was served his dinner and it is noted, 'Sweet only eaten.' The next entry records that the priest made another visit from 12.50 to 1.10 p.m., then notes: 'Officer Ironside to remove dinner dishes.' At the change of shifts at two o'clock, three officers signed the summary of their observations: 'Prisoner played cards most of the morning and spoke most of the time about his case, the Prisoner smoked most of my time on duty.' Was that all there was to it? What happened between the events that are recorded? What did Manuel say about his case? How did he feel? How did the officers feel?

Whatever inner turmoil Manuel may or may not have been going through, whatever his thoughts or plans or fears, none of it gets into this record. It deals solely with the basic facts and events. So it tells us that Manuel's need for cigarettes is met by the delivery of 20 of them at 2.01 p.m. Visits by a member of the Prison Visiting Committee, the governor, the chief officer and Officer McDonald follow. At 3.30 p.m., it is noted that he smoked two cigarettes. McDonald returns at 3.45 to make another visit and at 4.35 dinner arrives: 'Fish, Chips, Lettuce, Tomatoes, Bread and tea. Prisoner left all fish and half Bread.' The next note states that at 4.50 p.m., 'Prisoner smoked 2 cigarettes.' At 5.35, he was taken to be interviewed by the governor. He had not returned by the time the shift was relieved at six o'clock but the officers' summary on leaving was: 'Prisoner was very cheerful and talkative, he conversed continually about his trial and appeal, and appeared in good spirits during our tour of duty.' And only 14 hours left until he was to die.

At 8.10 p.m., Manuel saw his brother James for the final time; the meeting lasted ten minutes. Next Father Smith came to him again and after he had left, the prisoner was visited by the governor and the chief prison officer, then by the medical officer and the chief nursing officer, and then by another prison officer. Nothing of what transpired during these visits, nothing of the whys and wherefores, is mentioned. At 10 p.m., the shift, going off duty, records: 'Prisoner was very cheery and appeared to be very calm.' Admirable composure in the face of death – if the account is accurate.

Perhaps it is no surprise to learn that Manuel's last night seems to have been spent entirely without sleep. At ten o'clock, he is 'awake and talking cheerfully'. At one, tea is brought and 'Prisoner [is] still awake and talking of past experiences.' (One assumes his accounts of his experiences did not include anything about raping and murdering; otherwise, surely, a note would have been made?) At four in the morning, four hours before he is to hang, he 'reads old letters then destroys them. Continues to chat.' At 5.30 a.m., 'Prisoner goes to lavatory and has bowel movement. Played dominoes.' At 5.45, the chief officer arrives with the prisoner's clothes, the new suit he will wear to be killed. Well, he was always one for looking smart.

There were only two hours to go when the morning shift entered the condemned cell. The delegated diary keeper recorded that, as they did so, Manuel was 'sitting at the table playing dominoes'. He then rose, sat on his bed and smoked. At 6.25 a.m., he washed and dressed in his new suit. Ten minutes later, Father Smith entered the cell and the three officers withdrew. The chaplain's visit ended two minutes later. Between 6.50 and 7.15, 'Prisoner attended R.C. Religious service.' At 7.25, the medical officer and the chief nursing officer arrived. Manuel was offered a drink of whisky and accepted. Nothing more is noted until 7.50, except for the removal of dishes. Then Father Smith returns to stay with Manuel to the end. For weeks, the priest had been striving to persuade Manuel to confess his sins; he had had no success. When it was all over, he told a friend that Manuel was unlike anyone else he had ever encountered: the man seemed totally impervious to all his persuasion, arguments and suggestions. Father Smith did not reveal if, right at the end, Manuel did make his confession but, from what he said about him, it seems unlikely that he did.

The next bare entry, timed at 7.58 a.m., states: 'Entrance of Governor and Executioner. Prisoner addressed the Governor while executioner completed his duties.' An asterisk has been added to the penultimate sentence and, at the bottom of the page, the governor later wrote: 'Expressed his thanks to staff who looked after him, through me.'

The journal's closing entry summarises Manuel's final two hours: 'From 6 a.m. the prisoner smoked continuously and conversed freely on General subjects, also about a Visit he had from his brother last night. He was obviously under an immense emotional strain but in all respects remain [*sic*] calm, composed and quite cheerful to the end.' But can we believe it?

Manuel was taken out of his cell at 7.59 a.m. At the scaffold, the hangman and his assistant worked with such speed that Governor Anderson was able to report: 'The time that elapsed between the prisoner leaving the condemned cell and the drop was eight seconds.' Death was quick. Manuel was certified dead a mere thirty-two seconds after eight o'clock. Dr Anderson went down into the pit and Father Smith went with him to administer the last rites. When the hood was removed from Manuel's head, he anointed the dead man.

It was usual for there to be either silence or uproar in a jail at the moment of a hanging. One prison officer has recalled that Barlinnie's inmates simply went on eating their breakfast as Manuel fell to his death.

The bureaucratic and legal paperwork that a hanging necessitated was also dealt with speedily. At just seven minutes past eight, the governor sent a telegram to the Scottish Home Department to notify them that, after all the trouble and concern he had caused them,

'Sentence on Peter Thomas Anthony Manuel executed'. At 8.14 a.m., notice of the execution was posted on the prison gates and a black flag hoisted. Some 20 minutes after that, at 8.35, Father Smith, who had spent so long with Manuel, conducted the burial service. The strain on him was so great that he spent the rest of the day prostrate on his bed.

A person's funeral often reflects their status in society. The way in which the body is disposed of, the funeral rites and the style of hospitality offered the mourners are usually clear indications of the deceased's importance and financial worth. Manuel's body was buried, as the law required, within the prison grounds. His parents were excluded, denied any solace the rituals of their religion might have offered. The grave was unmarked, though its location was specified with great precision in the governor's formal report: 'against the West Wall of D Hall, 60 ft 2 in. from the south-west corner of the Hall'. (Years later, when new drains were being laid in the prison, their route was diverted to avoid his and other prisoners' graves.)

Less than an hour after the burial, at half past nine, the public inquiry into the execution was held before the Glasgow sheriff. Dr Anderson stated that he had seen Manuel hanged and then examined him: 'I found that he was dead.' One of those who had been present at the execution, a magistrate, stated that: 'Everything was carried out in the most satisfactory manner and expeditiously done.' His view was supported by another witness.

Finally, on 15 July, the formal public record of the event was published in the official journal the *Edinburgh Gazette*, where the Sheriff Substitute of Lanarkshire recorded that sentence on Peter Thomas Anthony Manuel had been carried out. Sentence carried out, corpse buried and all paperwork absolutely correct.

It was all over, all recorded in the proper formal documents, tucked away neatly in the files, as the Civil Service and the law required. A few days later, Sir William Murrie sent the governor a letter saying that: 'The Secretary of State and we officers in the Department appreciated how well he and the prison officers had performed their duties while Manuel was in Barlinnie.'

It was one thing to be thanked by the Secretary of State, quite another to be thanked for taking good care of him by Manuel himself. To the end of his days, the medical officer Dr Anderson recalled with revulsion the man's thanks, given seconds before he went to the scaffold. He was sure this was Manuel's final attempt to manipulate those around him, to leave them with a lasting sense of guilt and shame for what they were doing to him.

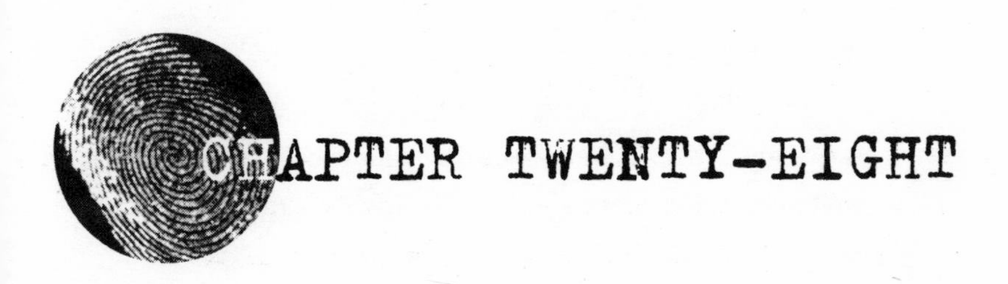

CHAPTER TWENTY-EIGHT

One question – appalling, fascinating, frightening – remained: had Manuel committed other murders? If so, how many and who had he killed?

The moment he had been safely hanged for seven murders, newspapers began to claim that he had carried out more killings. Now that he could no longer contradict anything they printed, they were free to scare their readers with the grisly notion that he had committed several more murders for which he could never be made accountable. Rival papers competed over the numbers; some claimed ten, others even more. In the death cell, the *Sunday Pictorial* claimed, he had admitted killing Anne Kneilands – not that there had ever been much doubt about that. Next, however, the paper revealed to its eager readers:

> Today, we are able to disclose that MANUEL MURDERED FOUR OTHER PEOPLE, making twelve in all. They were

> Glasgow spinster Anne Steele, Durham taxi driver Sydney Dunn and Soho prostitute Helen Carlin, and one person whose name the police will not reveal. AND MANUEL PLANNED TO MURDER THREE MORE PEOPLE.

This new information, the paper claimed, came from the police:

> Police also know that IF MANUEL HAD BEEN FREE FOR JUST ONE WEEK MORE, THREE MORE PEOPLE WOULD HAVE DIED. The man who killed – just because he liked killing – had compiled a list of future victims! The police know their names – but they will never reveal them. And today those intended victims do not know they escaped by a mere few days.

It seems that the paper hopes profuse use of capital letters will disguise a lack of supporting evidence.

In recent years, the number of deaths ascribed to Manuel has increased even further. Authors and journalists, including Harry Benson, who visited Manuel in Barlinnie, have claimed he killed 15 people, perhaps more. On the 50th anniversary of his hanging, one paper, *Scotland on Sunday*, said some experts thought the number of his victims was as high as 18. But did he really claim to have killed others? And if he did, was it true or was it another example of Manuel's grandiose, self-vaunting lies?

The claim that Manuel killed more than nine people (eight in the Glasgow area and one in Northumberland) was rejected by John Bingham in his *The Hunting Down of Peter Manuel*. He was repeating the view of Muncie, from whom he got most of his inside information. Bingham's nine must therefore be taken as the official view. He says of these other, suppositious murders: 'There is no evidence he perpetrated them.' John Bingham was the pen name used by Lord Clanmorris, who was a senior MI5 officer, used to sifting and evaluating evidence and choosing his words with care. The key phrase is 'no evidence'. He is not claiming absolutely that Manuel did not kill more people; only that the requisite evidence is lacking. This is a very similar statement to an earlier remark about the Barlinnie poison plot: 'There is *no ascertainable record* that such an attempt was made' to poison Manuel. That is, these things may have happened but there is no definitive proof. All this leaves open the possibility that Manuel had, in fact, committed other murders.

Manuel may have left us a clue in the form of remarks he made during his trial. Perhaps, in the heat of that contest for his life, he unconsciously let slip the true number of his victims: ten. In court, he said that the Glasgow police suspected him of *ten* murders and that when Superintendent Brown interrogated him shortly after his arrest he 'told me he knew I had committed *ten* murders'. Later that day, Manuel said, Goodall talked of the Kneilands, Watt, Smart and Cooke killings – eight in all – 'and . . . two other cases in Glasgow'. The number ten recurred when he cross-examined Brown.

'Did you tell me you were going to hang me for ten murders?'

'I couldn't tell you that.'

'Did you question me about ten murders?'

'I did not.'

During the trial, Manuel oscillated, for no discernible reason, between talking about eight killings and ten. Thus, at another point, again while examining Brown, he claimed that he had said, 'I am going to pin eight murders on you,' and later, 'You must confess to these eight murders.'

There are two obvious explanations for this appearance of the number ten. The first is that at the start of their investigations the Glasgow police really did suspect Manuel of killing ten people. Later, for a variety of possible reasons, including Manuel's confessions, they reduced the number to eight and charged him with those. Even if they suspected him of two others, good evidence – as Bingham indicates – must have been lacking. It's not impossible that the prosecution also thought that eight charges were enough: if Manuel was convicted of only one capital murder, he would hang and that would be an end to it.

The second explanation – which need not exclude the first – is that Manuel himself knew he had killed ten people and that his mention of the number ten was a conscious or unconscious indication of what he had done.

But if he killed ten people, who were the other two? The murder we can most confidently attribute to him is that of Newcastle taxi driver Sydney Dunn. A Durham coroner's jury judged that Manuel did kill Dunn. By the time the jury met, however, Manuel had been dead for over a fortnight and had no chance to defend himself.

The crime began at Newcastle railway station at about 4.30 on the morning of Sunday, 8 December 1957. A man sought a taxi to take him to Edmundbyers, an isolated moorland village about 18 miles south-west of the city. The first driver he approached passed him over to 36-year-old Sydney Dunn, who owned a black Austin saloon that he used as a taxi. He accepted the hire. Taxi and passenger set off into the night.

Later that day, a number of motorists noticed Dunn's car parked, almost out of sight, in a dip or gully beside the Stanhope Road about two miles from Edmundbyers. They seem to have taken no particular notice of it. Eventually, towards noon, a passing PC stopped and examined the car. Inside, he saw what looked like blood on the steering wheel. There was no sign of the driver. He alerted his colleagues.

According to a later report, the car's front and rear lights, the windows, windscreen and rear window, and the bulbs of the interior lights had all been smashed. Perhaps this was what first drew the constable's attention to the vehicle. Why this had been done and why nobody had taken any notice of the smashed-up car up to this point are the first of the many puzzles. Later, Bingham speculated that one might be the answer to the other: that the damage might have been done to make the taxi look like an abandoned vehicle, one not worth closer examination. According to another report, passers-by had probably assumed the car belonged to picnickers, as the area was locally famed for its scenery. Neither explanation is convincing. Picnicking on a cold December day would be unlikely and, in an era when cars were expensive and comparatively rare, an abandoned car in the country was highly unusual, as likely to attract interest as to deflect it.

A few hours later, the police began to search the area around the car. At about eight in the evening, a police dog led them to the body of Sydney Dunn. It was lying on the ground about 140 yards away from his car. There was blood on Dunn's throat.

A body found in the dark by the light of torches on a bitterly cold December night was always going to present problems. The investigation got off to the worst possible start: the police concluded that Dunn had committed suicide. They issued a statement saying that, although Dunn had suffered a wound to the throat, foul play was not suspected. They also said that Dunn's passenger from the railway station was not under suspicion. They asked him to get in touch. He never did.

As soon as the local pathologist examined the body, he saw what the police had missed: the unfortunate driver had been shot through the head and his throat had then been slashed. Suddenly, suicide became murder. The most serious of crimes had now to be investigated at a site that had already been trampled over by those searching for the body. The police withdrew their first statement and asked anyone who had been in the area early on Sunday morning to come forward. Nobody did.

In appalling conditions, they began to examine the bleak moors for clues. Heavy rain had already washed away traces left when the body had been dragged to where it was found, and the weather was worsening. It was important to find the gun and knife used in the killing but the task was horrendous. The searchers had to cover vast areas of rough and marshy terrain. Blizzarding snow obscured the ground as dozens of officers stumbled along lines of string marking out their search area, responding to orders yelled into the wind through loudspeakers. One of the dog handlers was sucked down into a bog and had to be saved by his colleagues. More help was needed. Troops from a nearby camp were drafted in to seek the weapons. They brought no fewer than 30 mine detectors. A few items were found that could have fallen from the dead man's pockets as he was dragged along but the gun and knife remained undiscovered.

Intensive local enquiries were started; a team of 12 detectives began visiting every house in the area. As they did so, they and their colleagues were aware that the murder did not seem to make sense. Why had Dunn been killed in such a remote spot? Theft could have been a motive if the victim had been robbed but his wallet was found on the ground and it contained five pounds in notes. If not robbery, was the killing motivated by revenge or hatred? If so, did that suggest some link between Dunn and his killer? Was someone local the murderer? None of it made much sense. Why had there been no sighting of the killer as he made his way away from the scene? Perhaps he too had met his death on the moor: a local paper speculated that he might have fallen into one of the many bogs and drowned.

In Newcastle, the police continued their efforts to locate anyone who had been near the station area about the time Dunn had picked up his fare. A train from Bristol had arrived at 4.38 p.m., one from Carlisle a little earlier. Had the killer been on one of them? One local paper said that it was thought that the killer might have arrived on what it called the Carlisle 'Paddy Train', which 'usually carries a large number of Irishmen'. Despite many enquiries, the police found nobody, Irish or otherwise, who could help them. They persisted; it was reported in early January that Irishmen were still being questioned about the crime.

The police's only useful witness was Thomas Green, the taxi driver who had been approached first by the suspect. Two days after the body had been found, he provided the public with the first detailed evidence about Dunn's passenger. He told a reporter that the man had 'a local accent, was about 24 years of age, 5 ft 8 in. tall and of medium build. He was wearing a dark suit but no hat.' This description was expanded the next day, 11 December, by the police. The man they were seeking was, they said: 'About 5 ft 8 in., swarthy, clean-shaven, with dark hair pushed back and appearing to be greased. The parting may be on the left. The man had a north-country accent and was wearing a dark single-breasted suit believed to be blue, light-coloured shirt and collar, dark tie and dark, loose raincoat.' Other information given to the press indicated that the murder gun was of British make, possibly old, and .32 or .38 calibre.

A couple of days later, a sketch of the suspect was released, based on the memories of Green and of Albert Younger, another taxi driver at the station. It was not much help, as the features were so general that they could have been almost any white male between the ages of 20 and 40.

Not only was there the problem of the two missing weapons but there was also the even more crucial question of how the killer had left the murder scene. Nobody had come forward to say they had seen anyone near where the taxi had been dumped. Despite widely publicised pleas for information, nobody had admitted to giving anyone a lift away from the area. This was perplexing. After all, it was reasonable to think that anyone hitch-hiking from a remote spot on the moors at around six o'clock on a Sunday morning would have been easily remembered. How then had the killer got away? One theory, arrived at because fragments of headlight glass had been spotted on the road about a mile away from the murder site, was that the murder could have involved at least two people: the passenger and the driver of another car. Perhaps Dunn's taxi had been followed and overtaken by the other car, which had then braked hard in front of it to cause a collision that damaged its headlights? When Dunn had stopped, he had been killed and the murderer had then fled in the second car.

The police began to test an alternative and rather more likely theory. If the suspect had a north-country accent, as taxi driver Green had stated, then perhaps he was a local man. If he was from the area, it could explain why he had asked to be taken to Edmundbyers and might also indicate an earlier contact with Dunn from which a murderous hate had grown. Local knowledge could also explain how the killer had been able to leave the murder scene unobserved. He could have made his way home across the moors by paths that were unknown to outsiders. Now the local community came under even greater scrutiny. Enquiry headquarters were moved to Stanhope police station and house-to-house questioning was concentrated on that village. By this stage, no fewer than 36 Durham CID officers were working on the case and 30 other officers were still searching the moors. Still, virtually no useful information was forthcoming. Finally, on 16 December, the local paper announced, 'Moorland People Talking of Murder at Last'. But whatever the previously silent locals might have said to the police, it was of no help. The murder remained a mystery; the weapons had still not been found.

There had, earlier on, been a brief flash of hope for the police. Two days after the murder, a 29-year-old man with an extensive criminal record – he'd committed no fewer than 228 offences – stole a handbag from a church in nearby Hexham. He then gave himself up and admitted he had killed Sydney Dunn. In court on 13 December, he stated: 'I surrendered myself to the police but not specially for this offence [the theft of the bag]. There are other offences of greater seriousness and I would like to be assured they will be dealt with.' He was remanded in custody. The police's brief hope that they had got the murderer soon faded. The man had a history of mental illness and soon admitted that, although he had genuinely believed he had killed Dunn, he now knew this was not the case. 'I admitted the Newcastle taxi murder,' he said. 'I honestly thought I did it.'

The enquiries seemed to be going nowhere and yet seven months later, towards the end of July 1958, the Durham coroner's jury determined that Peter Manuel had killed Dunn. How this came about can now only be reconstructed from fragments of information. Something, somehow, had alerted the Northumberland police to the possibility that Manuel could be a suspect. Four days after his arrest, on the evening of 18 January, he was questioned about the murder by Detective Chief Inspector Wilkinson of the Durham police force. Manuel's response was to deny everything.

We reproduce in full the statement he gave Wilkinson. It illustrates the way he created his alibis from a mixture of hard fact and total vagueness, hoping the apparent firm accuracy of one part will deflect attention from the lack of evidence in the other. For a man with such an excellent memory, he is curiously unclear about events that had occurred less than two months previously – or he was lying. Manuel starts with a firm rejection of any involvement in the Dunn killing:

> I deny that I am in any way responsible. I have never been to Edmunbyres [*sic*], I don't know where it is. The last time I was in Durham County was about 1942, when I was in an Approved School at St Peters, by Gainsford, Darlington. I was there roughly about a year, you'll get it all from Darlington. I was charged with housebreaking. That's the only connection I have had with Durham County. I have only once been in Newcastle that was between Christmas, 1942, and March 15th, 1943, when I ran away from Market Weighton Approved School. I have never been in that area since and I was certainly not in Newcastle on Sunday, the 8th December, 1957. I was released from Barlinnie Prison about 7 a.m. on Saturday, the 30th November, 1957, and I went straight home with my brother who had come to the prison to meet me. I went to see a football match that day and on the night time I went for a drink with my father and my brother. I cannot remember what I did on the Sunday, that is a dead day as far as I am concerned, the pubs are not open and I cannot remember

> who I was with on the Monday (2nd). I met Mr Dowdall, a solicitor from Glasgow, and he told me to meet him the following night in the same place. I met him again on the Tuesday night (3rd) in the lounge of the Whitehall Bar in Glasgow. A man called Mr Watt was with us. I was with Watt until about 7 a.m. the next morning. I met him again on the Wednesday night (4th) with Watt not for long, just to square one or two things up. These interviews were important to me, that is why I remember the dates so clearly, but I am not clear about the rest of the week. From the Thursday onwards they were just ordinary days, I was just knocking around. I am not altogether sure but I was probably in the house watching TV on the Saturday night (7th) and I was probably doing the same on the Sunday. I know I signed the National Assistance Board at Bellshill on the Monday (9th) some time in the morning. The fellow there gave me a lecture about my conduct. I have only got the one suit, black, and a pair of charcoal grey slacks. I also have a black jacket with a snowdrop pattern. I have a grey gabardine raincoat, single breasted, the Police have it now. I also have a big black overcoat.

Enquiries into the murder continued. On 22 January, Wilkinson, McNeil, Brown and Goodall interviewed another untried prisoner in Barlinnie. What they were seeking to discover cannot now be established. Perhaps he had been in contact with Manuel and had information for them. Manuel's claim that he had not been in Newcastle since 1943 was rejected by the Durham police. They brought Thomas Green and Albert Younger to Hamilton. An identity parade was held and they stated that Manuel was the man they had seen hiring Dunn's taxi. He was charged with the murder.

That crime, of course, had taken place in England and English justice would have to wait. If Manuel escaped conviction for the Scottish murders, he would be tried in England for Dunn's murder.

And so, in case he was acquitted, Durham officers were present at the end of his Glasgow trial, ready to take him south. The jury ensured that was not necessary.

The evidence that Manuel had been in Newcastle and had committed this murder was therefore never tested at trial. According to Bingham, Manuel had applied for a job at British Electrical Repairs Ltd in Newcastle early on Friday, 6 December, two days before Dunn was killed. The next evening, Bingham relates, he was seen in the railway station cafeteria. There was some physical evidence that seemed to tie him to the murder site. A brown suit and maroon pullover belonging to him were examined. The trouser turn-ups contained grass fragments from moorland terrain. A button and fibres found on the running board of Dunn's car matched ones from Manuel's jacket and pullover. Despite the rather Sherlock Holmes feel of this evidence – the detached button, the fragments of grass – the evidence was enough to convince the coroner's jury that Manuel, by then a notorious multiple murderer, had killed Dunn.

By any standards, the Dunn murder is extraordinarily strange. Consider what we know: early on the Sunday morning a man, making no attempt to hide his features, talks to one taxi driver and then goes off with another, having asked both drivers to take him to an isolated village on the moors. A couple of miles from Edmundbyers, the taxi stops for some reason (the meter was turned off when the car was found) and Dunn is killed. The killer not only shoots his victim but then slashes his throat. He does not bother to take the man's money. He drags the body away from the car and at some point he smashes all the windows and lights on the vehicle. Then he disappears from the scene of the crime. Was it Manuel?

Against the view that Manuel was the killer there is the description first offered by Thomas Green, who had said that Dunn's passenger had a north-country accent, was aged about 24 and 5 ft 8 in. in height. This description hardly fits Manuel: when he was not imitating an American, he had a strong Lanarkshire accent, very different from that of a Geordie. He was nearly 32 and a couple of inches shorter than the man described. Of course, memories and descriptions based on memories can be faulty and, as we have seen, after Manuel had been arrested, Green and another driver identified him as Dunn's passenger. What's more, Manuel greased his hair heavily, as did the man described by Green. But then so did tens of thousands of other men.

Even if we accept the identification and the forensic evidence (the traces of grass and the detached button), there still remains the most puzzling aspect of the crime: its apparent senselessness. Even Bingham, who was convinced Manuel was the killer, says: 'It was an amateurish botched up murder, curiously out of keeping with Manuel's other killings.' Indeed, this murder was totally different from his sly, stealthy shootings of sleeping victims or his violent assaults on young girls. Would he have killed in this way? Why would he have wanted to go to Edmundbyers? Why would he have wanted to kill Dunn? Why would he have smashed all the car lights and windows? Why would he not have taken the five pounds Dunn had in his wallet? None of it makes any sense.

A flimsy, partial explanation of the crime has been offered. It has been suggested that Manuel had asked the driver, in his strong Scottish accent, to take him to Edinburgh and that Dunn misunderstood him. Then, when Manuel realised they were stopping at Edmundbyers, he lost his temper and in a fury murdered Dunn. But why would Manuel want to go to Edinburgh anyway? After all, he lived about 50 miles from that city. And if he was the killer, how on earth did he get away without being seen?

The matter remains mysterious. There is, however, one factor that may support the jury's decision that Manuel was the killer. This is the curious destruction of the car lights and windows. If this was not done to make the car look like a dumped derelict vehicle or to cover up some clue, such as fingerprints on one of the surfaces, then it might have been done as an assertion of power, to vandalise. This was certainly a characteristic of Manuel's crimes. He liked to spoil things, defile other people's treasured homes, destroy their tidiness and cleanliness. Perhaps, then, if he did kill Dunn, smashing up his taxi was an act of the same vicious sort. Perhaps. Even if we accept this, though, the motive for killing Dunn remains obscure, the way the killer escaped from the moors unknown.

Whatever the truth of the matter, in early August 1958 the chief constable of Durham wrote to the Director of Public Prosecutions to say that, as Manuel was dead and the inquest on Dunn concluded, 'The matter is now satisfactorily concluded as far as this county is concerned.'

The second murder for which Manuel is a strong suspect, the possible tenth in all, is that of Anne Steele, who was beaten to death with a poker as her horrified neighbours stood powerlessly outside her front door. Killing by striking or shooting to the head was certainly a Manuel trademark but it is by no means unique. It is clear that Glasgow police thought it was possible that Manuel had killed Steele. However, they could never obtain any evidence that he had been in her flat. Superintendent Brown, after Manuel was hanged, told a newspaper that he thought Manuel might have been the killer but that he had never questioned him about the matter, adding that he had no right to do so.

And were there more victims? Manuel himself may have boasted that he had killed other people. One paper said he had killed the London prostitute Helen Carlin but there was never any evidence to link him to this 1954 crime. A Barlinnie prison officer recalled in a 2008 television programme that there had been a story going round that Manuel claimed that at Blackpool he had pushed a car with a couple in it into the sea. This seems certain to have been another Manuel fantasy.

As for all the others, the two or three or even seven or eight more, there is no proof of any sort: just rumours, wild stories, dread-filled imaginings, some of them almost certainly encouraged by Manuel himself. The rumours were free to grow uncontrollably because by the time he was hanged he had ceased to be regarded as a human being and had become the embodiment of evil.

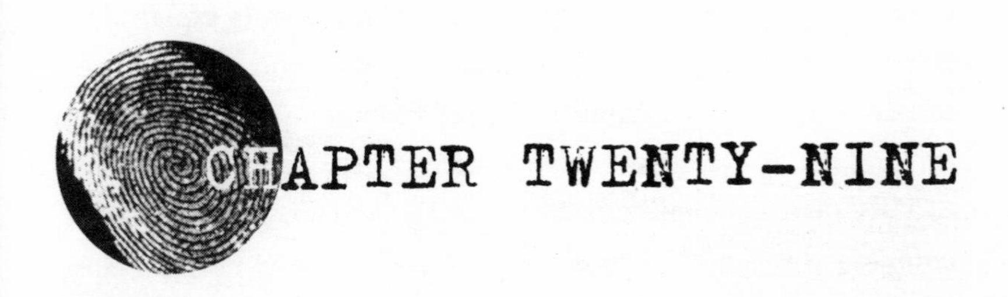

CHAPTER TWENTY-NINE

Manuel quickly became almost a mythological figure in Scotland. In the streets, young girls skipped to the rhyme:

> Mary had a little cat,
> She used to call it Daniel,
> Then she found it killed six mice
> And now she calls it Manuel.

Mothers threatened naughty children that Manuel would get them if they did not behave. The popular press immediately contributed to this mythologising of the murderer. In writing about the case, the papers had to answer some unavoidable questions. Why had he committed his murders? Was he sane or mad? If he was sane, what was the motive for his crimes?

They quickly decided he was sane. In taking this view, they were able to quote Lord Cameron's remark, 'A man may be very bad without being mad.' But, by depicting Manuel as sane, the papers also implied that he was a rational being who must have known what he was doing. If this was so, what could explain his terrible actions? The papers made much of the fact that Manuel had been an aggressive and violent criminal since the age of 12. They emphasised the early physical and sexual assaults he had carried out. Because he had done these things when he was so young, they suggested, the evolution of his behaviour could not be understood in any rational terms. They decided that there was only one satisfactory explanation: Manuel was an inhuman monster, a born killer whose actions were totally inexplicable in terms of normal human motivation. He was evil and that was an end to it – no further explanation was needed.

They attributed non-human characteristics to him. One of the most emphasised was his 'coldness'. In almost all of these press accounts, Manuel is referred to as 'cold-blooded' and 'merciless'. That is, he is depicted as the opposite of a 'real, warm human being'. The cliché of the 'cold-blooded killer' fits this situation perfectly. The headline on the account published under the name of Alex Brown in the *Daily Express* in October 1958 was: 'As Dawn Breaks I Arrest the Icy-Eyed Little Killer'. It was stressed in the newspaper articles and in the books subsequently written about him that Manuel showed this profoundly unnatural coldness in situation after situation.

It is undoubtedly true that he did display an extraordinary coldness that struck people at the time. Lord Cameron told his son that Manuel was the coldest person he had ever encountered and Ranald Sutherland commented on this characteristic too. It is also undeniable that Manuel showed no empathy towards others. This seems to have been an aspect of his belief in his own vast superiority. Whatever its root, it certainly helped the press to depict him as less than human.

Manuel was given other non-human characteristics: he was supposed to be able to see in the dark. The attribution of this ability to him must stem from his strong preference for going out during the hours of darkness to commit his crimes. He was accustomed to moving about by back ways, along railway lines and by hidden routes. He was someone, in other words, who literally ignored normal human boundaries, not only in how he moved through the night but also in what he did in the shielding darkness.

Manuel was thus depicted in the press as someone whose actions were totally aberrant, unnatural, inhuman. Several other factors contributed to the general belief that Manuel was exceptionally evil. The most obvious was the sheer number of his murders. At a time when there were about fourteen murders a year in Scotland, it was almost beyond understanding that one man had killed nine people within two years and five in the short time between 8 December 1957 and 1 January 1958. Public feelings of bewildered horror were increased by claims that he had killed even more people.

Second, revulsion at Manuel's crimes was increased by the range of his victims and the different ways in which they were killed: Kneilands was battered to death with dreadful brutality, Cooke strangled with her own bra, Vivienne Watt probably tortured before being shot, Dunn shot and his throat slashed, the others shot as they slept. Several different sorts of people, one of them a young boy, all of them callously murdered in various manners: it made the situation seem even more inexplicable.

Third, there was the fact that five of his victims had been shot as they slept. We are at our most unguarded and vulnerable when we sleep; but asleep in our own beds in our own houses, we also assume we are as safe as we can be. Manuel's silent night-time break-ins and apparently motiveless murders seemed a complete inversion of the proper order of things. If a man, his wife and child cannot sleep safely in their own beds, where can they ever be safe?

Finally, there was the extreme disparity between the violence of the killings and any apparent gain to the killer. Dunn was not robbed; little or nothing was stolen from the Watts; the absolute maximum Manuel could have got from the Smart house was about £40; Cooke and Kneilands were clearly killed for reasons other than theft. This was a time of growing economic prosperity. Men like Watt and Smart were able to own their own bungalows, get cars. Yet all this could be snatched away in a few seconds, all their hopes, the lives they had built up destroyed for no understandable reason.

The same was true of the killings of Dunn, Kneilands and Cooke: why should their lives and those of their loved ones be destroyed? There was no sense to it. The only way to explain it was to look on Manuel as a manifestation of evil. He had ceased to be human; he was now 'the Beast of Birkenshaw'.

* * *

The morning of Manuel's execution had been particularly arduous for Dr Anderson. He had watched as the man who had been in his care died in the execution chamber and had removed the hood to examine his body and pronounce life extinct. He had attended the funeral service and gone to Glasgow Sheriff Court to give formal evidence of the execution of the death warrant. When he returned to Barlinnie that day, his friend the Reverend Russell Anderson, the prison chaplain, called upon him to console him. Over a cup of coffee, the reverend observed, 'I know I'm not supposed to say this, but I'm glad he's gone.' It was a sentiment that resounded across the whole country.

BIBLIOGRAPHY

UNPUBLISHED DOCUMENTS HELD IN THE NATIONAL ARCHIVES OF SCOTLAND

AD24/61 trial transcript PM murder trial
AD24/60/1–5 Crown Office Criminal Appeal P. Manuel
AD24/62 Crown Office Criminal Appeal P. Manuel
AD24/62/1–4 Crown Office Criminal Appeal P. Manuel
AD24/62/5/1–2 Crown Office Criminal Appeal P. Manuel
AD24/62/6/1–2 Crown Office Criminal Appeal P. Manuel
AD24/62/7/1–2 Crown Office Criminal Appeal P. Manuel
AD24/62/8/1–2 Crown Office Criminal Appeal P. Manuel
AD24/62/9 Crown Office Criminal Appeal P Manuel
HH60/703/1–2 Murder Cases Peter Manuel
HH60/704–8 Murder Cases Peter Manuel
JC1958/26 Trial Papers Peter Manuel
JC34/2/178 Peter Manuel papers relating to appeal against rape conviction
JC 34/5/57 Peter Manuel appeal papers conviction for HB and previous

JC34/5/60 Peter Manuel appeal papers conviction for HB and previous
JC34/5/243 Peter Manuel appeal papers conviction for murder, etc.
HH15/295/2 Death watch journal Peter Manuel
SC37/50/20 Minute book HCJ Edinburgh sentencing of Martin David Hart and Charles Tallis
JC13/155 HCJ minute book conviction of Samuel McKay
SC35/37/11 Sheriff Court minute book convictions of Joseph Brannan
SC36/56/209 Hamilton Sheriff Court book conviction of Charles Tallis HB Explosives, etc.
JP16/5/10 Airdrie Burgh court record of fine for BoP Samuel Manuel 1953
HH57/672 Disturbances at Peterhead Prison
HH12/44 Johnnie Ramenski in Peterhead
HH12/25/25 Prison journal Barlinnie prison
JC15/57 Minute book of HCJ Glasgow showing 1946 rape trial
SC37/50/20 Hamilton Sheriff Court minute book; Blantyreferme HB trial minutes
SC35/37/12 Showing conviction of David Knox
HH16/644/1 Trial of Patrick Carragher

PUBLISHED SOURCES

Books

Bingham, John, *The Hunting Down of Peter Manuel*, Macmillan, 1973
Muncie, William, *The Crime Pond*, Chambers, 1959
Wilson, John Grey, *The Trial of Peter Manuel*, Secker & Warburg, 1959

Periodicals

Baird, John A., 'Forensic Psychiatry in its Time and Place', *The Journal of the American Academy of Psychiatry and Law*, Vol. 32, 2004
The College Courant, Whitsun 1963
Hansard, 3 March 1993
John Mack, 'Full-Time Miscreants, Delinquent Neighbourhoods and Criminal Networks', *The British Journal of Sociology*, Vol. 15, No. 1, March 1964
Psychiatric Bulletin, Vol. 23, 2003